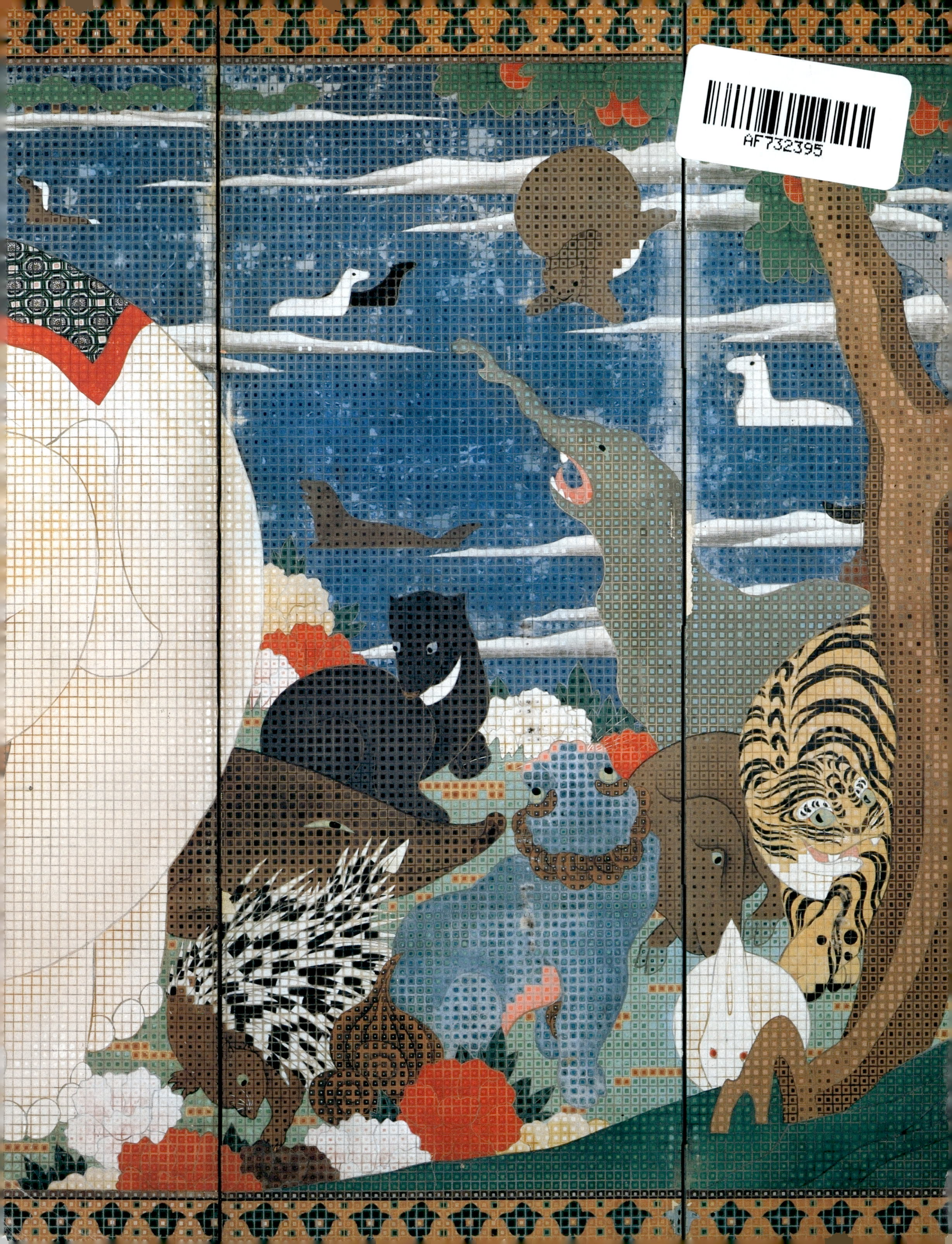

Masterpieces from the Shin'enkan Collection

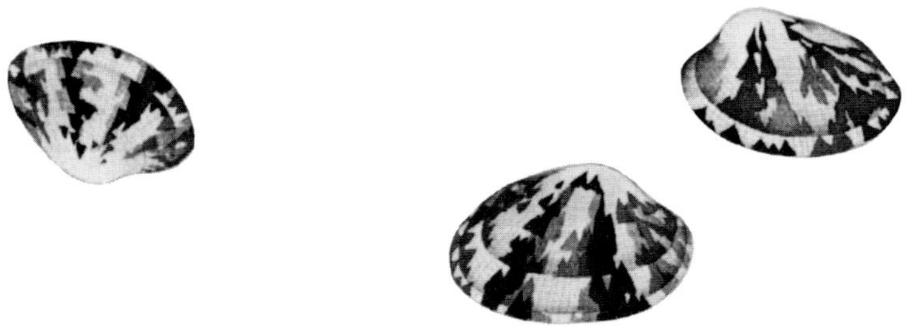

Masterpieces from the SHIN'ENKAN COLLECTION

Japanese Painting of the Edo Period

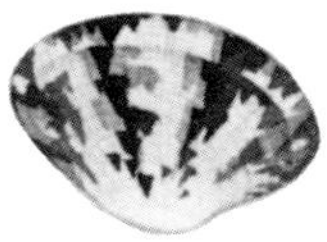

Los Angeles County Museum of Art

Harper & Row, Publishers, Inc.
New York Philadelphia San Francisco London Mexico City
Sao Paulo Singapore Sydney

Cover: *Birds, Animals, and Flowering Plants* (plate 66, detail)

Published by Los Angeles County Museum of Art
5905 Wilshire Boulevard
Los Angeles, California 90036

A trade edition of this catalogue has been published for distribution in the United States by Harper & Row, Publishers, Inc.
10 East 53rd Street, New York, New York 10022
for distribution in Canada by Fitzhenry & Whiteside Limited, Toronto and for distribution in the United Kingdom by Thames and Hudson Ltd, London.

Editor: Mitch Tuchman
Designer: Deenie Yudell
Production artist: Eileen Delson
Text set in Simoncini Garamond by Continental Typographics, Inc.
Chatsworth, California
Printed in an edition of 7,000 copies on Espel paper by Nissha Printing Co., Ltd., Kyoto, Japan.

Photo credits: plates 1-6, 8-11, 13-17, 19-20, 23, 25-26, 28, 30-32, 34-43, 45-46, 48-63, 67-68, and 70-74 reproduced courtesy of Seeg Publishers, Inc.; plates 7, 12, 18, 21-22, 24, 33, 44, 47, 64-65, and 69 reproduced courtesy of Osaka Municipal Museum; plate 27 photographed by Peter Brenner, Los Angeles County Museum of Art; plate 29 photographed by Haruo Sohba; plate 66 photographed by Morio Kanai.

Library of Congress Cataloguing-in-Publication Data
Los Angeles County Museum of Art
Masterpieces from the Shin'enkan Collection.
1. Painting, Japanese—Edo period, 1600-1868—Exhibitions. 2. Price, Joe D.—Art collections—Exhibitions. 3. Price, Mrs. Joe D.—Art collections—Exhibitions. 4. Painting—Private collections—California—Los Angeles —Exhibitions. I. Title.
ND1053.5.L67 1986 759.952'074'019494
85-24152 ISBN 0-87587-128-3
85-45953 ISBN 0-06-430161-3 (Harper & Row)
ISBN 0-500-27420-7 (Thames and Hudson)

The essays "Joe Price and the Shin'enkan Collection," "A Personal Explanation of the Shin'enkan Collection," and "A Pavilion for Japanese Art at the Los Angeles County Museum of Art" are adapted from essays that appeared originally in *The Shin'enkan Collection of Japanese Painting,* published in Japan in 1984 by Kyoto Shoin, Inc.,

This exhibition and its catalogue are presented by the Los Angeles County Museum of Art in association with the Shin'enkan Foundation.

Contents

Foreword

The Edo period (1615–1868) was an age of political stability and economic prosperity in Japan. Authoritarian rule enforced the isolation of the country from the rest of the world and mandated a rigid class structure in an attempt to prevent change. But the attempt was futile. Large metropolitan centers grew, and the rise of an affluent mercantile class did bring enormous change in society just as new patrons brought significant change to the arts. The years from 1600 to 1850 were the most innovative for Japanese painting with more than a dozen schools continuing revered traditions or exploring new directions. The best of both these aspects are richly represented in the Shin'enkan Collection, assembled over thirty years by Mr. and Mrs. Joe D. Price.

The Shin'enkan Collection is considered the most outstanding repository of Edo-period painting in the Western world. It consists of more than three hundred scroll paintings and screens, particularly from the latter part of the period (1759–1810). Of the highly imaginative Kyoto individualists, Itō Jakuchū, Soga Shōhaku, and Nagasawa Rosetsu, each is represented from his formative years to his maturity. Virtually all the leading masters of the Rimpa school are included, with the works of Sakai Hōitsu and Suzuki Kiitsu held in depth. The painters of the Shijō School are also strongly represented, particularly by the works of Mori Sosen. In addition, the collection includes impressive holdings by genre and ukiyo-e artists as well as examples of Buddhist painting and the Nanga and Nagasaki styles.

Mr. and Mrs. Price have honored the Los Angeles County Museum of Art with the gift of their Shin'enkan Collection. In addition, they have given the museum an original design and partial funding for a Pavilion for Japanese Art that will house Shin'enkan and the museum's Japanese art collection.

Paintings of the Edo period were conceived by the artists as the only decoration in a room or tokonoma alcove. Not only was each piece meant to appear alone, it was to be illuminated by nothing more than the delicately changing light of the sun. No conventional museum space, no matter how beautiful, could display the art in this way. A completely new concept was required. For this reason, the Prices commissioned Bruce Goff to develop a plan for a building for which the art, not the collector, was the "client." The Pavilion for Japanese Art embodies that concept.

This dual gift, the collection and building design, will make the museum a major center for the study and appreciation of Japanese art in the United States.

The challenge that remains is to raise the additional funds needed to construct the extraordinary home for this most extraordinary of collections. We look to the community at large to make this possible and hope that this first in-depth preview of this magnificent collection will justify that support.

Numerous talented people contribute to the making of an exhibition and its catalogue. In addition to the donors, Mr. and Mrs. Price, it is a pleasure to acknowledge the contributions of George Kuwayama, senior curator, Julia F. Andrews, assistant curator, and Hollis Goodall-Cristante of the Far East Art Department; Myrna Smoot, assistant director for Museum Programs; Mitch Tuchman, managing editor, and Deenie Yudell, head graphic designer; Bernard Kester, who designed the installation; Dr. James Peoples, assistant director for Operations, and his staff; and the Press Office, led by Pamela Jenkinson Leavitt, which ably disseminates information about our exhibitions to the museum-going public.

In Japan we are indebted to Takefumi Masuda of Seeg Publishers, Inc., for much of the photography that appears in the catalogue and for his assistance in facilitating its publication. Atsushi Wakisaka, curator of paintings at the Osaka Municipal Museum, dated many of the paintings in the Shin'enkan Collection at the time of that museum's 1985 exhibition of works from the collection.

Earl A. Powell III
Director

by Yūzō Yamane

JOE PRICE AND THE SHIN'ENKAN COLLECTION

It was in the fall of 1970, at the airing of the treasures of the Imperial Household Collection in Kyoto Palace, that I first encountered Joe Price. I was in poor physical condition at the time, a result of the stress of student disturbances occurring on Japanese university campuses. But every year it was my practice to take advantage of the opportunity to see the imperial treasures when they are aired in the fall, and so I went to Kyoto as usual. At the airing two years earlier, I had spent an entire day examining a pair of eight-fold screens with fan paintings depicting the *Tales of the Hogen and Heiji Insurrections* while doing research for the volume *Sōtatsu and Kōrin* in the *Genshoku Nihon no Bijutsu* (Japanese art in color) series published by Shogakukan. This time (in 1970), I had heard that the set of thirty paintings by Itō Jakuchū called *The Colorful World of Living Beings* were to be shown in the room adjacent to the one in which I had seen the Hogen-Heiji fan painting screens.

When I worked at Kyoto Imperial Museum (now Kyoto National Museum) from 1944 to 1951, I enjoyed looking at Jakuchū's ink painting *Vegetable Nehan*, which is in that museum's collection. I also admired Jakuchū's ink paintings in Rokuon-ji temple and *Roosters and Hens*, his highly colored sliding-door paintings with gold-leaf ground, in Saifuku-ji temple. In my university lectures I would point to the Saifuku-ji paintings as the post-Kōrin paintings that best use a solid gold-leaf ground for the composition. However, when it came to the set of thirty Jakuchū paintings in the Imperial Household Collection, which I had only seen in reproduction published several at a time in various books, I had only gone so far as to identify Kōrin's compositional influence, such as evidenced in *Chrysanthemums by a Stream*. In the small room where I was now viewing them, the thirty paintings were hung close together side by side on three walls. Each painting was marked by an astonishing thickness of paint, tightly filled space, and a unique use of color. After looking at several of the paintings I was overwhelmed by their power, and I began to feel almost faint. My poor physical condition and low energy level may have been partially responsible, but an overpowering atmosphere pervading that room proved to be too much for me, and I had to withdraw. Looking back on it, it doesn't seem surprising: it was unreasonable to try to view all at once and in a cramped space all thirty paintings into which Jakuchū had poured his heart and soul for ten years.

While I was examining other imperial treasures in another, more spacious room, a staff member told me that a foreigner had just burst into tears while viewing the thirty Jakuchū paintings. Looking out into the corridor I saw my colleague, the art historian Yoshi Shirahata, coming out of the room in which the Jakuchū paintings were hung, and she explained to me that she had brought along to the airing a Mr. Joe Price, the American collector of Jakuchū paintings. I don't recall whether I was introduced to Mr. Price at that time, but even today the sight of him looking with such intensity at those paintings is fresh in my memory. Impressed by his great energy, I left so as not to disturb him.

At the time of the great Jakuchū exhibition at Tokyo National Museum in 1971, I was hospitalized because my chronic hepatitis had taken a turn for the worse. I was sorry that I was therefore unable to see the Jakuchū paintings in Mr. Price's collection that had been borrowed for the exhibition. But in my hospital bed I read the March 1971 special Jakuchū issue (no. 255) of the art magazine *Geijutsu Shinchō*, which contained an article by Mr. Price entitled "A Collector's View of Jakuchū" and an article by Yoshi Shirahata called "Joe Price and Jakuchū." Later, in the October issue (no. 262) of the same magazine, I read the transcript of a symposium on the topic "A Reassessment of Jakuchū" in which the participants were Joe Price, Teiji Chizawa, and Tadashi Kobayashi. Through these articles I was able to learn in some detail how Mr. Price looked at paintings and what he thought about them, and about the special features of his Shin'enkan Collection. I learned that he was an engineer by training and that he chose paintings entirely on the basis of his own intuition; that he considered Jakuchū to be an extremely individualistic painter, but not an unorthodox one; that he thought Jakuchū was close to Kōrin in terms of artistic lineage; and that he thought highly of Jakuchū for his deep understanding of nature and his solid pictorial structure. I agreed wholeheartedly with all of these opinions. But we differ on one point: Mr. Price considers *Chrysanthemums by a Stream* in the Imperial Household Collection series to be Jakuchū's greatest masterpiece, while I give that place of honor to *Roosters and Hens* in Saifuku-ji. Perhaps this difference in opinion is due to something more personal and complex than differences in perception or taste. In any case, from Yoshi Shirahata's article I came to understand why Mr. Price shed tears of joy upon seeing the Imperial Household Collection's Jakuchū paintings, for she reported that to view these works had been his dearest wish for many years.

The first opportunity I had to see several paintings from the Shin'enkan Collection was at the epoch-making Rimpa exhibition at Tokyo National Museum in 1973. By that time my health had recovered to the point where I was just barely able to resume my teaching at Tokyo University, but as this important exhibition was in my area of specialization I made many trips to view it. I was strongly attracted to the Shin'enkan paintings on display, in particular to the pair of hanging scrolls, *Paulownia and Maple* (plate 25), by Suzuki Kiitsu. Although the subject matter is lyrical, I saw in this pair of paintings a sober modern quality not to be found in the work of his teacher Sakai Hōitsu. I was deeply

Sakai Hōitsu
The Thirty-six Poets on a Field of Flowers and Grasses
(detail, plate 18)

impressed at this proof of the sureness and acuity of Mr. Price's eye. As I wrote in my book *Sōtatsu and Kōrin,* I had not thought much of Rimpa painting after Kōrin. In the case of Hōitsu—with the exception of his masterpieces *Summer and Autumn Grasses* (a pair of two-fold screens) and *Moon and Autumn Grasses* (a six-fold screen)—I felt something was lacking in his work. I felt this even more strongly when it came to Hōitsu's student Kiitsu, whom I thought of as merely a weak follower of his teacher. But this exhibition, whose extensive coverage of Kiitsu was probably a result of the exposure of Professor Tadashi Kobayashi and his colleagues to the Kiitsu works in the Price collection, was to me a great shock and eye-opener.

After my experience with the Rimpa exhibition, I resolved to undertake a five-year project: a comprehensive and exhaustive series of books to be called *Rimpa Kaiga Zenshū* (Rimpa paintings). Mr. Jirō Enjōji, then president of the *Japan Economic Journal,* offered to sponsor this project, which also involved Nobuo Tsuji, Tadashi Kobayashi, and Motoaki Kōno as editors and writers. The plan was to conduct research and gather material for three years, starting in 1974, and then to publish a total of five massive volumes in the final two years: *Sōtatsu School,* volumes 1 and 2, *Kōrin School,* volumes 1 and 2, and *Hōitsu School.* Some of these scholars had kept a respectful distance from the difficult problems of Sōtatsu and Kōrin, but in the belief that these artists' work was essential to an understanding of the history of early modern Japanese painting, I persuaded them to participate. My hope was to publish all of my own research on Sōtatsu and Kōrin for the benefit of future research on these artists, while my younger coauthors would be able to examine with fresh eyes the post-Kōrin artists to whom I had previously paid little attention. Our overall goal was to trace Rimpa carefully from its origins through its later developments and on this foundation to study the originality and legacy of each individual artist.

In the spring of 1975 we paused in our investigations within Japan in order to travel to America to examine and photograph Rimpa paintings there. Although my physical condition was not good, I very much wanted to see Sōtatsu's folding-screen masterpieces *Matsushima* and *Dragons and Clouds* in the Freer Gallery of Art in Washington, D.C. Nobuo Tsuji was in charge of planning for our trip, and he laid out an itinerary in which we would start in San Francisco and Los Angeles, proceed to Oklahoma to spend four or five days at the Price residence, and then continue on to New York and Washington, D.C. My three colleagues had become close friends with Mr. and Mrs. Price over the years, but I had met them only once, in Kyoto, where we had dined together and where I had observed them purchasing a large painting of a tiger at an art dealer's shop. I thought that it would be too great an imposition on the Prices for us to stay as long as four or five days so that I could rest, but word came from them that they were waiting to welcome

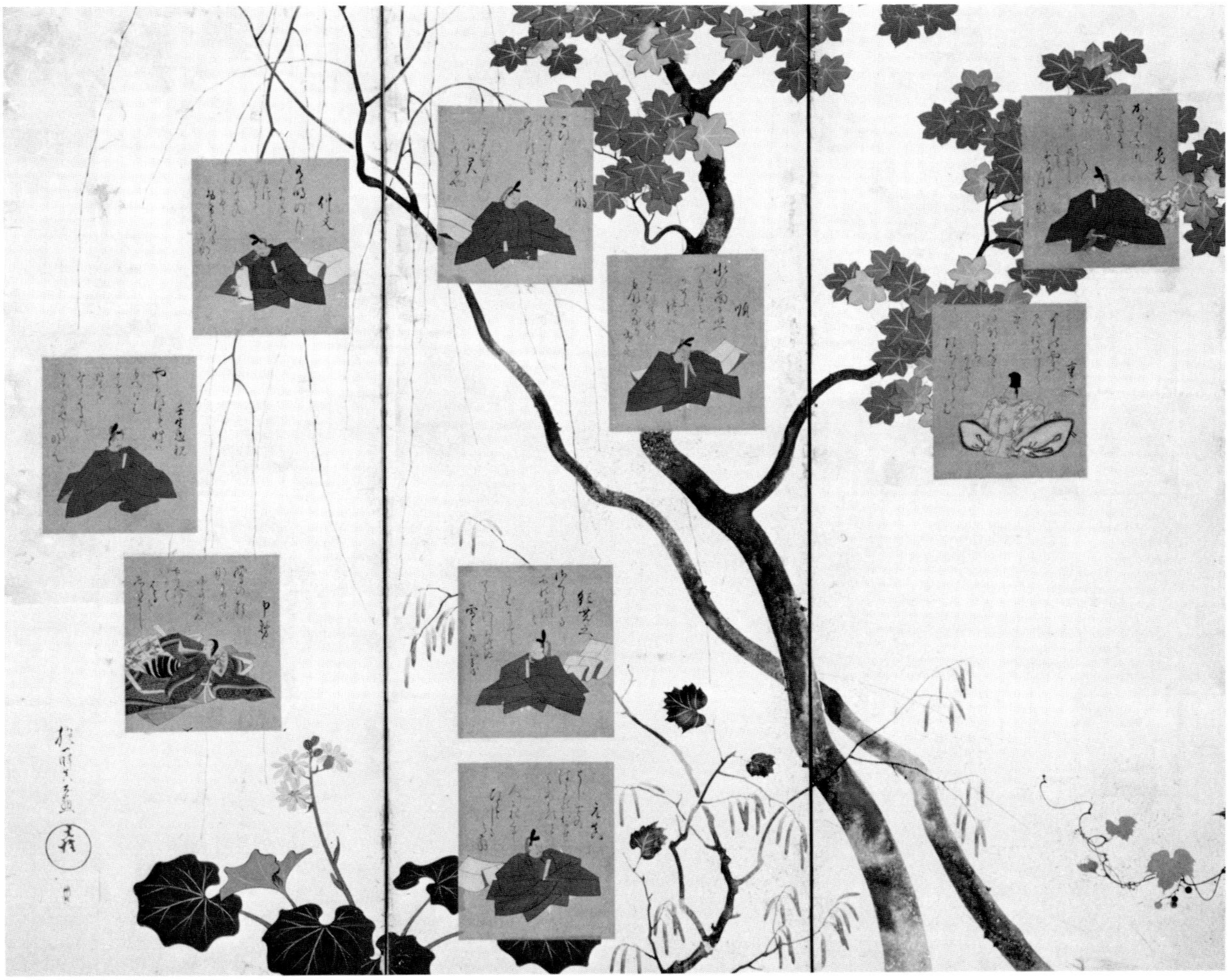

us, and I decided it would be best for my health if I followed this schedule. Tsuneo Takeda joined us as an associate member, and with my daughter Yumi, who came along to act as a nurse for me, our group came to a total of six.

The Price residence in Oklahoma was extremely modern in design and located on a vast estate, the size of which is almost impossible to conceive in Japan. The architect was Bruce Goff, who was inspired by the celebrated Frank Lloyd Wright, the man Joe Price credits with teaching him to appreciate nature. But in every corner of the house one could sense the wishes and concerns of the client himself. First, there was a large entry hall, then, to the right a large space for entertaining visitors, to the left a family area, and finally the largest area was devoted to the Shin'enkan gallery. All of these separate areas were closely linked by the multiple use of acute angles in the roofs. Every day we spent the morning and afternoon viewing and photographing paintings, the late afternoon taking walks or fishing in the lake on the grounds, and the evening relaxing near the open bar and discussing art and life. In this way we enjoyed the wonderful hospitality of Joe and Etsuko; I will never forget the happiness of those five days spent with them. But before I become too absorbed in the happy memory of that visit, I would like to move on to the collection itself.

In line with the purpose of our trip, we began by looking at the Rimpa paintings. As Mr. Price has written in his own articles, the viewing gallery was designed so that each screen or scroll could be seen independently and under natural light. When we viewed the Hōitsu screens *The Thirty-six Poets on a Field of Flowers and Grasses* (plate 18) from across the pond that occupied the middle of the gallery, I recalled the time I had seen the famous sliding-door paintings *Maples* and *Cherry Trees* in Chishaku-in temple in Kyoto when they were still displayed in situ. The late afternoon light had reflected off the hill in the garden onto the temple pond and then into the rooms that held the paintings: the gold leaf in the screens had shone faintly in that soft light. I remember thinking how subtly radiant gold leaf could appear under such conditions. What an original design was required to produce the same effect in a gallery setting. When I looked at Mr. Price, he was smiling and chuckling at my reaction. The others, who were photographing up close, began to back away from the screens as if in a trance, and I worried that they might fall into the pond. But it would be probably just as enjoyable to view the paintings while swimming! These screens are certainly Hōitsu's masterpieces.

After viewing the Rimpa paintings, we moved on to those by Jakuchū, Rosetsu, and Shōhaku. Some members of our group were as captivated by those paintings as I was by the Rimpa paintings. Behind every work in the Shin'enkan Collection, I felt the keen eye and firm principles of Mr. Price.

I must confess, in ending, that when, a few days later and in good health, I stood before the Sōtatsu *Matsushima* screens at the Freer Gallery, I wept tears of joy at seeing them at long last, just as Mr. Price had in the Kyoto Palace when he saw the Jakuchū paintings for the first time.

by Joe D. Price

A PERSONAL EXPLANATION OF THE SHIN'ENKAN COLLECTION

Nearly four hundred years ago in the tiny island nation of Japan, an art form emerged which became virtually an island itself in the world of art.

In early times the eyes of Japan seemed always to be directed beyond its ocean. The Japanese people were forced by their educated and ruling class to submerge their own inherent tendencies to those of their huge neighbor, China. Indeed they imitated the customs and art of China to such an extent that many people today consider all Japanese art to be merely a copy of the Chinese. But that is a mistake. The Japanese are not a people who could be content forever with someone else's culture. Moreover the rulers of Japan who had supported the introduction of the Chinese way of life began slowly to lose their authority. Power was shifting from the imperial court and its advisers, and they were being replaced by the fighting soldier, the samurai.

The samurai lacked both the education of the older ruling classes and the historical learning of the Buddhist church, which were both steeped in knowledge of China. Samurai were mounted knights versed in the military arts of the sword and the horse. As their power grew, so did their influence in the arts. The great leaders of the warrior clans rejected both the iconographic art of ancient Buddhism and the severe canons of Zen aesthetics; these were too somber, to austere, for their cruder tastes. They decorated the interiors of their gloomy castles with the glitter of gold, gold that reflected the thin light filtering through the heavy shutters, gold that reflected the shimmer of lamps and candles. The samurai built their capital where Tokyo now stands and called it Edo. Believing that society could be protected from change, they closed the ports of Japan to the outside world. In such a state of seclusion, Japan was able to recover from the devastation of its civil wars and begin a 250-year-long period of unprecedented peace and internal development. This was the age known as the Edo period.

Within the cocoonlike isolation of this tiny island society, the artists, freed from the dictates of outside influence, reached back to a time prior to those restrictions and resumed an art that was peculiar to their heritage. They copied little from the world outside Japan, since it scarcely existed for them. What they developed was an art form unique in content and style, an art form purely Japanese.

The art of the Edo period is made up of many schools and styles. One of these schools came into existence in

Sakai Hōitsu
Bird and Flowers of the Twelve Months
(detail, plate 21)

response to the interests and demands of the merchant class, a most unlikely class to produce a lasting art, since the merchants were considered at that time to be the lowest of the low: base, uneducated, and interested solely in the "misdeed" of profit. But they had soon appropriated most of the wealth and begun to demand as well an art of their own. What emerged from this unlikely source was an art that expressed the new mood of affluence, an art that was simply and purely decorative, intended for no purpose other than to delight the eye.

The question most often asked about the Shin'enkan Collection is: Why did I like this art, and what made me begin to collect it? That question I can answer. The one I cannot answer is: Why didn't anybody else?

How did an engineer living in the central part of the United States, with no training in art and no knowledge or experience of the Orient, become so fascinated with these obscure painters of Japan? My higher education was limited to six years of the study of engineering. Repetitious, concerned only with what had already been proven, it emphasized memorization and neglected originality.

After leaving the university, I talked myself into an assignment as the local engineer on one of my father's building projects. He wanted to erect a one- or two-story ranch-style office building; the architect to whom I introduced him tried to talk him into a building of fourteen stories. In my father's own words, they compromised on nineteen. The architect was Frank Lloyd Wright, and the building that emerged was the Price Tower, a soaring, copper-sheathed structure that now stands as a memorial to these two great men.

Frank Lloyd Wright explained to me, with infinite patience, the fascination of nature. I learned from him to appreciate the growth of things. Sometimes we would take a walk across the prairie, and Mr. Wright would stoop to pick a flower and explain its structure, how each part functioned and was shaped to serve its particular purpose; or he would find a simple object, such as an empty turtle shell, and give it his attention for an extended period. I remember his saying, "Do you spell *God* with a capital *G*? Well, I spell *Nature* with a capital *N*."

The artists of the Edo period obviously had the same fascination with nature, the same love for understanding how and why things happen. Certainly, if their calligraphy had used capitals, the Japanese too would have spelled *Nature* with a capital *N*.

I was never taught to love Japanese painting, but I was taught to love the things the Edo painters themselves must have loved. Through Frank Lloyd Wright I learned that it was possible to gouge out a hillside, then take brick, stone, lumber, and tile and construct a man-made structure that, when complete, makes the hillside seem more a part of nature than it had been before. If, once the structure is there, you try to imagine it gone, the hillside would appear

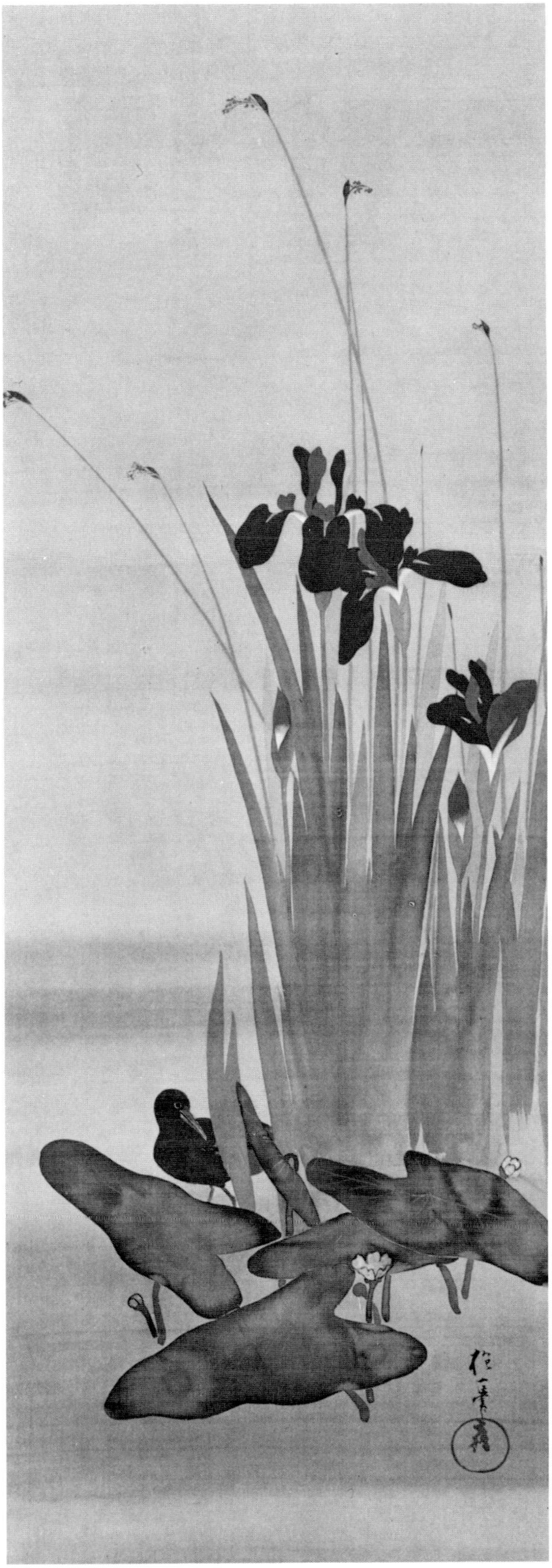

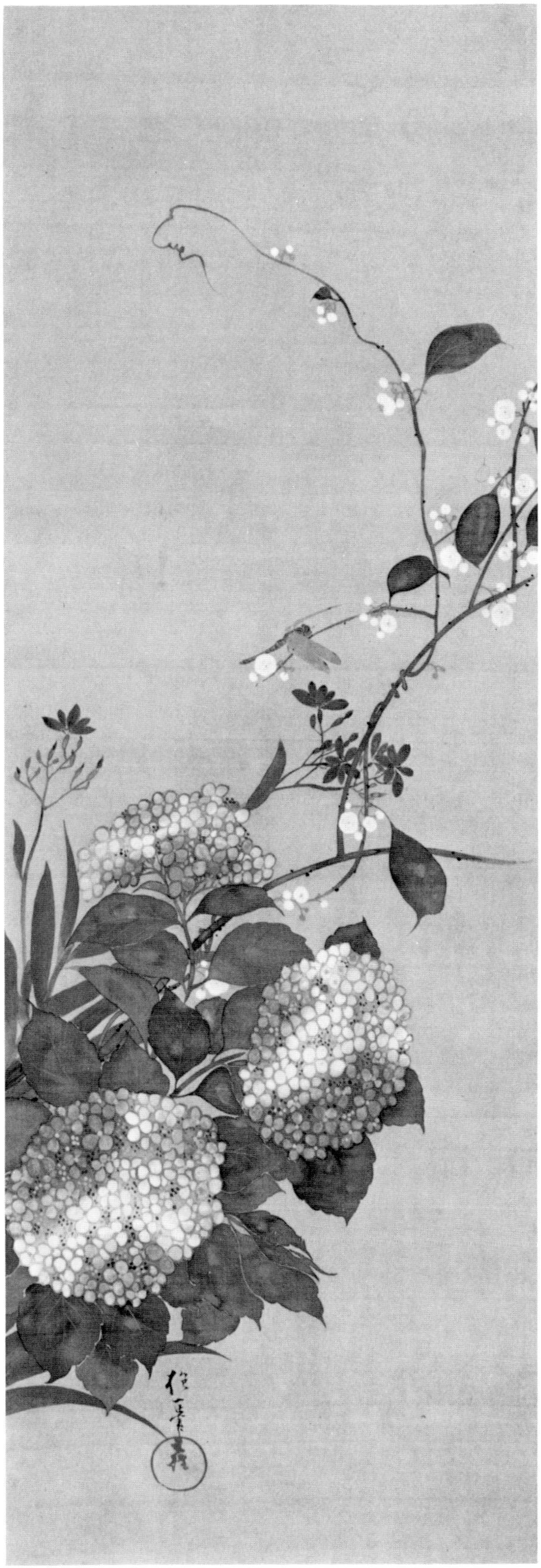

naked. This enhancement of nature with human creation is what the Japanese have managed to do for more than a thousand years. From the magnificent Ise Shrine through the Katsura Imperial Villa and down to simple teahouses, they seemed to surpass nature as a creative force. They could take a pine tree and mutilate it—cutting it, twisting it, plucking it—until all that is left is its essence; but what remains looks more like a pine tree than anything nature could have made on its own.

This ability to reconstruct nature and even appear to improve on it is an essential characteristic of Japanese Edo painting. It is surely the answer to the often-asked question about what attracted me to that art; it is surely what caught my eye and sparked my love for it. In contrast to my engineering education, the discovery of Japanese art and the search for these seemingly forgotten paintings became a delightful preoccupation.

On an early trip to Japan I traveled extensively to the outer provinces, along the Japan Sea coast. There the immense value of space was obvious. Each and every piece of land was in use. Even the sides of the railroad embankments were terraced for rice paddies. Every corner was frugally planted, and in the tiny villages all the houses were crowded together to preserve precious space. Space became so important, so valuable that to waste it was unthinkable. Yet every single house, no matter how small or cramped or crowded by other houses, had a garden. The space occupied by this garden could easily have been roofed over to have made another entire room for the obviously over-crowded living quarters. But no, beauty was far more important than mere convenience. It is this appreciation of beauty that surely has accounted for the development of the art of the Japanese.

In the fifties and early sixties I was not "collecting" art, but only occasionally buying paintings that pleased me. At first I was not even conscious that they were Japanese; they were just paintings that excited me. In fact I had accumulated art for probably ten years before someone finally read the signatures and asked why I only collected Japanese art, why only from a fifty-year period out of the two thousand years in their painting history, and why only six artists. I had never realized this was so. An architect friend had once shown me a book containing reproductions of thirty paintings by Itō Jakuchū. Ever since I had dreamed of some day seeing a real painting by him; and now, to my amazement, I was told I already had several in my collection, purchased unsuspectingly since the signatures were undecipherable to me.

My first venture to Japan was in 1963, when a planned short trip ended as a rather lengthy one. This art that I had come to love was everywhere. It was beautiful, it was plentiful, and it was almost totally unappreciated.

Over the following ten years I was often asked, "Why do you like only modern art?" Two hundred years old, and it was considered only "modern," base, common, and below the dignity of scholarship. Even woodblock prints, which were produced in editions of hundreds, brought more respect and higher prices than did the individual paintings of the same period and by the same artists.

Luck plays an immeasurable role in collecting. Not only was I in the right place at the right time, but I was also fortunate enough to discover later that most of my original purchases were genuine, although there was no reason to expect that they should have been. I seldom subsequently made a mistake in collecting those particular artists. Once the skill of an artist and the style of a school can be assimilated, there is no reason ever to purchase anything of lesser quality. Nevertheless, I did buy some artists the hard way, by constantly improving upon the fakes first purchased. An example is a putative Rosetsu painting of a crow on a branch. At first glance, from a distance, every feather seems in place, and the bird is alert with the pride of his species; yet on closer inspection one sees that there are no individual feathers, just a few amazingly quick strokes of the brush. Although the artist has undeniable talent, the silk has the suspicious look of the Meiji period. But most damning of all is the knowledge that only experience brings to the collector: that this is just not the way Rosetsu paints crows. He paints crows like the ones on the elephant in plate 44. How nice it would be if there were no signature on the crow painting; then I could still prize it as I did on the day it was purchased. Or better yet, if only it could have retained the signature of the real artist, we could search out more of his works and give credit where it is due.

It is the fantastic skill of the artist that makes this art of the Edo period particularly appealing. The skill goes beyond their superb utilization of space—that asymmetrical placing of things—and the painter's control of nature. It depends upon the facility with which he transposes this vision onto his medium. Serious students started learning to paint when they were first able to hold brushes, and they would practice for twenty to thirty years before approaching the perfection of their masters. Only then were they allowed to paint for patrons or for sale. Under such discipline, the artist developed his techniques and the control over his medium to virtual perfection. There is no excuse for any part of a painting not to be perfect in every detail if it was produced by an artist who is known to have attained this level of ability. Remember, we are dealing with a period of nearly three hundred years, during which a great many artists were studying their craft every working moment of every day of their lives; and yet so few have emerged from this mass for posterity to remember. In three hundred years, with such intense, concentrated study, if those few are all that have emerged whom we can readily remember, then we know that those few must be capable of perfection; we must at least rank them with those artists in the West whom we respect and admire. In other words, would we accept a sloppy painting with Rembrandt's name on it? Or a painting by Michelangelo in which the figures are stiff? Or Leonardo, or

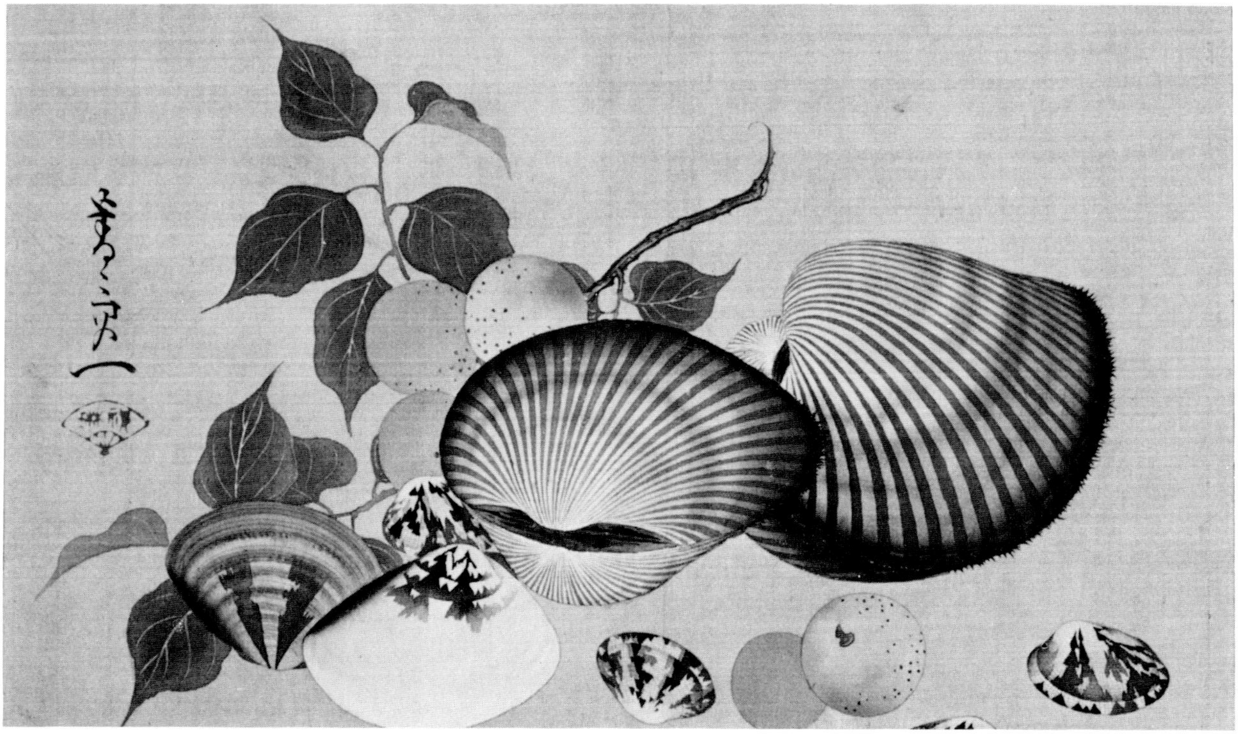

Velazquez? Then why should we continue to accept paintings by Kōrin, Sōtatsu, Hōitsu, Jakuchū, Kiitsu, Rosetsu, Ōkyo, or Sosen when those paintings contain imperfections, when even one of the brush strokes wavers, when two strokes of the brush cross each other, or when the shape bounded by two strokes is not as important as the strokes themselves?

There are three magic words to beware of when you are collecting Japanese paintings: *young*, *old*, and *drunk*. Dealers use them to excuse a poor painting. But in reality that is all it is, a bad painting; the work of a master never needs an excuse. Whenever you hear one of these three words used to describe a work of Edo-period art, you are almost certainly listening to someone excusing some deficiency in the painting. The artist's earliest works may be imitations of his teacher's style and may even be direct copies, but his skill with the brush should nearly match his teacher's, otherwise he would never have been allowed to paint. Many masters would even sign a student's work to show their satisfaction. The greatest compliment a student could give his master was to be better than the master, since it was the teacher who received the credit for the student's success.

In most paintings of the period we are discussing, no two brush strokes should ever cross. The ink tones are so thin that the crossing of the strokes would leave a darker spot. There should be only one layer of pigment on any scroll, since it had to be flexible enough to roll up for storage. Not only was the artist limited by such practical necessities, he also had to be proficient in loading the brush with ink, for the stroke might begin to dry and become solid, or the reverse, or both. At the same time he had to control the brush both in direction and in pressure to vary the thickness of

Suzuki Kiitsu
Seashells and Plums
(detail, plate 26)

the stroke while directing its path along predetermined shapes without outlines or guides. This had to be done with total control and certainty, since no stroke could be changed, no mistake covered up, no error eradicated.

Notice the areas that are not painted, the resultant shapes left between the brush strokes, between leaves or petals of a flower; these leftover shapes are as important as the painted forms themselves, and sometimes on gold screens the untouched gold even dominates. These shapes should all form exciting movements that are never static and never repetitious. In Edo painting some of the greatest art is that part which is not painted.

In genre screens pay particular attention to the spaces between the figures, which should dance and be alive; if they "just happen," if the areas between are just accidental, then the screen is just not very good. Any competent artist can paint a figure, but only a master can place that figure so that it complements the whole rather than existing solely as an independent shape. Look closely at the hands and feet of the participants in the scene. No matter how small the figure, these extremities should portray their functions; are the hands grasping the spear or relaxed in dance? Only a great artist can express this inner strength. The hands of a monkey must grasp a vine, not simply lie on it. The claw of a rooster must seem to cling to the soil, alive; it must support the weight of the rooster while obviously gripping the ground or limb; or if lifted from the surface as in a step, it should be relaxed without stiffness. In other words, the extremities should express the complete nature of the action.

If these skills are not enough to confront an artist, think of his problems with compositions. Scroll paintings are usually very tall; fans have a peculiar arched shape that has to be filled; screens are huge and are usually divided into six panels. These screens usually must also be painted as pairs, making a total of twelve panels in all; not only that, they must fold to support themselves, since they are freestanding, usually in the center of the room. Each fold in a screen creates a vertical line that cuts through the painting, so that the artist, in order to keep this line from being foreign to the composition and obstructing its feeling, must design each of the panels as a complete composition in itself. (It need not be pictorially complete, but in balance it must be total.) To make the problem even more complex, every other joint in the screen folds backwards, thereby making the gap much thicker and more pronounced; so the artist must make every pair of panels a more dominating composition than each of the single panels. By mastering these challenges in composition and proportion, the artist has now made the cracks caused by the hinges in the screen into integral parts of the painting.

The method of studying to be an artist, through apprenticeship to a master, can be compared somewhat with the education of an athlete. He searches out the finest coach and absorbs from him all he can teach. The athlete does not try to invent a new way of running but instead tries to improve upon his master's. If he is someone special, if he has something unique within himself, he can go beyond what he has been taught and can cut a fraction of a second off a record. By the same means the Japanese artists have created an evolving art, reaching back hundreds of years, to which each artist adds his special contribution, going beyond his master and adding something uniquely his that did not exist before. His training could also be compared with the training of a surgeon: it takes many years of study and practice before he is ever allowed to operate. The artist must similarly serve his time learning to mix inks, learning the use of a brush and how to load the ink on the brush, as well as rules of proportion, aesthetics, and discipline. Only when he is fully competent in his master's eyes is he allowed to paint.

This Edo art that is contained in the Shin'enkan Collection is free from overtones of religion, intellectual meanings, or dictatorial stylistic conventions. The paintings are so purely related to the heart of nature that their inherent beauty and delicacy can be appreciated by anyone without the aid of scholarly explanations or religious disciplines. That is why an engineer from Oklahoma could fall in love with them.

The argument that an Edo collection is a limited collection is just not valid. Edo art is an island in the art world: it does not connect to any other style, since it developed in near-total isolation from its neighbors. It is an entity in itself. Every time I have listened to suggestions that the collection should be "rounded out and expanded," the result has almost always been a mistake and usually a disaster.

Of course, Edo art does not consist only of painting; there are other forms to appreciate, such as ceramics, lacquer, and woodblock prints, not to mention Kabuki and flower arranging. But basically I was too late for the collectible ones among these; they were already sought after and therefore far out of my price range at that time. It was, and is, inconceivable to me that a woodblock print, one of many near-identical prints, should cost more than an original painting by the same artist.

The Edo paintings that I was able to purchase in the fifties and sixties were relatively inexpensive compared with paintings of earlier periods, and most certainly when compared with prices after 1971, when the Tokyo National Museum had its Jakuchū exhibition. But they were still beyond my means at the time. I was constantly in severe debt because of this art. I do not remember buying a painting that I felt I could easily afford, and every single one hurt. Each painting cost more than I could afford, but always just less than what would have been impossible for me to pay. Surprisingly, however, as soon as the decision was made to purchase and the painting arrived at my home, its cost ceased to interfere with the enjoyment. Never once have I hung or shown a painting because of its price; it was always because of its beauty.

The Shin'enkan Collection is limited to paintings for the reasons stated above. Also the collection is somewhat lacking in early paintings with famous names attached to them. There are many screens from this early period, but they are mostly unsigned, and, in any case, no one can argue about whether a painting is genuine if it has no signature. Then the argument can only be over its quality as a painting, and that argument is fun. I have never yet seen a signature that made a painting beautiful.

In the closed society of the times, several schools of painting kept their attachment to the outside world. Prominent among these were the Buddhist school, including Zen, and also Nagasaki school painting and later the scholar-painters of the Nanga school. These, although represented in the collection, are very limited in number, since they focused their philosophies upon reviving Chinese techniques. Nanga painters supposedly attempted to hide their ability to produce a fine brush stroke, in order to retain their "amateurism," and therefore they were ashamed of that skill I admire most.

In 1971 the Tokyo National Museum held an exhibition of the works of Itō Jakuchū. The exhibition was a huge success. The Japanese people had always appreciated Edo-period culture; it was only the paintings that they ignored. Bonsai, flower arranging, Kabuki, puppet theater, the tea ceremony, and many festivals were pure Edo; and the television and movie theaters were full of samurai epics. In modern times it was not until this Jakuchū exhibition that the general public had been treated to an exhibition of pure beauty and joy in nature in a national museum. The catalogues were sold out during the first week, and a second huge printing was sold out before the exhibit closed. Any magazine that appeared on the newsstands with a picture in it from the exhibition was immediately sold out, while the earlier months' issues remained available.

Two years later, probably because of the display of interest in Jakuchū, the Tokyo National Museum decided for its one hundredth anniversary to hold the now-famous Rimpa exhibition. From that day on, Edo painting of quality disappeared from the art market. For seven or eight years after the Jakuchū show, it was almost impossible for me to find paintings I liked. A few, yes, but none of great importance. During that period I concentrated on acquiring study piece paintings to use to explain the difference between the true paintings of an artist and those done by his students under his orders and instruction and those done as out-and-out fakes. These pieces have given the collection its depth; they form its heart and make it unique. Here is one place to study how an artist grows, to see copies of original paintings and then original paintings by those who produced the copies.

The most striking aspect of a painting, the aspect that catches the eye first, is usually the composition, and this

Itō Jakuchū
Figures, Birds, and Flowers
(detail, plate 65)

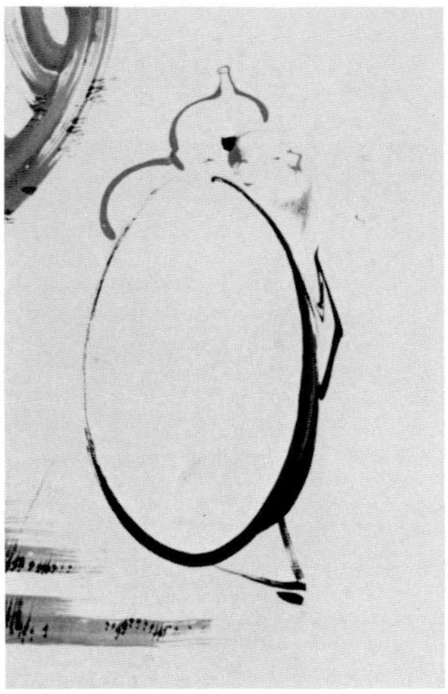

happens to be the easiest part of a painting to copy. The skill required to place a subject in the same place, to arrange its shape in the same form as its originator did, is trivial. What is not easy, what gives the copyist real trouble, is duplicating the skill that underlies the brushwork of the great Edo-period artists.

A great master's lines need never overlap since he has absolute control of his brush and the ink with which he has loaded it. It is easy to explain the difference between a poor imitator and a man whose life is his art, one who studied and practiced until he could control the flow of the ink, the pressure of the brush and its direction simultaneously. If an artist is capable of making a brush stroke that begins narrow and slightly dry, becomes more and more substantial, even massive, then dwindles away to a wispy thread—all so controlled that its direction forms an almost perfect ellipse — if an artist has the talent to produce such a line, why should he ever paint a lesser one? Once he has learned perfection (and he reaches this plateau before he ever completes a painting), why should he exhibit less? It takes no more time to produce a beautiful line than a sloppy one, only more skill. It does not take less effort to produce a clumsy painting than one with crispness, elegance, and a beauty that commands our attention, only less talent. There is no excuse for any single part of a painting to lack perfection if it is produced by an artist who has attained that level of ability.

The deficiencies of this kind of imitation can be easily spotted by simply seeing and knowing the actual ability of the artist being imitated. But what precautions can be taken against paintings that are not clumsy, that are beautiful in their own right, and that can fool even the experts when the original painting from which they were copied is not around for comparison?

Most artists of the Edo period learned to paint by imitating their masters. When the student approached the skill of the master, the paintings he produced would be very difficult to differentiate from those of the master if they were not indeed signed by the student. Sometimes, as mentioned, the master even signed the student's painting to bestow his highest compliment and approval. If the great artist liked a painting well enough to sign his own name to it, how can we as collectors not accept it also? What we do need to concern ourselves with, however, are the paintings that are fabricated with the sole purpose of defrauding the buyer.

One of the best ways to learn to distinguish between highly skilled fakes and the original works of a master is to first find the man capable of producing those fakes: someone who paints in the style of the master, seems to have the skill of the master, and yet is not known as an artist in his own right.

Jakuchū is as close to being original as it is likely for a Japanese artist to be. Being a loner, he was not obligated to the strict boundaries of any particular school and developed his own style, which evolved from his predecessors but in total is quite peculiar to him. The fact that he was not a part of a recognized school could help explain his obscurity during the time I was collecting him. He differed from his contemporaries, but not merely in order to be different; it was just his way of expressing fully what he saw in nature. His works were not, that is, deliberately "different": they were just more explicit and freer in form than those of his predecessors. His style is very powerful, its strength springing from a precise knowledge of his aims and a discipline devoted to expressing the nature of his subjects. He is driven by a desire to represent nature and the chicken and other animals that he knew so well and respected. He was known to have kept numerous fowls in his backyard and was constantly studying them. Jakuchū was a serious man, and his works resulted naturally from this seriousness. The priest Chikujo Daiten (1717–1801) wrote of him:

> Keiwa [Jakuchū] as a young man never liked studying. He had no talent in calligraphy. He was hardly versed in anything that can be called an accomplishment. All the pleasure of music and sensuous experience that an ordinary man would seek did not at all attract him. All the wealth, profit, and success that dazzle the people of this capital he totally ignored. He did not even cast one glance at them. By nature he would prefer to be alone, exhausting himself all day long in painting. Thirty years of immersion in painting was to him like one full day.*

His major works, although often seemingly wild in composition, have a precision and a premeditated design that are virtually architectural. His paintings were seldom subtle or mysterious. They concentrated instead on bringing out the inherent nature and essence of the object. A great many paintings are going around that bear Jakuchū's seal, done in sumi (ink monochrome) style with a humorous, carefree attitude. Some of them are very good paintings. But the one argument one can always make against them is that the subject, usually a chicken, is a caricature of itself; it does not take itself seriously. The brush strokes are good, the composition is fine, but the pictures are not serious in relation to nature; the chickens' feet are only there, they are not gripping for support, they are not even holding on, let alone able to bear the weight of the rooster. Could a man so dedicated to nature and the true essence of his subject paint such paintings? Could a man so serious about painting ever produce less than his best?

One answer to this peculiar type of painting (especially to the extremely good examples) which lack the "signature" of Jakuchū in the painting style itself but do have his seal in the lower corner, is that they could be by a painter named Jakuen. He seems to have mastered his teacher's brush, but not his preoccupation with representing nature. Jakuen seems to have been much more interested in composition than in accuracy, in technique than in reality. He paints

*Quoted from an article on Jakuchū by Yoshiaki Shimizu

roosters with feathers coming out of other feathers instead of from the body of the rooster. One of his paintings shows a rooster, beautifully drawn with an imaginative use of space, but the snow on the limb is not even disturbed by the weight of the rooster.

Why would an artist who had worked so long and arduously to develop the same skills as a great master not be content to sign his own name? Why would his own skills not be sufficient to sell a painting? In Jakuen's case he was probably not a professional painter but only a priest working with an unselfish master whom he watched and imitated without having been formally taught or instructed in the mysteries of why the master painted in that way. In his case the copies were innocent and probably even initiated by Jakuchū. But other cases may be less innocent.

It is generally believed that the talent to copy or imitate Edo painting did not extend far into the Meiji era. Japan, after Commander Perry arrived with his black ships of iron, which moved without sails, seemed to set aside those things particularly Japanese in its mad rush to absorb the Western technology that had been denied them through the years of isolation. Artists blindly adopted Western perspective and shading; besides, the newly imported oil pigments could now be used to cover mistakes. High technical skills that took a supreme effort and long years to perfect would no longer be required. How nice it would be if indeed we did not have to be concerned with Meiji fakes. But we do. Artists working in the Japanese style and taste were no longer appreciated, but a few continued to do so, refusing to abandon the past and doggedly striving still to produce perfection in the same way as before. But they probably found that there was no demand for their product. Here could be the source for highly skilled, complex forgeries.

Look closely at the scroll painting portraying a tiger in narrow format (plate 50), ignoring its pedigree and date. Whose style does it immediately call forth? Could this be Maruyama Ōkyo? If it were signed Ōkyo, would you accept it? Most scholars have been fooled by it when the real signature was hidden. And, most amazing of all, it is dated to the thirty-first year of Meiji, or 1898. This should be terrifying to all collectors of Edo painting.

There are a great number of "Ōkyo paintings" around which do not live up to our expectations of him. Ōkyo had immense capabilities and skill, and certainly many of the paintings bearing his signature should not be blamed on him. His reputation should not be diminished by those paintings that contain his name but not the quality expected of such a great master.

Could this tiger painting then be the key to the source of some of these numerous paintings bearing the imprint of Ōkyo without quite the perfection that Ōkyo is known to have possessed? It is signed Ōyō, and as noted, dated Meiji 31 (1898).

Since Ōyō is virtually unknown, could he possibly have painted only one painting in his lifetime and then died young before he could become famous in his own right? Could he have studied the style of his ancestors, made the supreme effort to learn this competence, and then just vanished? Not at all. We have another tiger (plate 52) which dispels such notions, and this one is dated Meiji 43 (1910), almost within our own lifetime. This means that his painting career lasted at least thirteen years, and unless all he ever did was paint tigers in narrow format, there must be a lot of Ōyōs around and probably, unfortunately, with Ōkyo's name on them.

Let us look again at these tigers, ignoring the actual signatures. If these paintings had instead borne the signature of Maruyama Ōkyo, would we have questioned that they were his?

First, are we blinded by the clever composition? Who else but a great master could conjure up such an original and striking idea? But composition, as we suggested earlier, is the easiest part of a painting to imitate. Cleverness is often used to cover up a lack of technical skill. It is how the artist executes this composition that matters.

Looking closely, we find that each individual hair on the tiger in Ōyō's work is painted rather coarsely. Only on the bridge of the nose do they form any pattern; the other hairs are rather repetitious. This alone is not enough to cast doubt. Only one thing does, and it is not something the painter did, but something he did not do. There is not a single stroke of the brush—in the hairs, in the facial expression, or in the claws—that any simple craftsman could not have made. Nowhere in the painting can there be seen a line that makes the viewer feel a great master accomplished it. Remember that fact: it is the only clue that could raise the specter of doubt.

To repeat, a clumsy painting can be disclosed as a fake by what the artist does; a good painting can become suspicious by what the artist does not do.

This fact becomes even more apparent when these paintings are placed beside the one that probably inspired them (plate 51). The most vivid impression now is how flat the new painting makes the two previous tigers appear. The Ōkyo tiger emerges from between the confines of the silk brocade and seems to project beyond its borders.

The hairs now become fur, and there is no sign of the coarseness that was apparent in the Meiji paintings.

The brush strokes in the claws are magnificent, and those of the nose give it a crispness and a lifelike feeling.

The expression of the two Ōyōs becomes blank, while the other one's eyes seem to glow as they glare at the viewer.

Ōkyo was indeed a master of realism and certainly knew how to handle depth. The tiger in plate 51 shows a tremendous improvement in this area.

The two paintings that originally appeared to be perhaps by the hand of a master simply fall apart. They become what they deserve to be: products of an intent to imitate a previous creation without adding anything. A real artist never tries simply to reproduce but always to improve on what went before. Once he stops attempting to make a painting better, to improve it, to add that little something he has to offer, then he ceases to be an artist.

Fortunately, because Ōyō used his own name in signing the two paintings, it has not been necessary to disprove either of them as a painting by Ōkyo. The question was only: What would we have said if the two paintings had had Ōkyo's name on them? Individually, they would have been difficult to question. When we place them together and realize that they are absolutely identical, then, no matter how competent they may be, it is apparent that a great artist did not paint them, for no one with the abilities we have discussed would ever reproduce identically a painting he had done before. There must be significant changes somewhere within the picture: no real artist reproduces himself line for line.

Now, do you feel you can tell a real Ōkyo from an Ōyō? The problem is, who can be positive that the painting in plate 51 is in fact really an Ōkyo? It has Ōkyo's name on it, but all that is certain, all we actually *know*, is that it is far, far superior to those two tigers signed Ōyō.

The Shin'enkan Collection was assembled with emphasis on the effect of the art alone. Quality of beauty and precision of line were dominant, consistent threads throughout. It was collected free from outside teachings, so no prevailing influences or tastes of the time affected it. My lack of ability to speak or read Japanese was certainly an advantage; it forced me to select by the artist's skill, not by his name. Even today, when I find a painting I never ask who painted it; for when a painting has quality, a great artist produced it.

I may have given the impression that in my early collecting days no one appreciated Edo painting but me. This is of course an extreme simplification and exaggeration. One of the exceptions was a scholar, Miss Yoshi Shirahata, who, on retiring from the Kyoto National Museum to take up teaching, said, "Now that I am no longer required to be the one to give permission to export, I would like to meet the American from Oklahoma who is buying all these beautiful Edo paintings." We met by Lake Biwa and drank sake together and became good friends. She is the one who explained to me that Itō Jakuchū once had a studio where he painted some of his greatest paintings. He called it Shin'enkan, the "house of the faraway heart."

Thanks to her, many of Jakuchū's paintings will be preserved in a new Shin'enkan: a house for losing your heart.

by Joe D. Price

A PAVILION FOR JAPANESE ART AT THE LOS ANGELES COUNTY MUSEUM OF ART

There has never really been a museum designed just for Japanese paintings, only replicas of Western museums, where all art competes for wall space. Twelve years ago I asked Bruce Goff to design a public museum for the Shin'enkan Collection. There were no museums as we know them in the Edo period and thus no earlier successful solutions to provide inspiration. To create a building for the display of Edo art, an entirely new concept had to be developed. What makes the art most beautiful in the space: that was the most important consideration. Together we worked backward from the ordinary architectural design process by designating the art itself as the client.

Japanese paintings of the Edo period were designed to be the only decoration in a room. No painting of the period ever had to compete with any other; and since it did not have to compete, it could be as simple and delicate as the artist's skills permitted. This delicacy makes it imperative that the paintings be displayed without a covering of glass and be illuminated by a soft light like the light that passes through the paper walls of old Japan.

Mr. Goff was not limited to the use of native Japanese materials or traditional shapes, and after eight years, just shortly before his death in 1982, he completed the design for the Pavilion for Japanese Art at the Los Angeles County Museum of Art. By working backward, by starting with the individual painting and proceeding from there outward, the viewer becomes secondary, his convenience a minor concern; the shape of the building just followed the dictates of the art.

In the Pavilion for Japanese Art the viewer will see the paintings first from a distance and will be able to see each one alone. The painting will be proteced by space, and glass will not be necessary. There will be no bright spotlights to shine on the paintings, for electricity was not in existence at the time they were painted; therefore the viewer will still be able to have those exhilarating moments when the sun passes behind a cloud, the gold becoming subdued, and then bursting forth again as the cloud moves on. The viewer will be able to enjoy the painting as the artist who created it intended it to be seen.

The building is divided basically into two parts: the display area, which is subservient to the art and in which the art will be perpetually exhibited in frequent rotation,

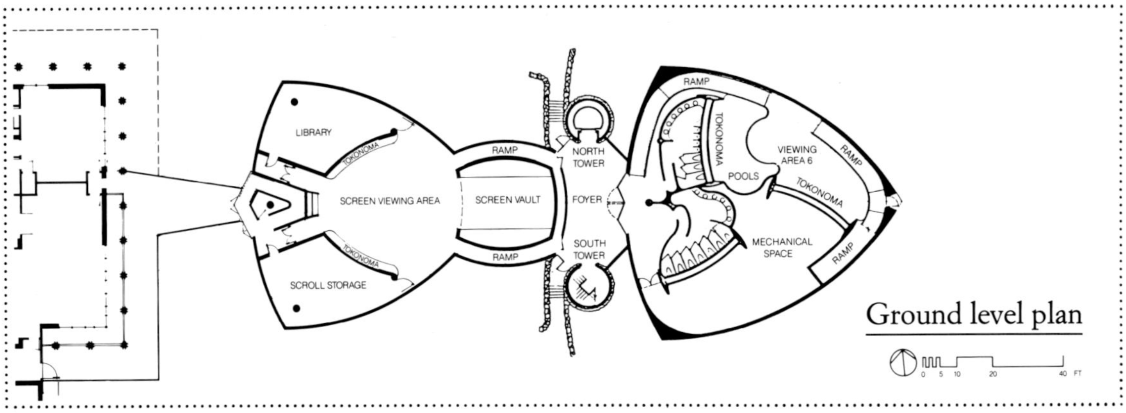

Ground level plan

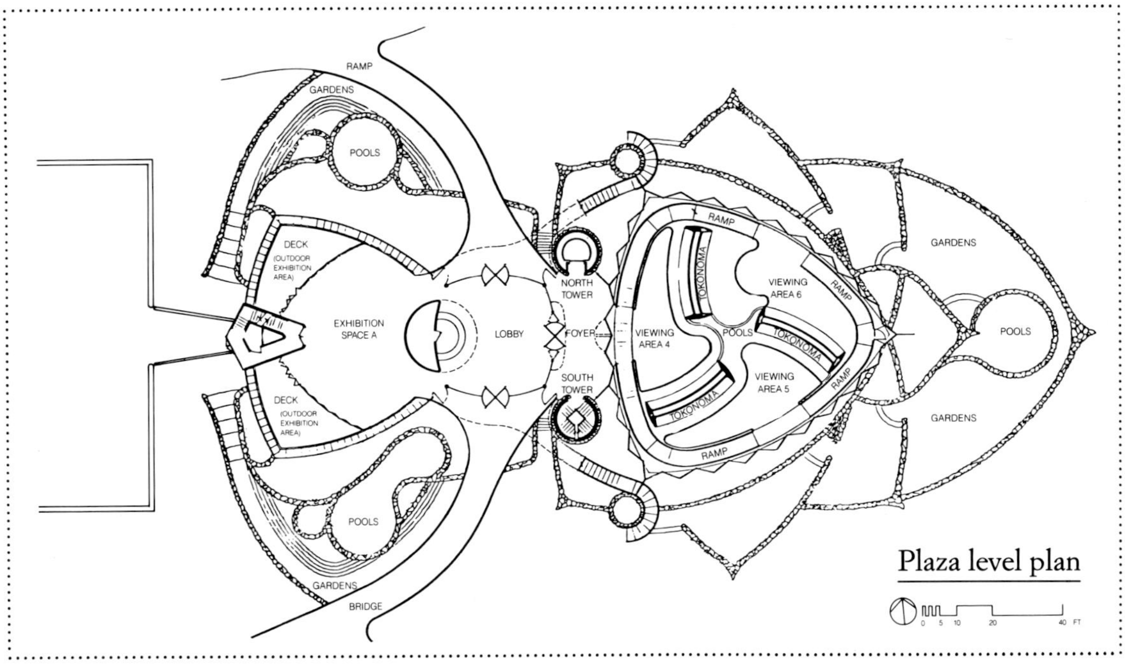

Plaza level plan

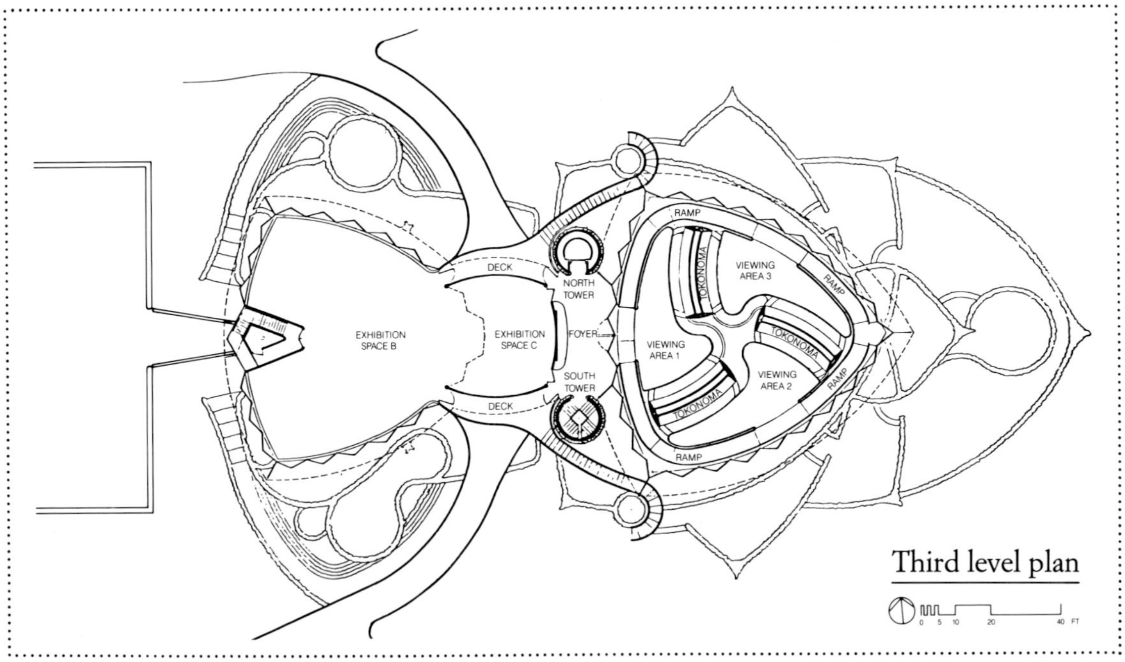

Third level plan

and a storage and study room, where the paintings will be available for intense scrutiny not possible while they are on display.

The actual function of the building is relatively simple. The viewer will take an elevator to the top viewing area and will walk down through six platforms, each four feet lower than the preceding one. They are connected by gentle ramps in the rounded corners, but in the viewing areas the floor is level. Three freestanding, curved structures will contain the paintings. These are separated from the platforms by open space for the protection of the art. A pair of six-fold screens can be shown on one side of the protected structure, generally the side curving toward the viewer, and these screens can be seen from as far away as sixty feet. On the reverse side of this curving structure, seen from the next platform, which is four feet lower than the preceding one, movable partitions can be inserted to form separate tokonomalike spaces. Because of the backward bend of the overall curving shape, each scroll hanging in its space can be seen as an isolated painting. Five or six scrolls can hence be placed in this way, and yet each one will have its privacy.

If the viewer descends all six floors–remember that they are four feet below each other and that as he completes the first three he has descended twelve feet and is now underneath the topmost floor–the sixth viewing area is a "grotto," surrounded by water, where the viewer can sit and rest and contemplate a golden screen reflected in the water.

The roofs of the structure are suspended from cables that are strung from round columns. This method allows the interior of the building to be virtually free of obstructions. It also allows the application of a nonsupporting skin of translucent walls, duplicating the light that would be obtained through paper shoji doors. The light will vary with the seasons and change with the weather, and the viewer will have the opportunity to experience this change.

Naturally, in this setting the art is to be experienced, not studied. To scrutinize the paintings in detail, the scholar must come when the art is not on display (there will be twelve changes a year). A seminar room, opening onto the storage vault, contains the screens. Since most screens are in pairs, provision is made to store the two halves on opposite sides of the vault, so if requested by scholars each half of the pair can be simply pulled out and opened without the danger of lifting or carrying. Scroll storage is in a separate room to the left of the vault; and provision for a library, to the right. Paintings shown in storage will therefore be seen at their best by those people who love them the most.

It is my desire that the paintings of the Edo period be seen in quiet contemplation, unobstructed, in a setting that illuminates their beauty under conditions as close as possible to those that the painters intended. I believe that this art, when seen under these conditions, will be recognized at last as among the world's most beautiful visual experiences and one of the finest creations of man.

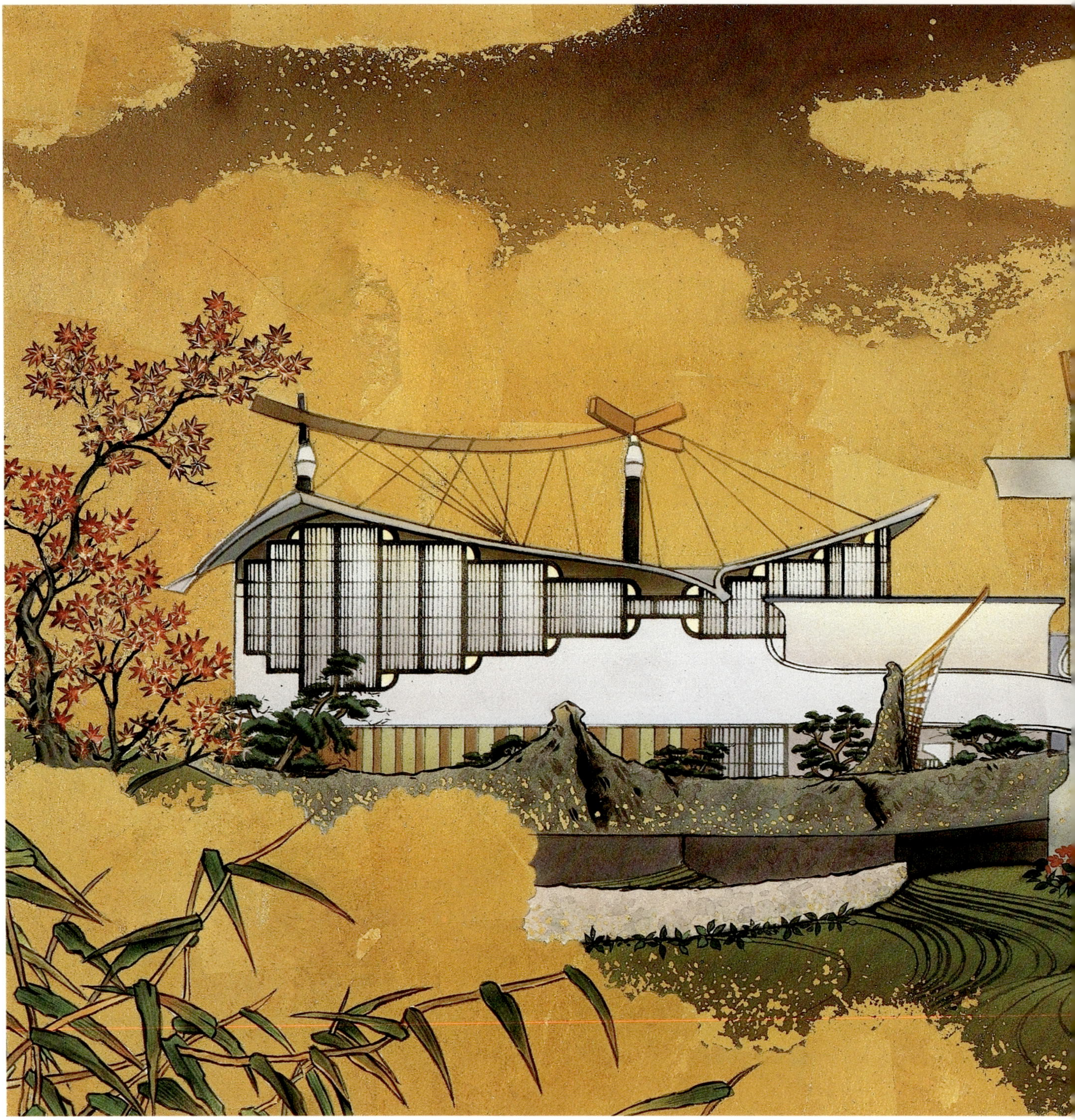

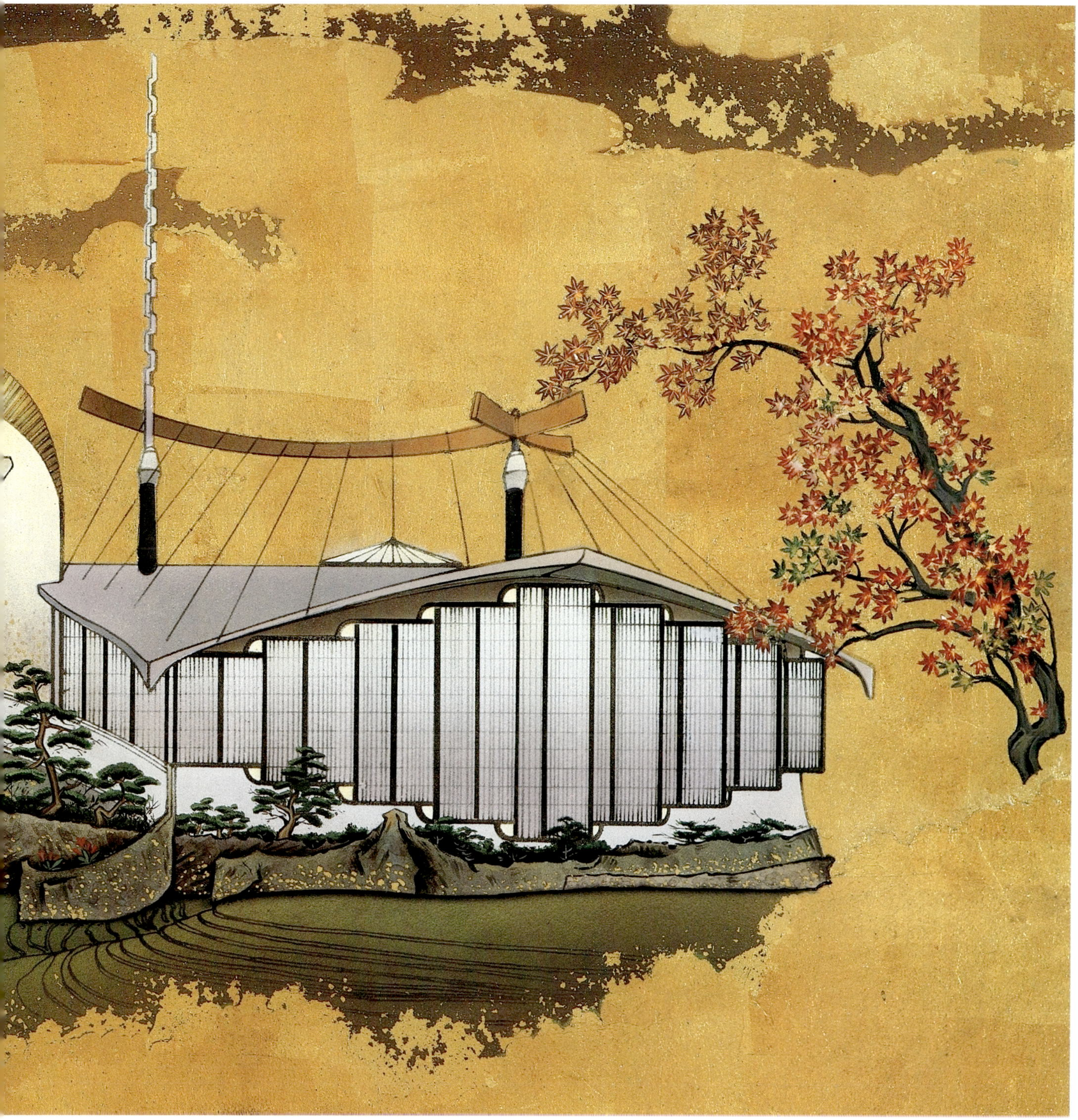

The Pavilion for Japanese Art at the Los Angeles County Museum of Art

Decorative, Genre, and Narrative Screens

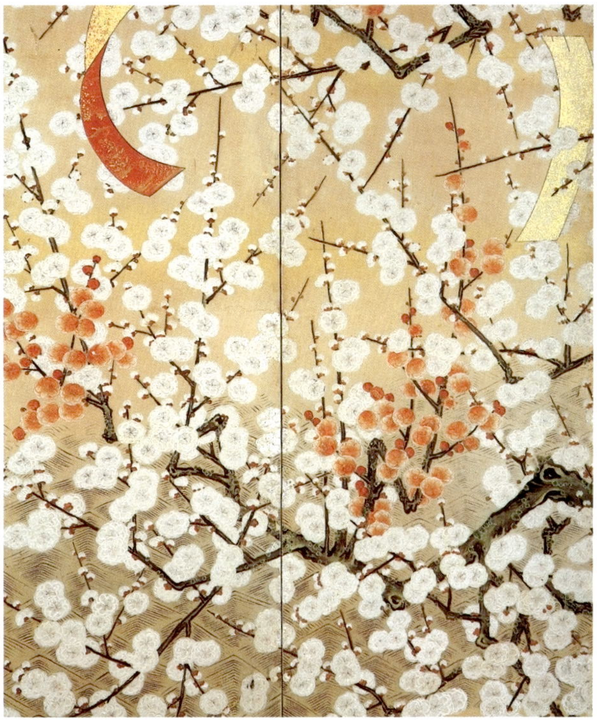

The Japanese word for folding screen, *byōbu*, literally means "barrier against the wind." A pair of folding screens not only cut the drafts in winter but served the all-season function of creating a private space in which ceremonies, poetry gatherings, conversations, weddings, and births could take place. Byōbu were also used at outdoor festivals and cherry blossom-viewing parties. It is this architectural use of the folding screen as a freestanding, movable partition or partial enclosure that makes it fundamentally different from other Japanese painting formats.

Most folding screens consist of six panels, although they are sometimes of two, four, eight, or ten panels. They vary in height from about six feet to the two-foot "pillow screens" that were placed on the tatami mat around a sleeper's futon bedding. Folding screens were usually painted in pairs, but single screens are not unknown.

Birds, Pines, and Camellias beside a Waterfall (plate 1) is the earliest painting in this exhibition, the sole pre-Edo-period work, and an important example of late-Muromachi-period (1392–1568) ink painting in the style of its greatest exponent, Kanō Motonobu (1476–1559). Rapid calligraphic brushwork and the dynamic rendering of the pine and cascading water create a circular movement that takes place almost entirely in the foreground.

The succeeding Momoyama period (1568–1615) is celebrated as the golden age of screen painting, both for the boldness of Momoyama design and for the lavish use of gold leaf and dust. This is reflected here in an early Edo-period painting, *Pheasants amid Bamboo and a Blossoming Plum Tree* (plate 2), in which a tremendous flowering plum, almost pinioned between three vertical bamboo, twists up and out of the picture frame and then reenters to extend across the entire length of the massive eight-fold screen. In Momoyama and Edo bird-and-flower screens, clouds of gold leaf helped to integrate shallow pictorial space and strong right-to-left movement: *Cranes* (plate 3), *Birds and Flowers of the Four Seasons* (anonymous, plate 4), and *Birds and Flowers of the Four Seasons* (Unkoku Tōteki, plate 5). Gold leaf also served to brighten otherwise gloomy interiors.

Because most screens were made in pairs, the artist often created a contrast or tension between the two screens. This frequently takes the form of a seasonal progression (plates 4 and 5) or a contrast between stillness and movement, in which, for example, a flock of cranes are shown quietly resting and feeding in the right screen and noisily flying off in the left (plate 3). The scene shown may be a continuous panoramic view of the four seasons (plate 4) extending across all twelve panels of both screens or a single, crystalline moment in time: *Ginkgo Trees and Fish Trap* (plate 7). Another approach is to pack the surface of both screens with a riot of blossoms; in the case of *Red and White Blossoming Plum Trees* (plate 8), plum blossoms in celebration of the advent of spring.

Folding screens, with their wide expanse, are ideal for the depiction of narrative. An entire story may be told in a series of individual scenes (*Shutendōji Ogre Tale*, plate 9), or one incident alone may be illustrated (*Tale of Genji: Battle of the Carts*, plate 12).

Genre scenes are another favored subject, either by themselves or as background to another event, such as the procession of a *daimyō* (lord) and his retinue (*A Daimyō's Procession through Seta*, plate 11). A separate category of genre paintings on screens is that of Shintō shrine festivals. In *Kasuga Wakamiya Festival* (plate 10), the only known screen depiction of this famous festival, the procession is shown rhythmically winding its way across both screens before entering the shrine at the upper left of the right screen.

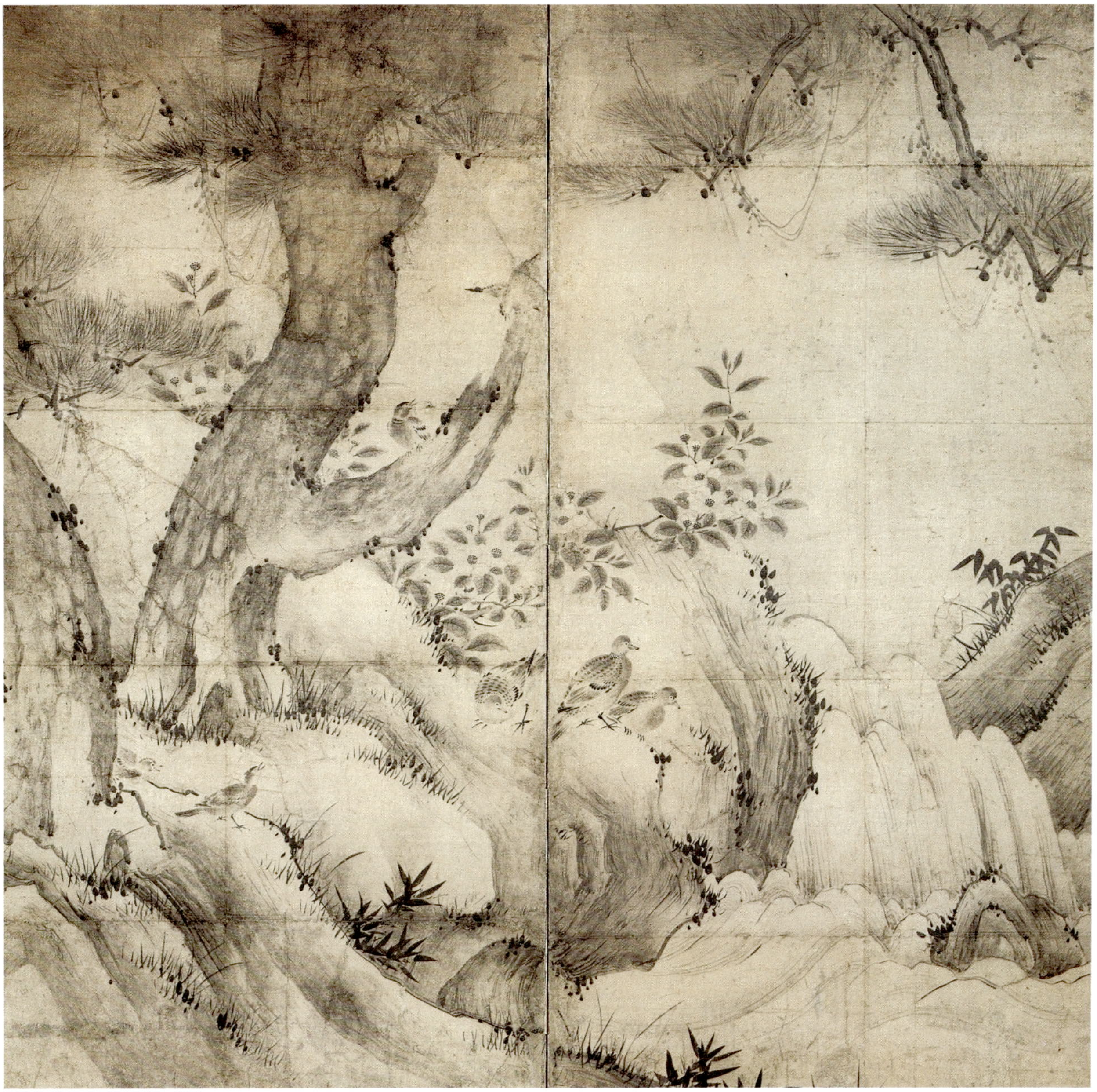

1
Kanō Motonobu (1476 – 1559)
Birds, Pines, and Camellias beside a Waterfall
Two-fold screen
Ink on paper
170.2 x 172 cm
(67 x 67¾ in.)

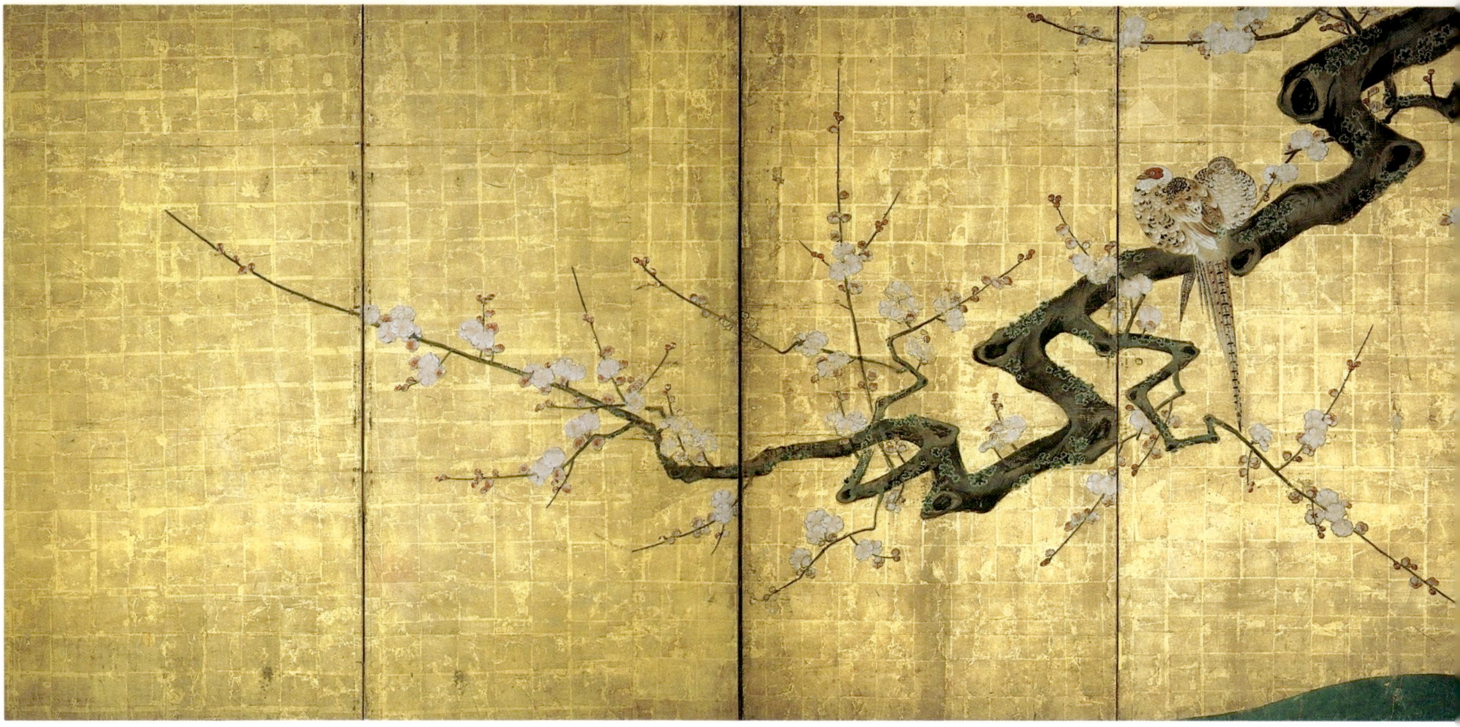

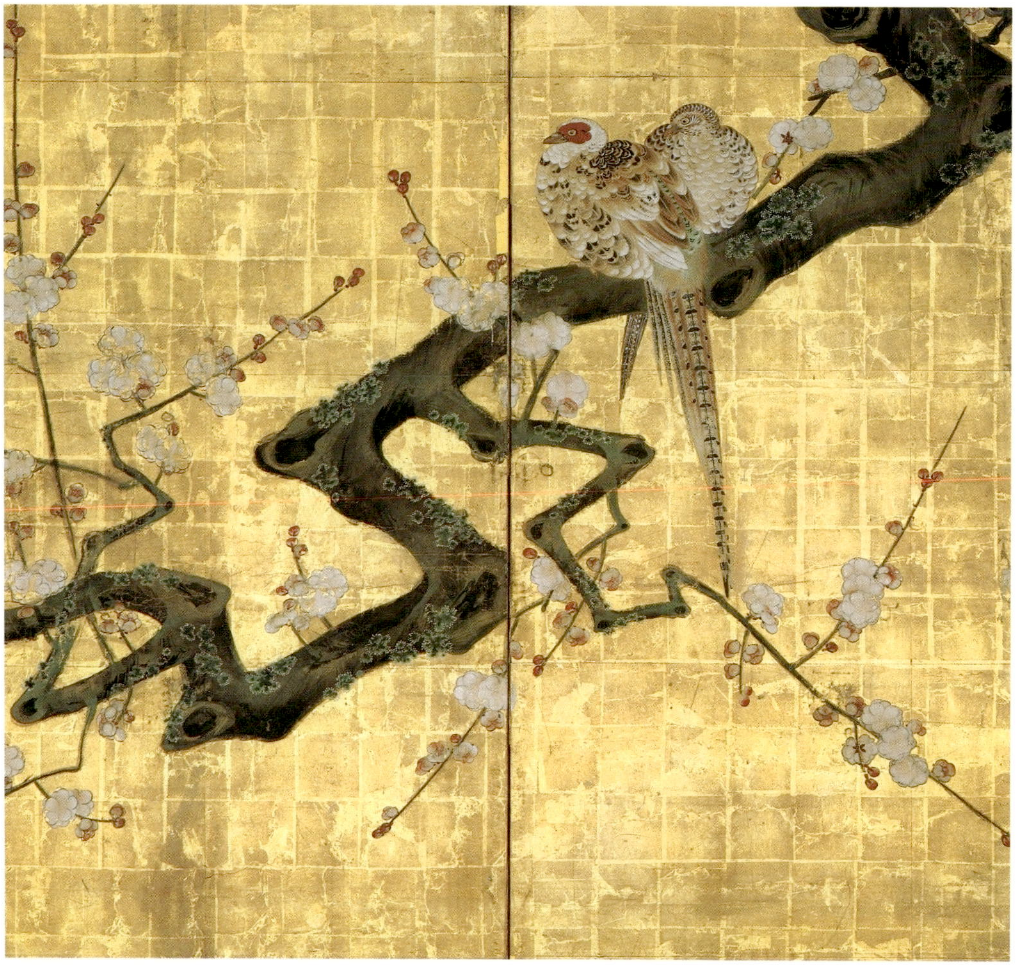

2
Anonymous
Pheasants amid Bamboo and a Blossoming Plum Tree
Seventeenth century
Eight-fold screen
Color with gold ground on paper
167.8 x 703.2 cm
(66$\frac{1}{16}$ x 276$\frac{13}{16}$ in.)

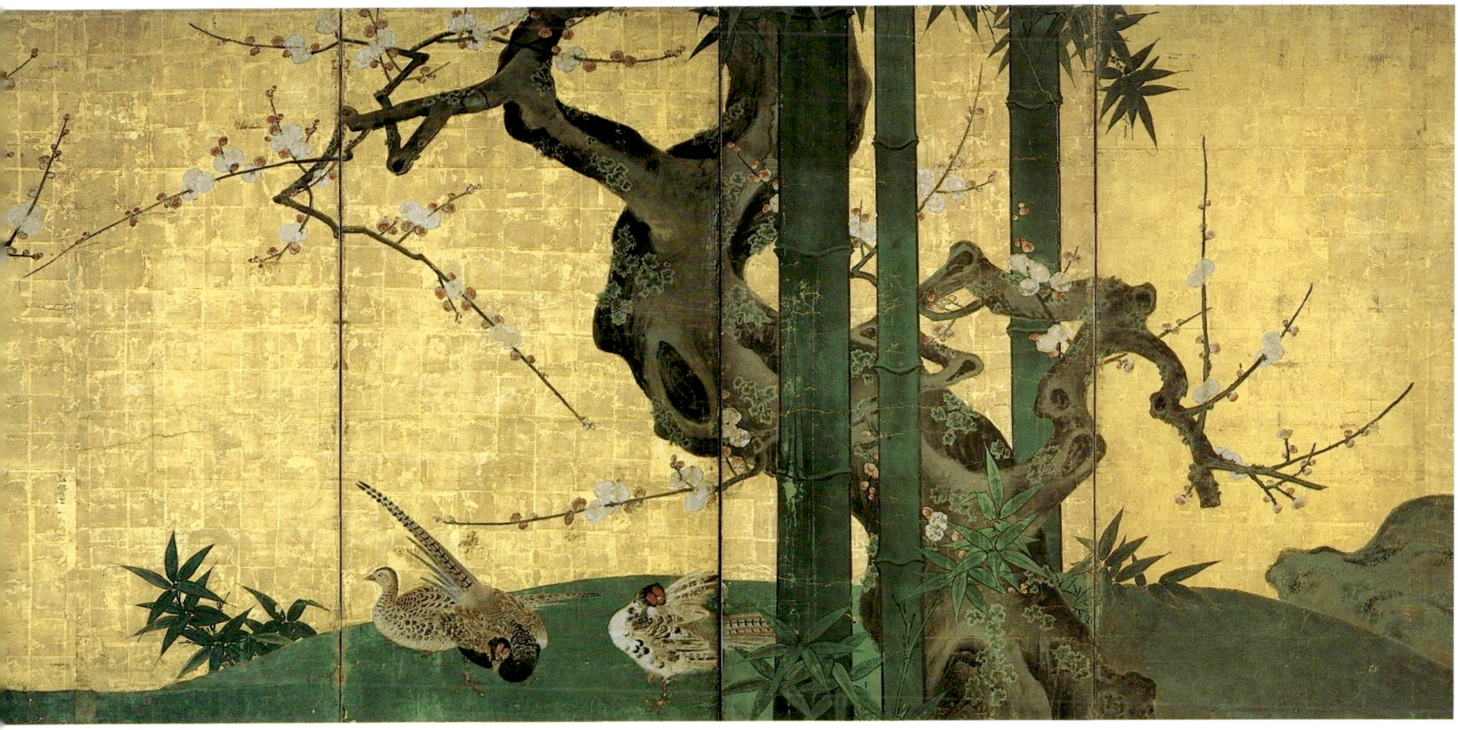

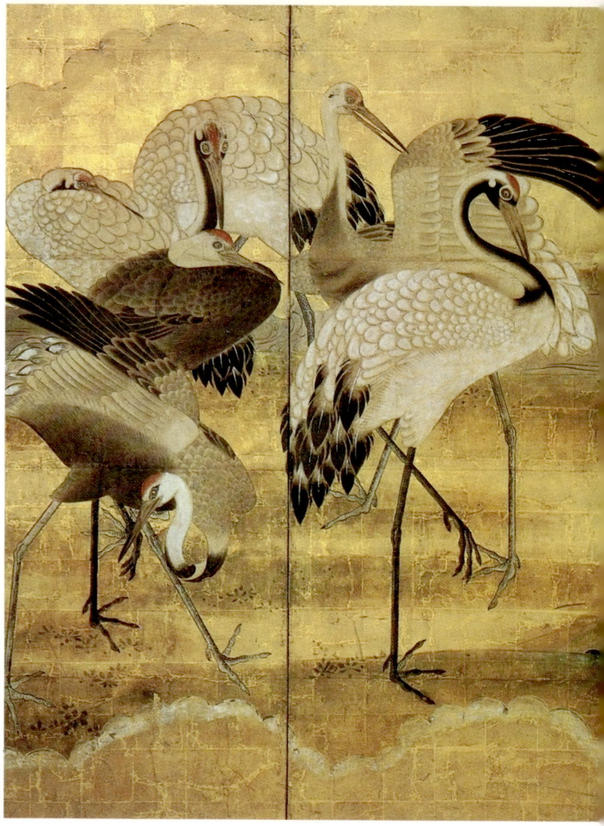

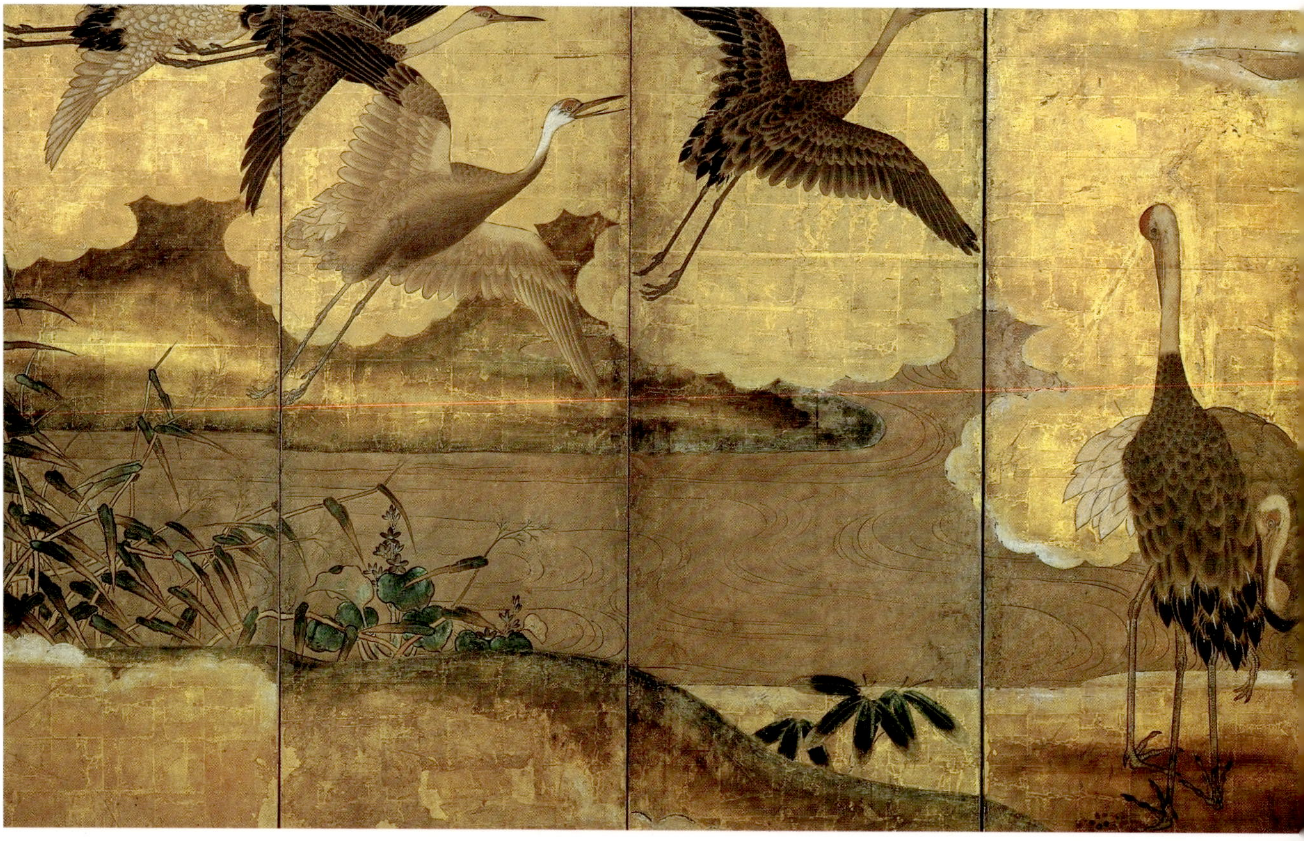

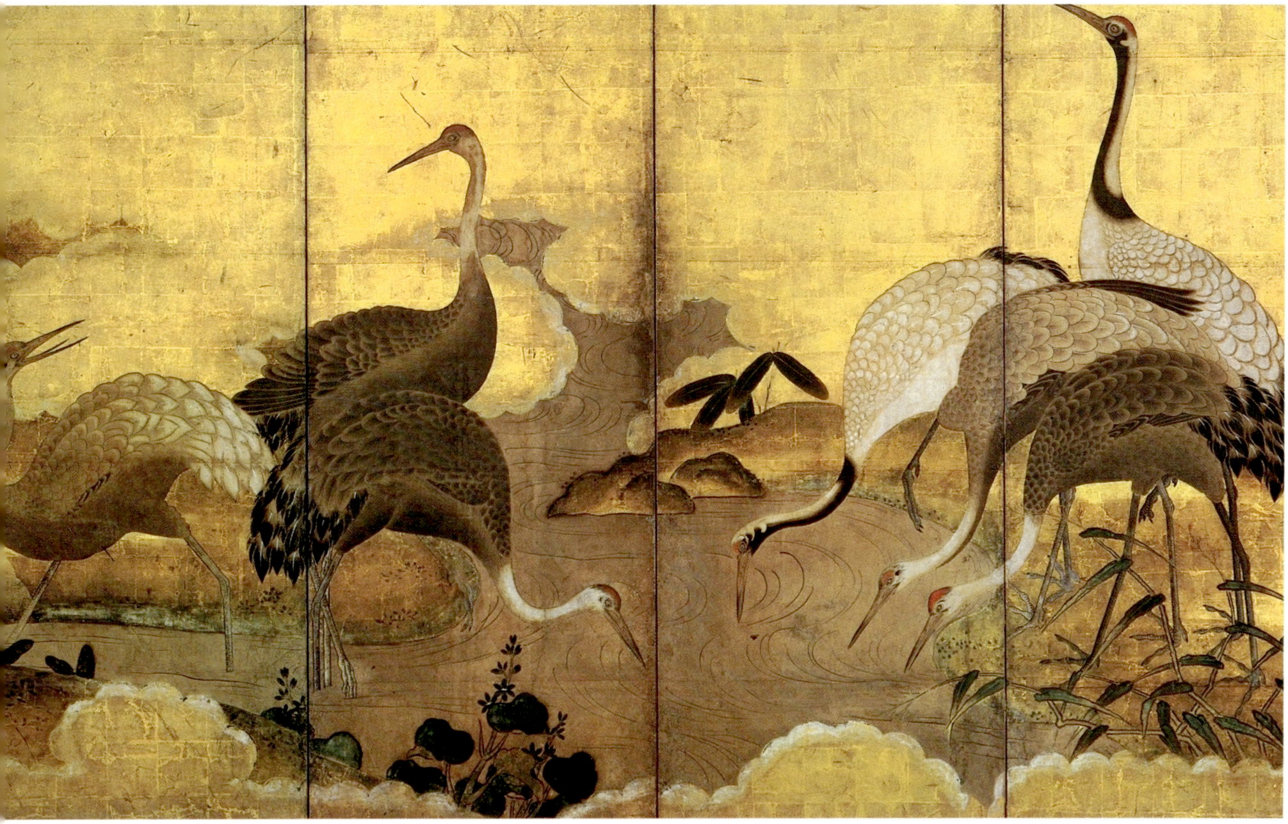

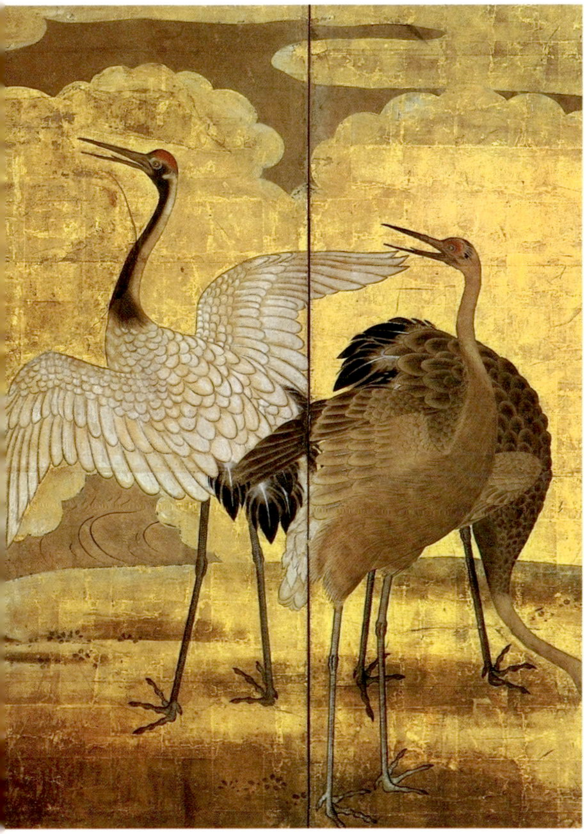

3
Anonymous
Cranes
Seventeenth century
Pair of six-fold screens
Color with gold ground on paper
Each 147.1 x 353.8 cm
($57\frac{15}{16}$ x $139\frac{3}{8}$ in.)

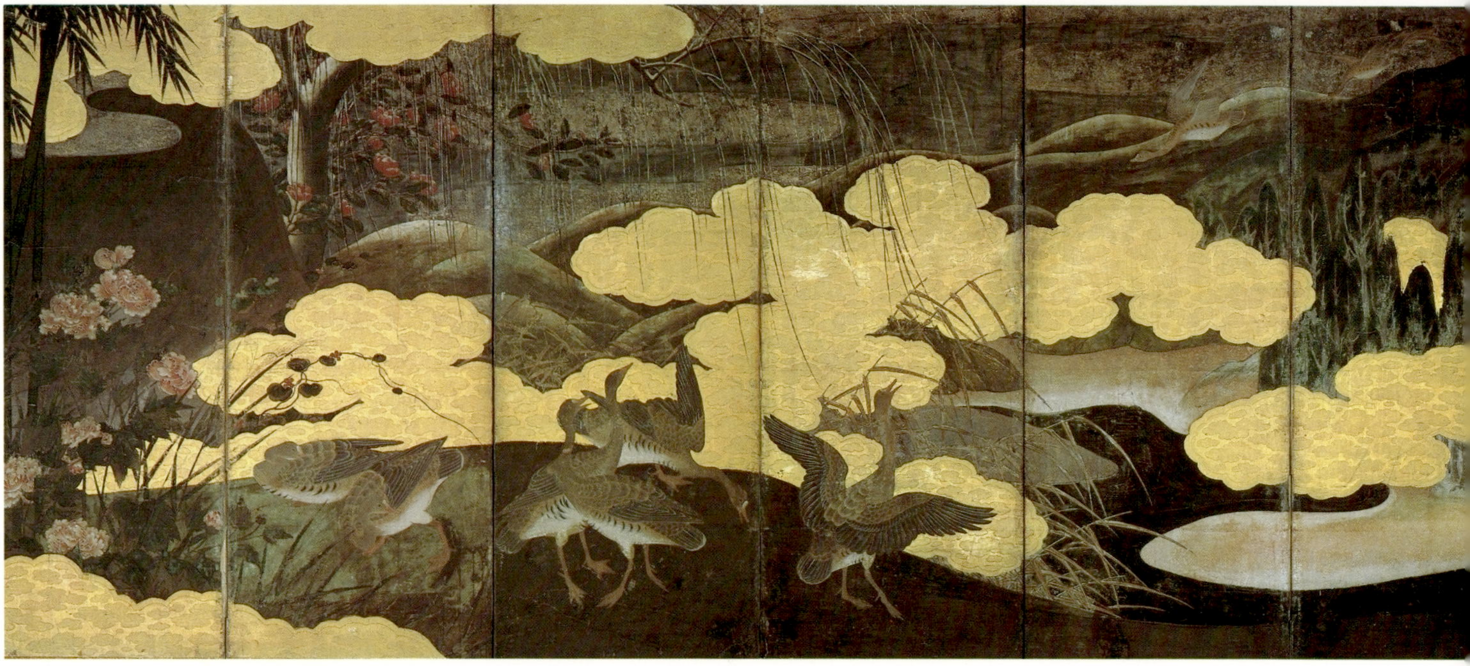

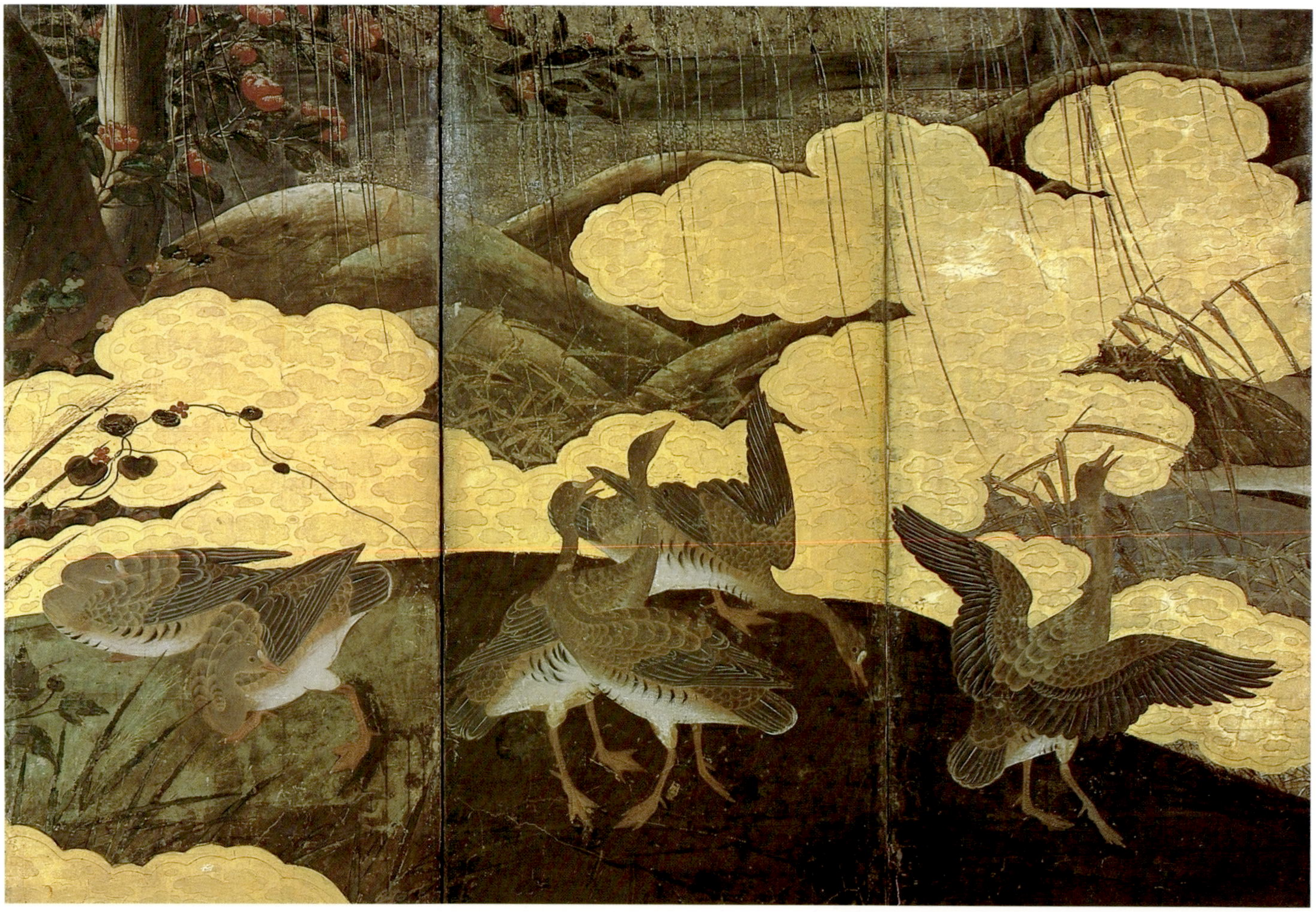

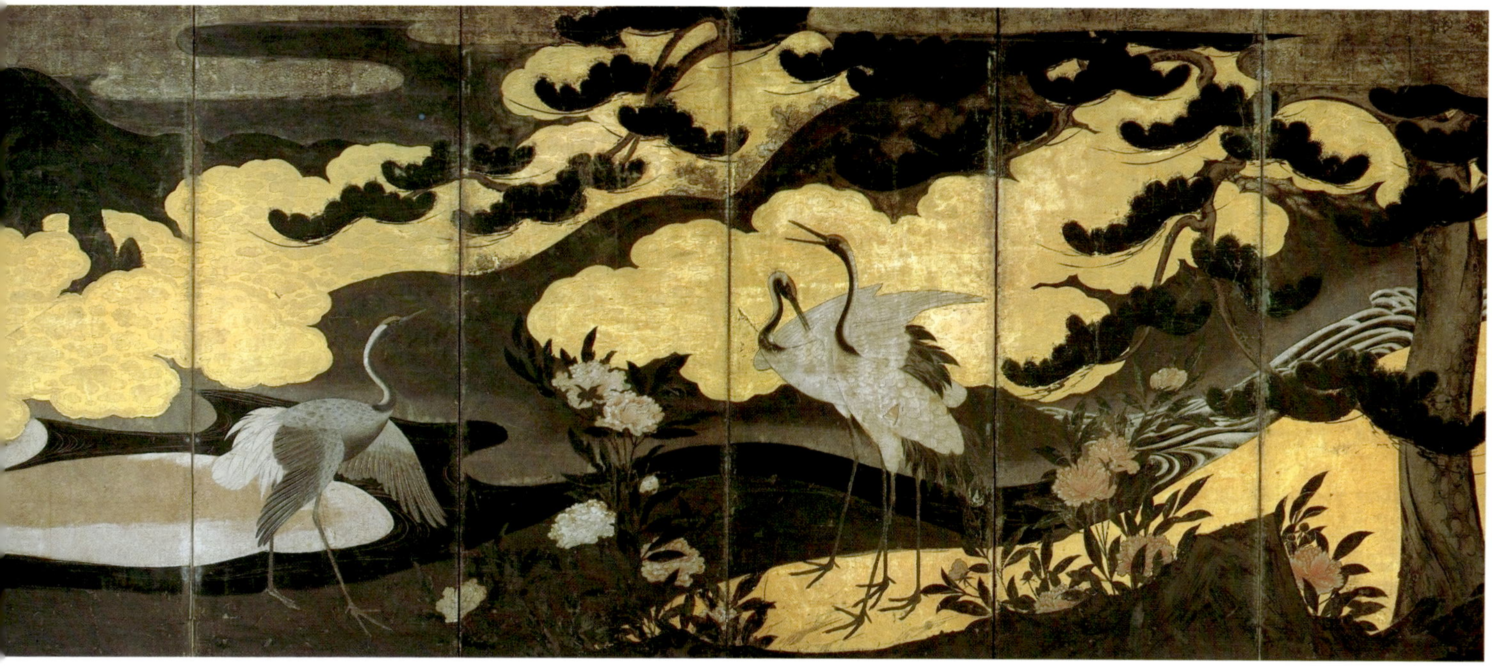

4
Anonymous
Birds and Flowers
of the Four Seasons
Seventeenth century
Pair of six-fold screens
Color on paper
Each 151.6 x 364.0 cm
($59^{11}/_{16}$ x $143^{3}/_{8}$ in.)

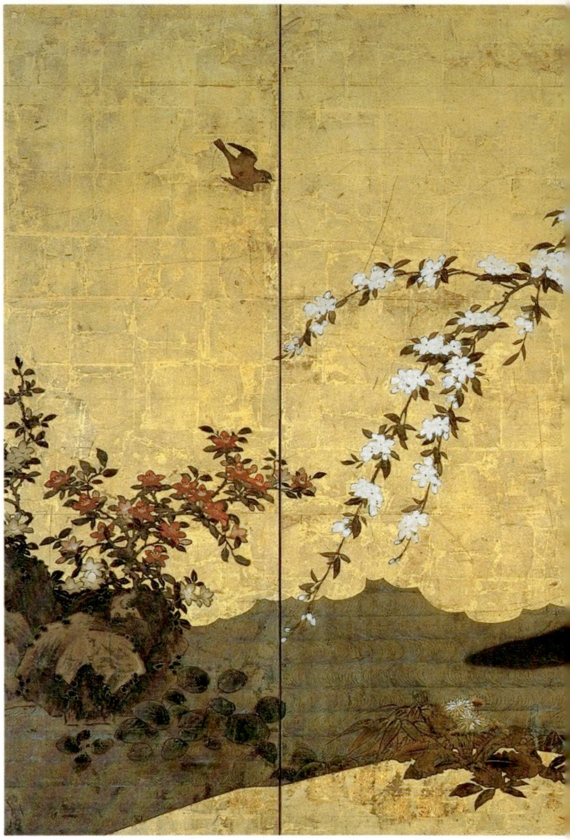

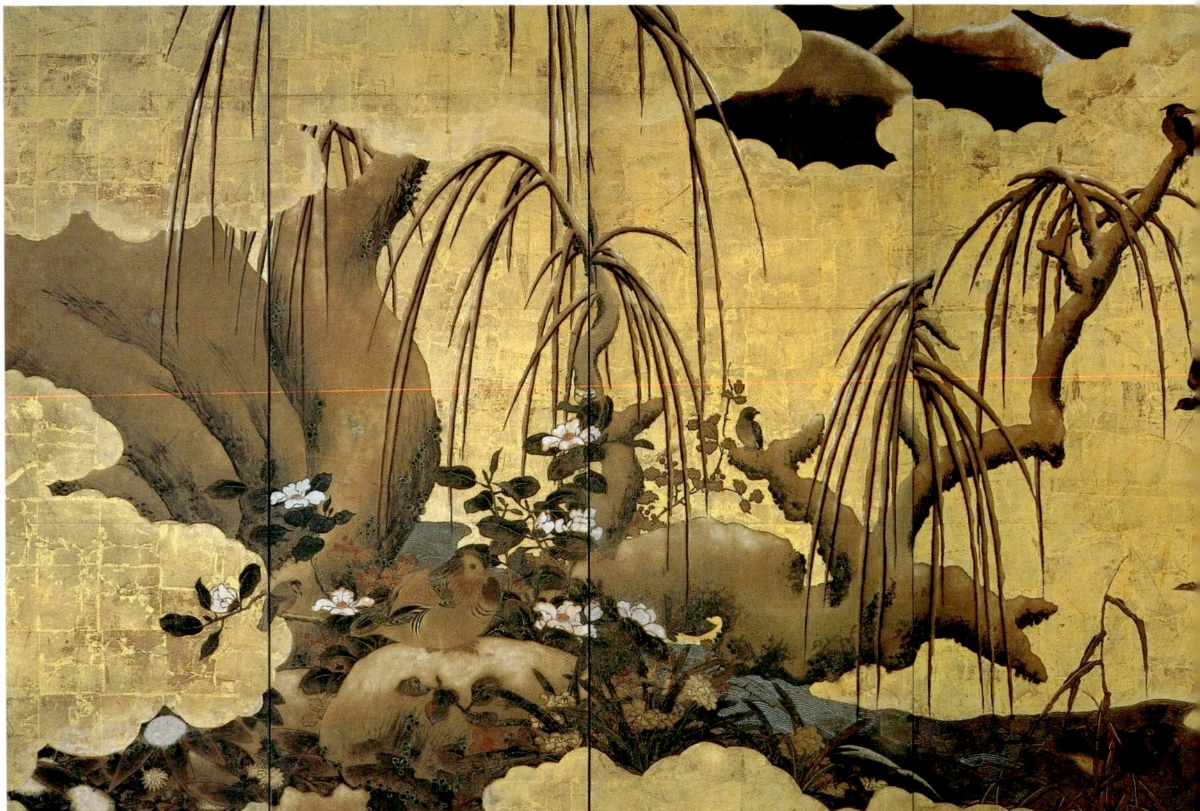

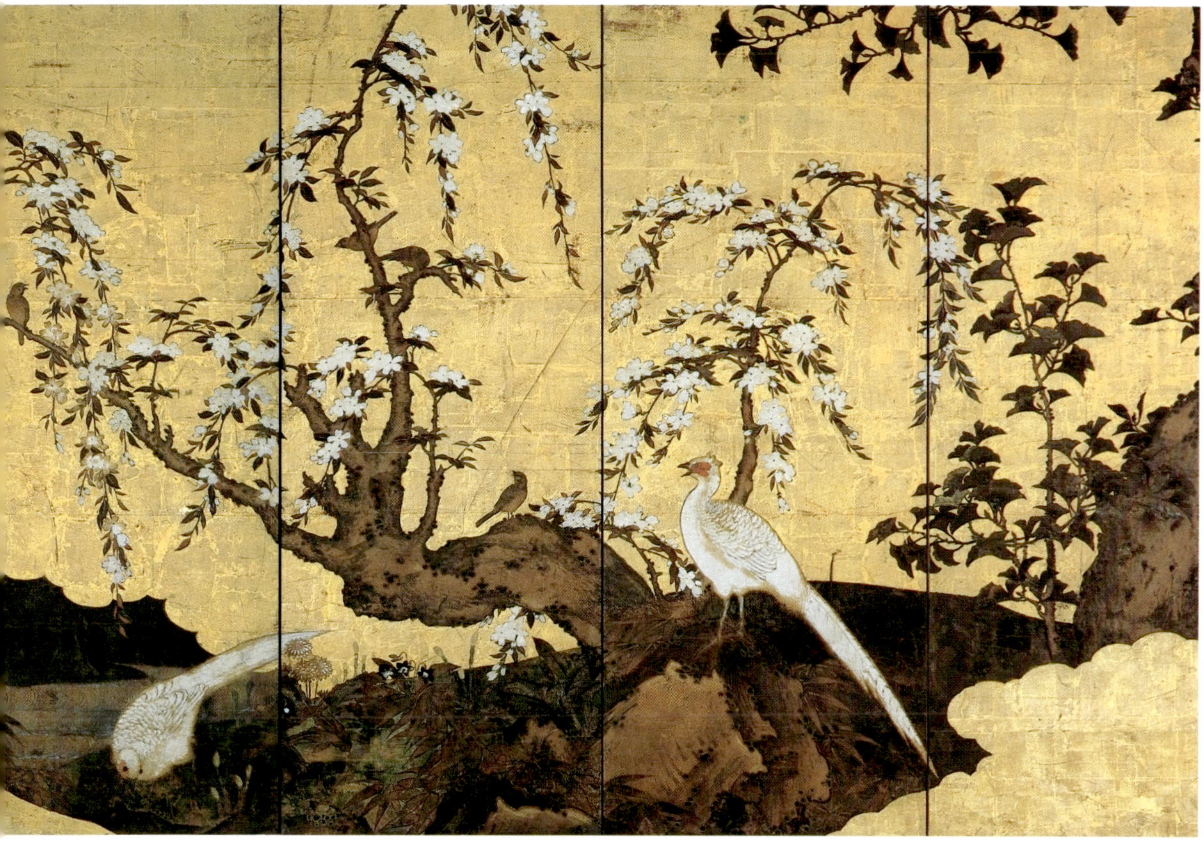

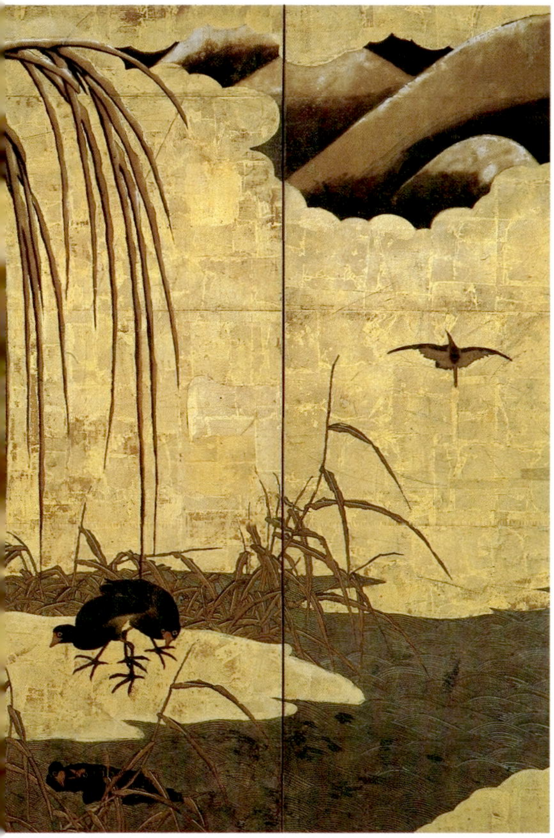

5
Unkoku Tōteki (d. 1626)
Birds and Flowers
of the Four Seasons
Pair of six-fold screens
Color with gold ground on paper
Each 129.6 x 295.2 cm
(51 x 116⅛ in.)

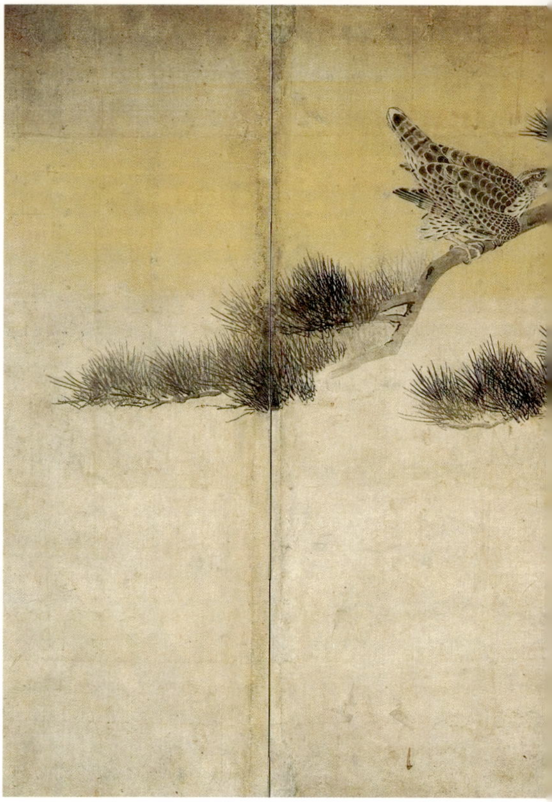

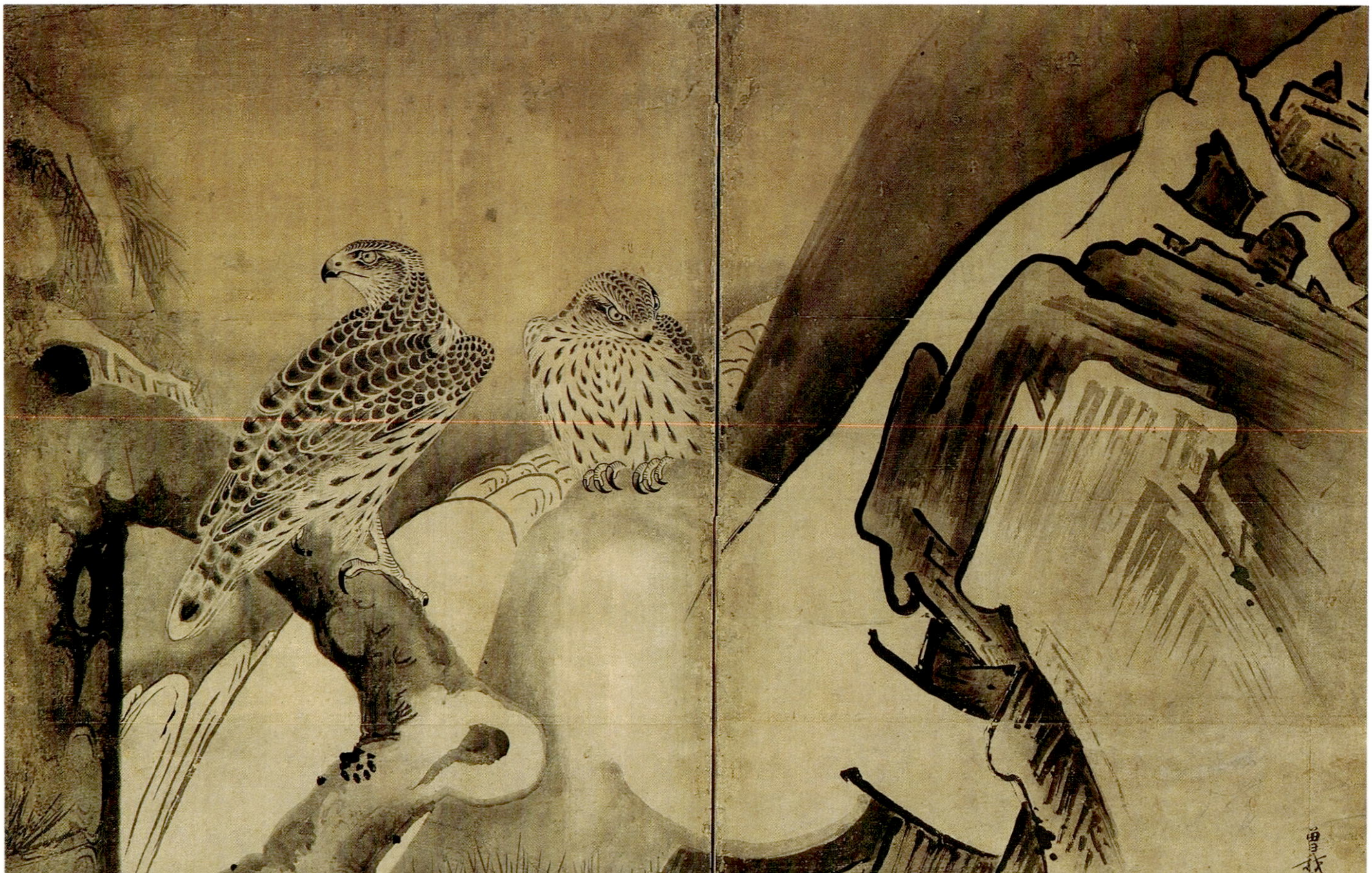

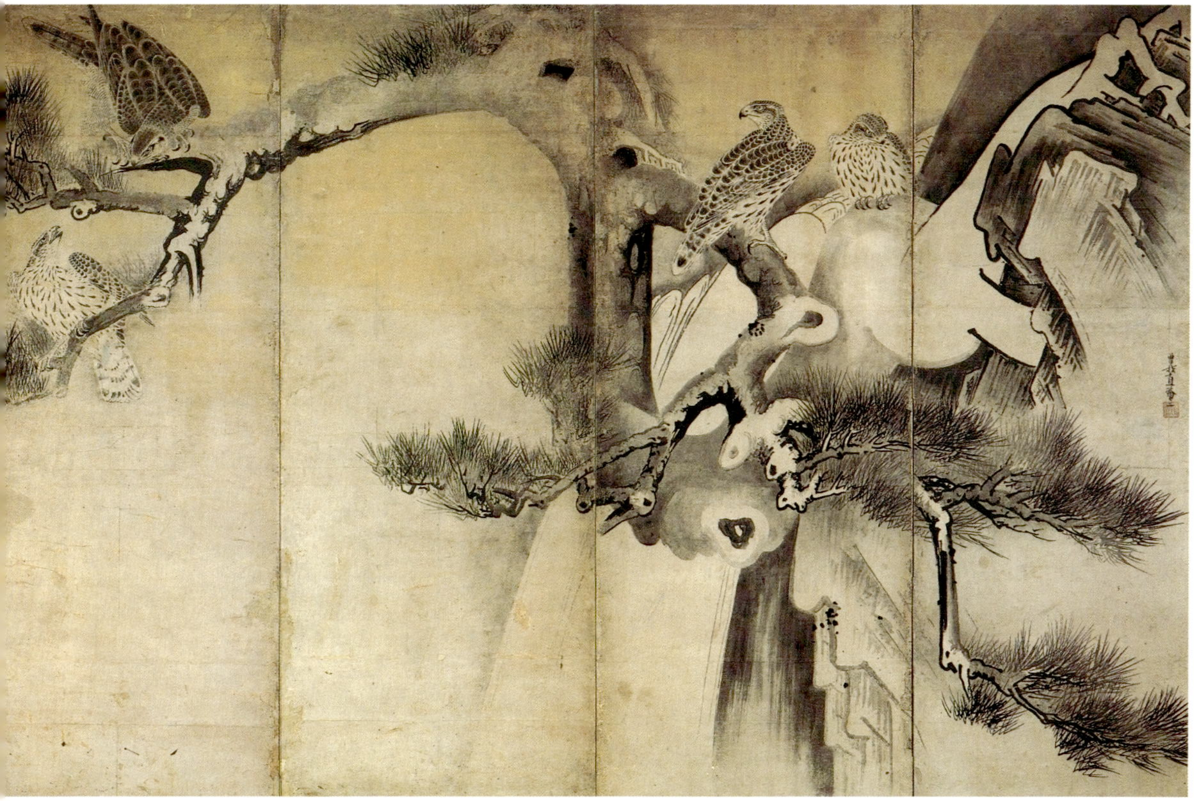

6
Soga Nichokuan
(fl. first half 17th century)
Hawks and Pine Tree
Six-fold screen
Ink on paper
154.1 x 359.3 cm
(60 11/16 x 141 7/16 in.)

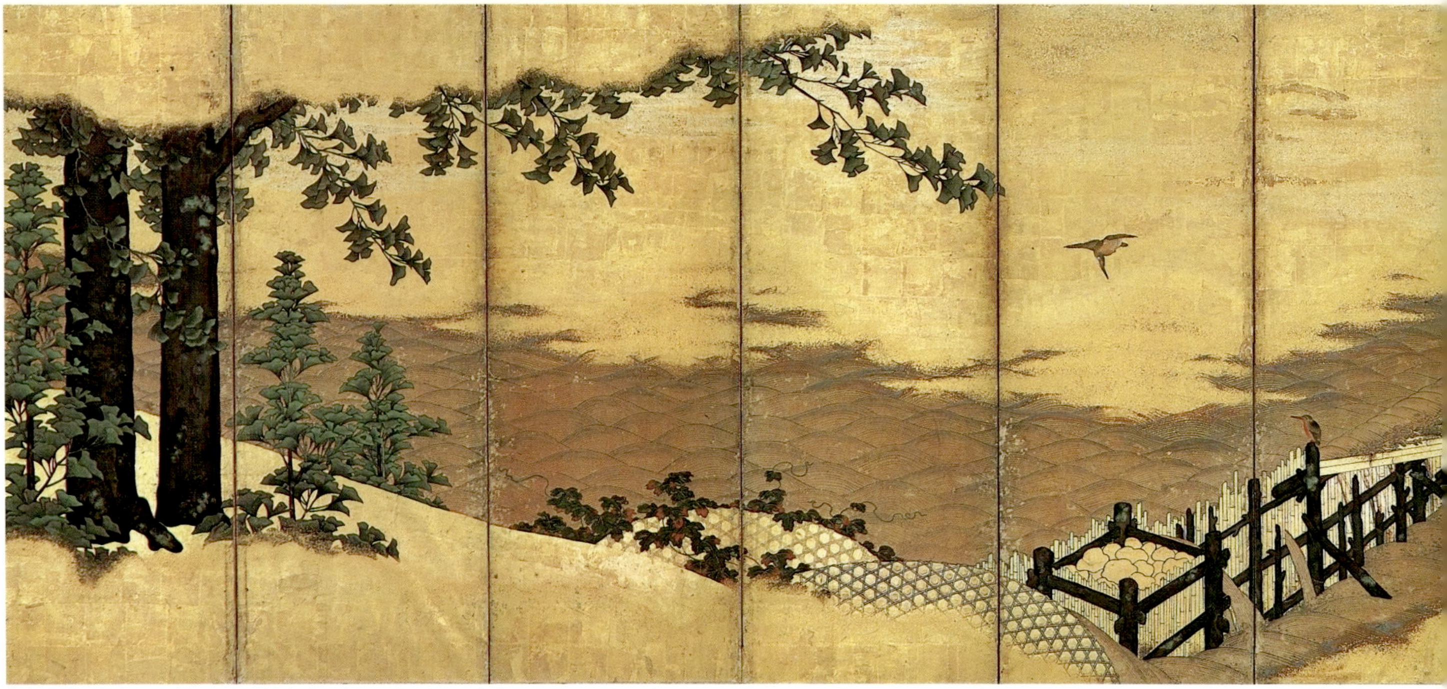

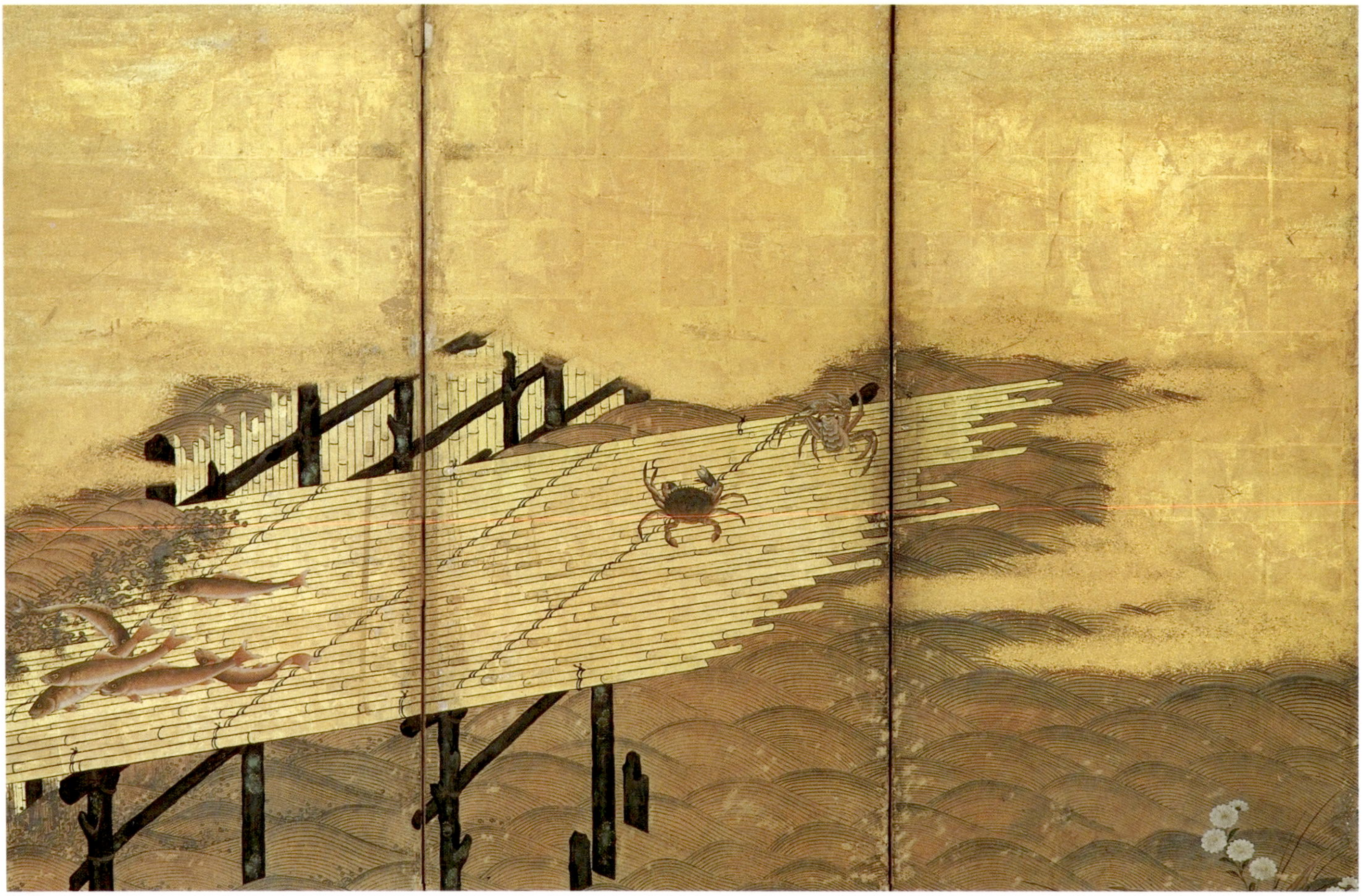

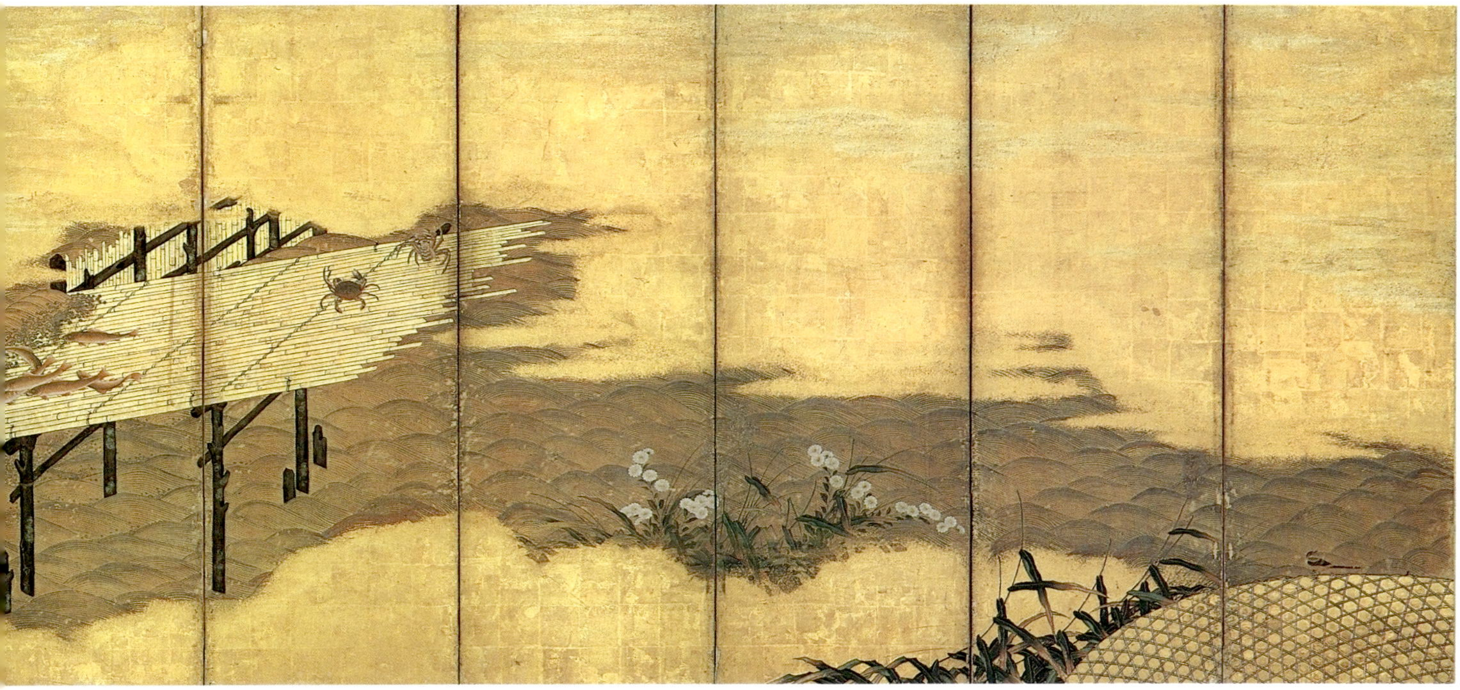

7
Anonymous
Ginkgo Trees and Fish Trap
Seventeenth century
Pair of six-fold screens
Color with gold ground on paper
Each 163.1 x 361.6 cm
(64¼ x 142$^{5}/_{16}$ in.)

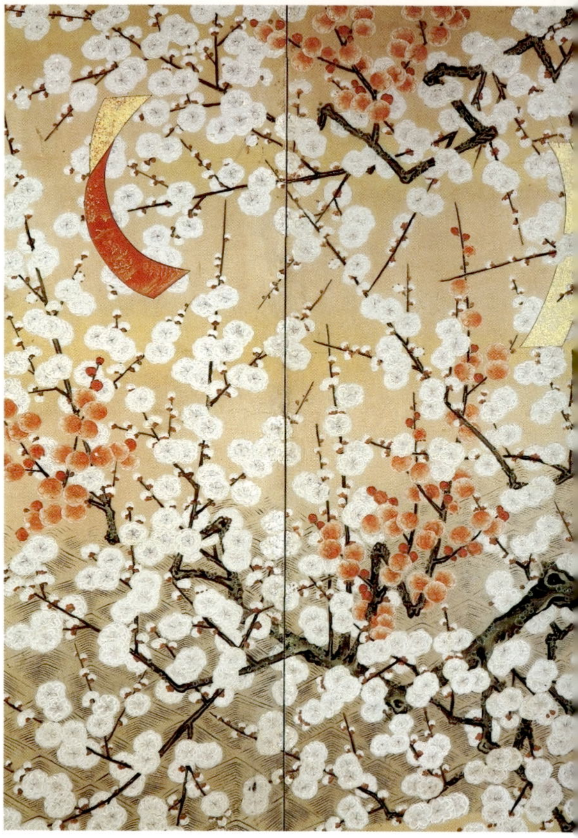

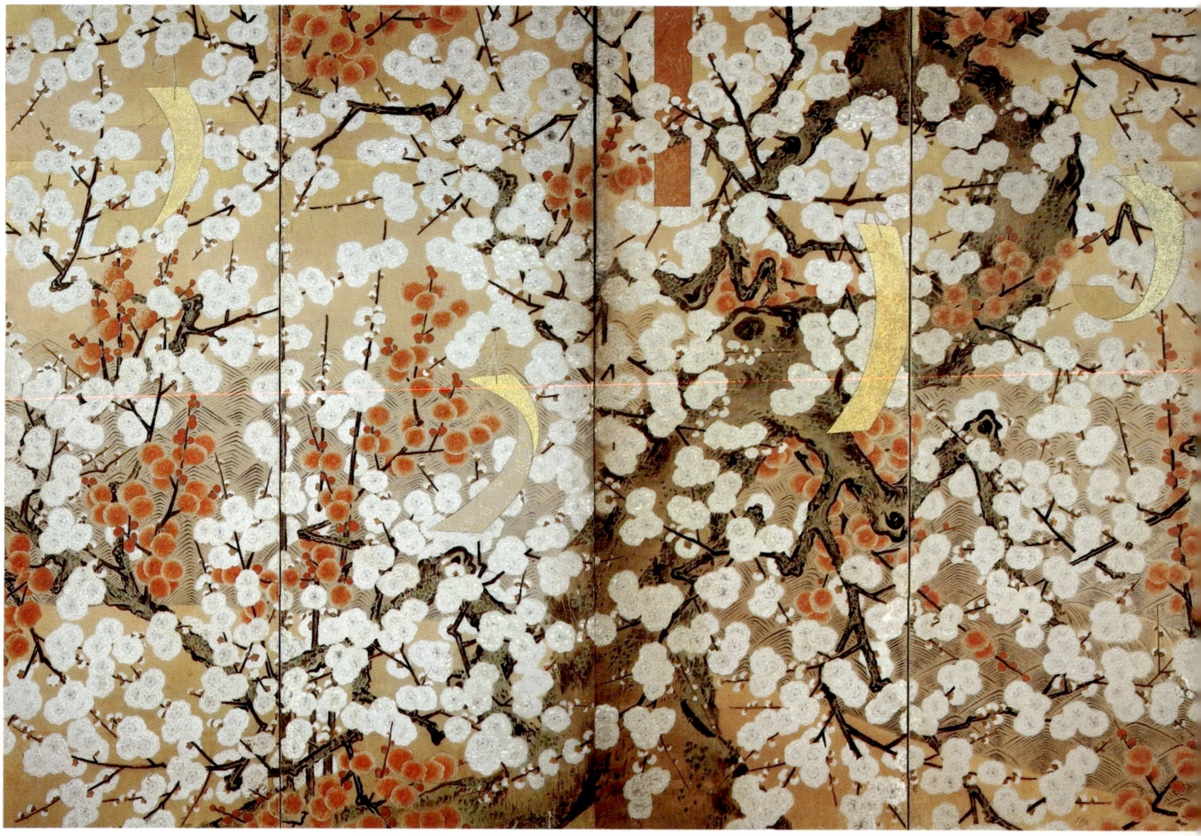

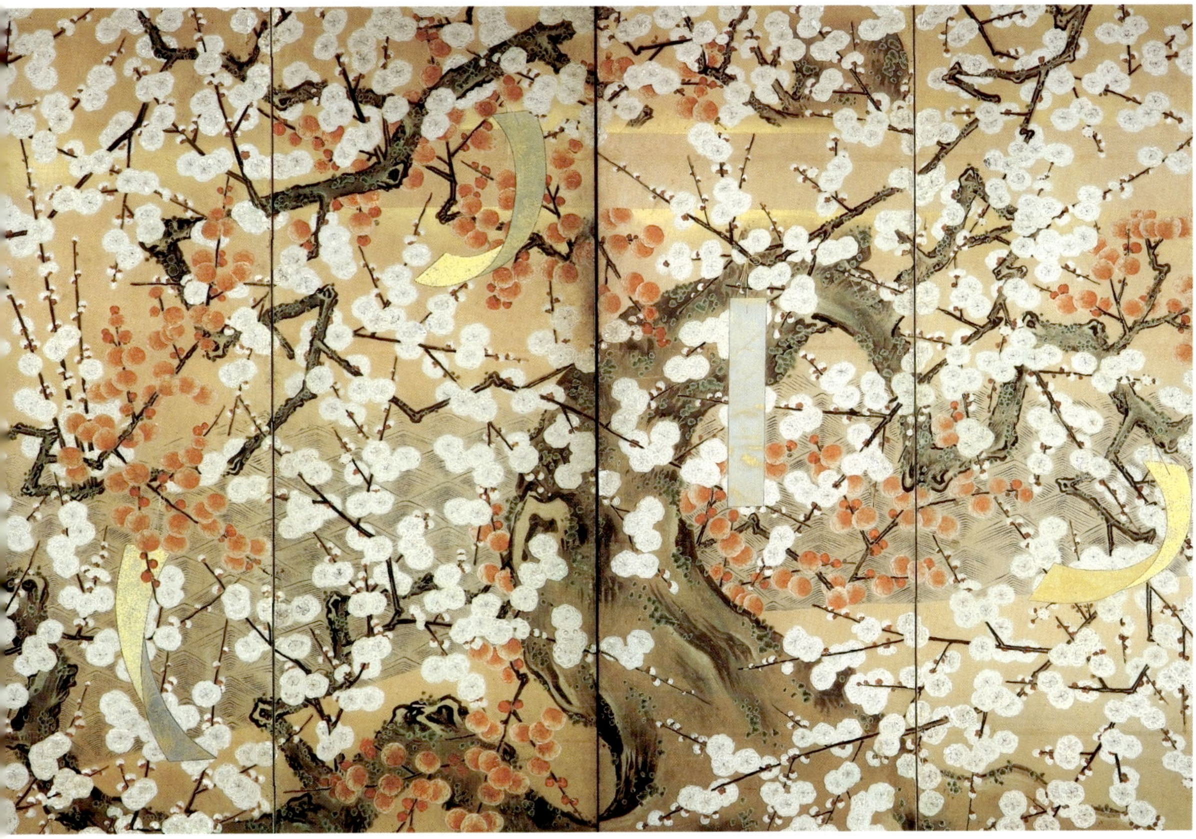

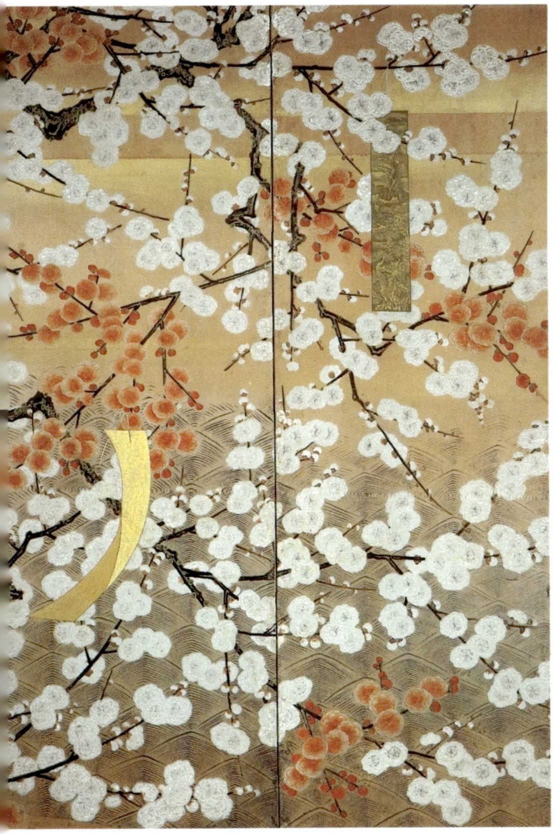

8
Anonymous
Red and White
Blossoming Plum Trees
Seventeenth century
Pair of six-fold screens
Color on paper
Each 153.3 x 346.8 cm
(60⅜ x 136 9/16 in.)

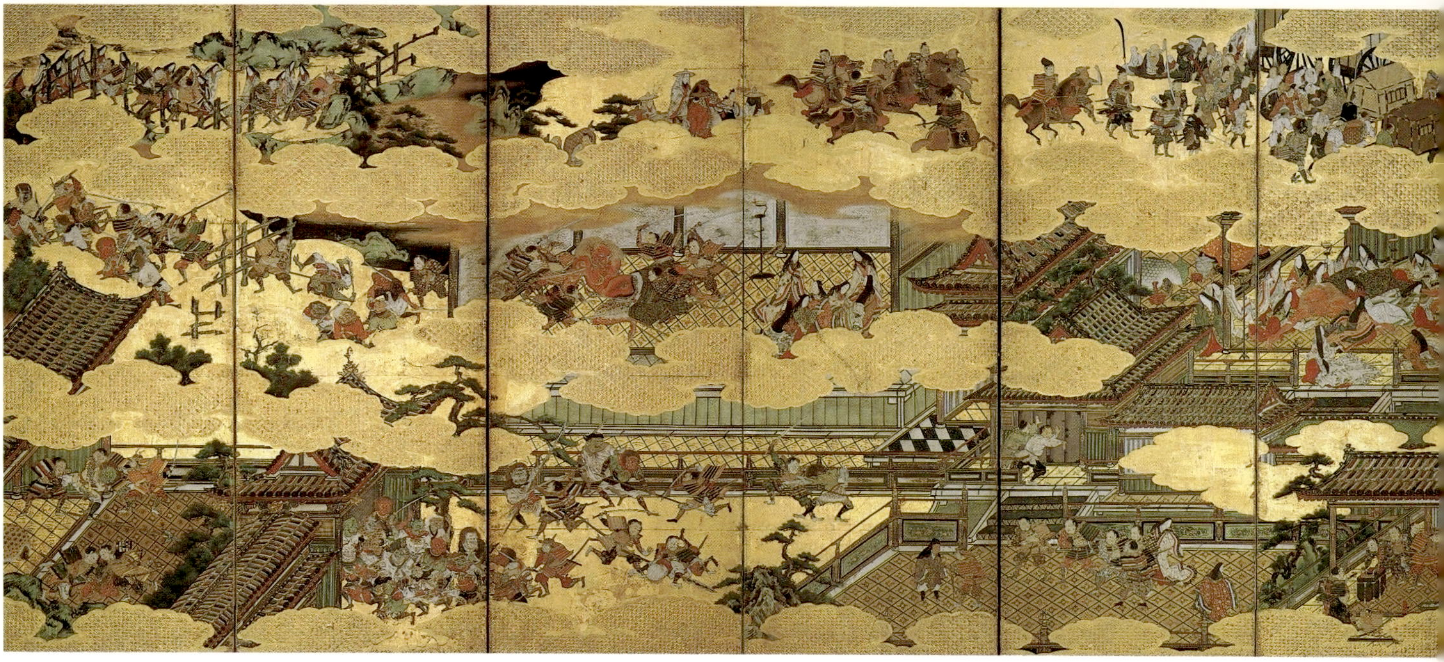

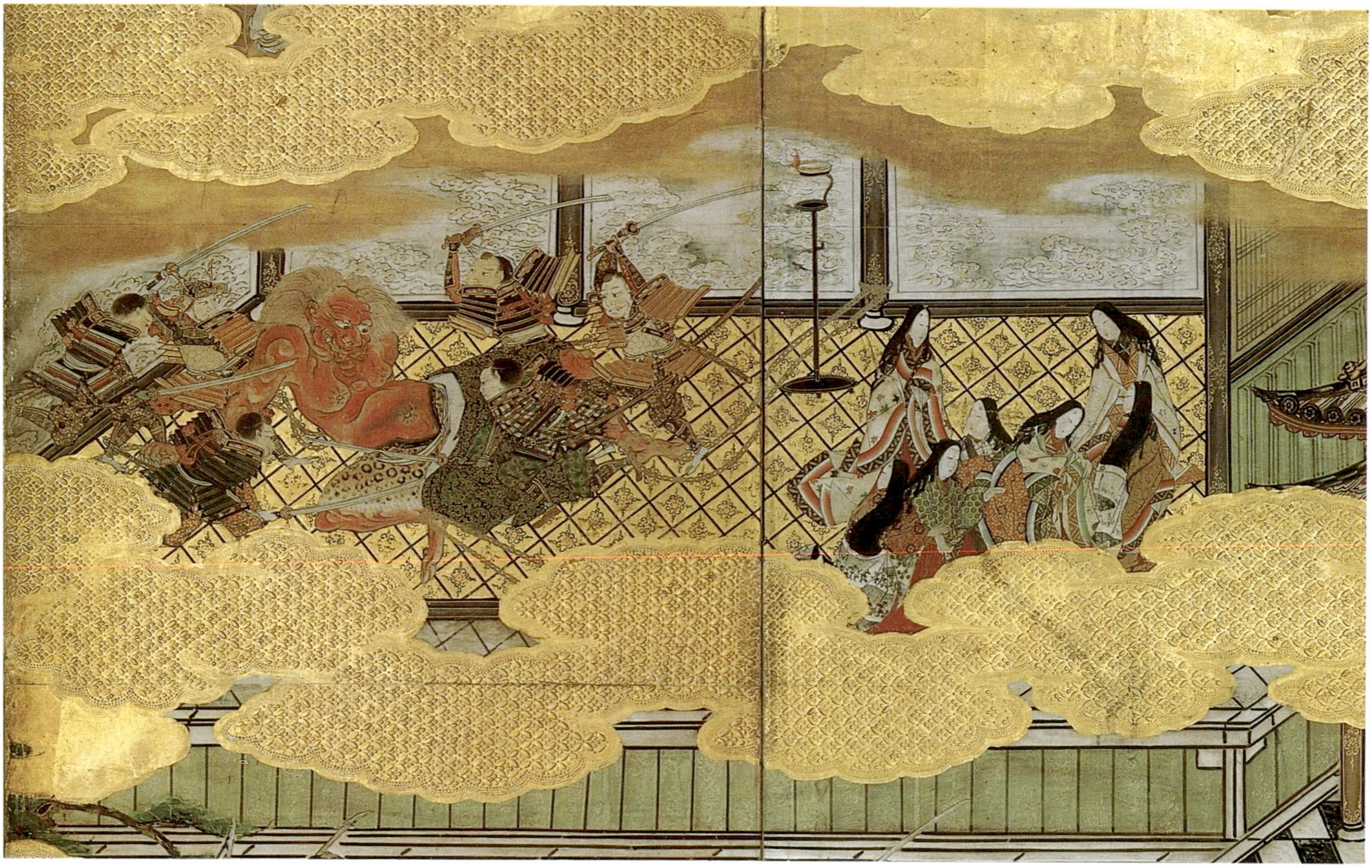

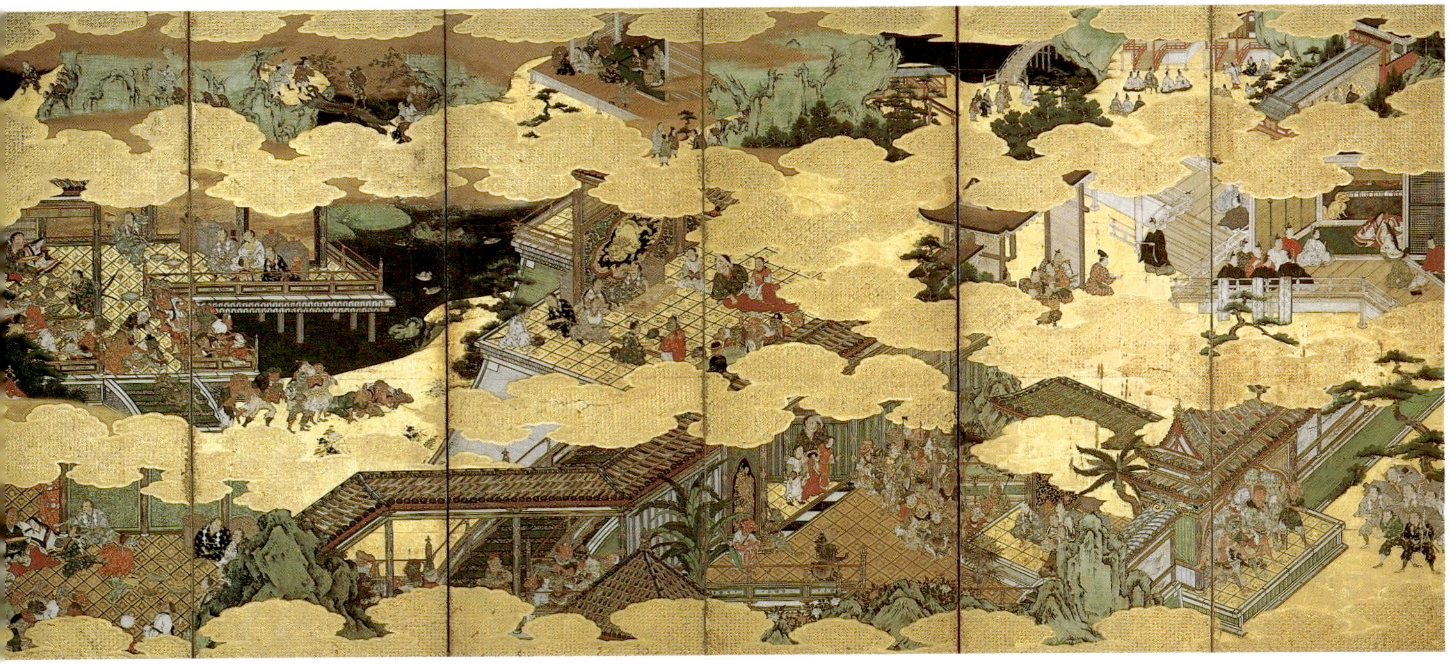

9
Anonymous
Shutendōji Ogre Tale
Seventeenth century
Pair of six-fold screens
Color with gold ground on paper
Each 156.0 x 360.6 cm
(61⁷⁄₁₆ x 141⁷⁄₈ in.)

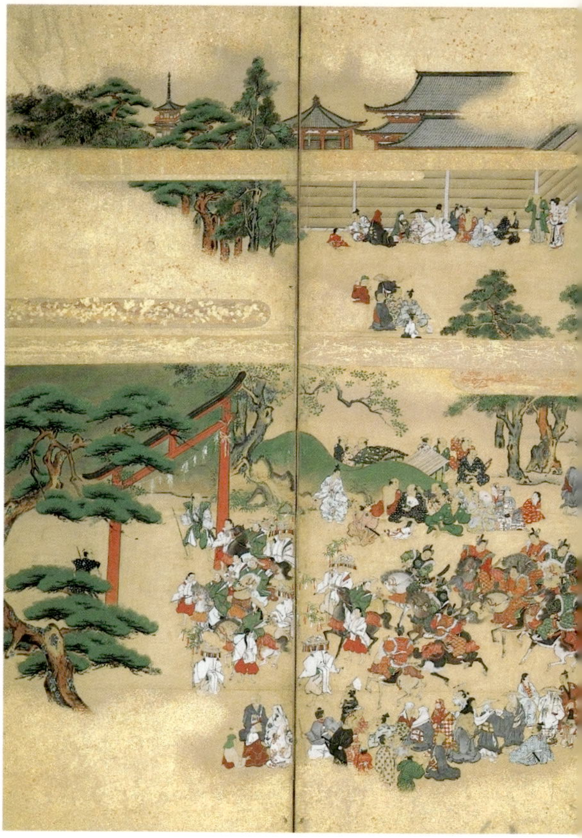

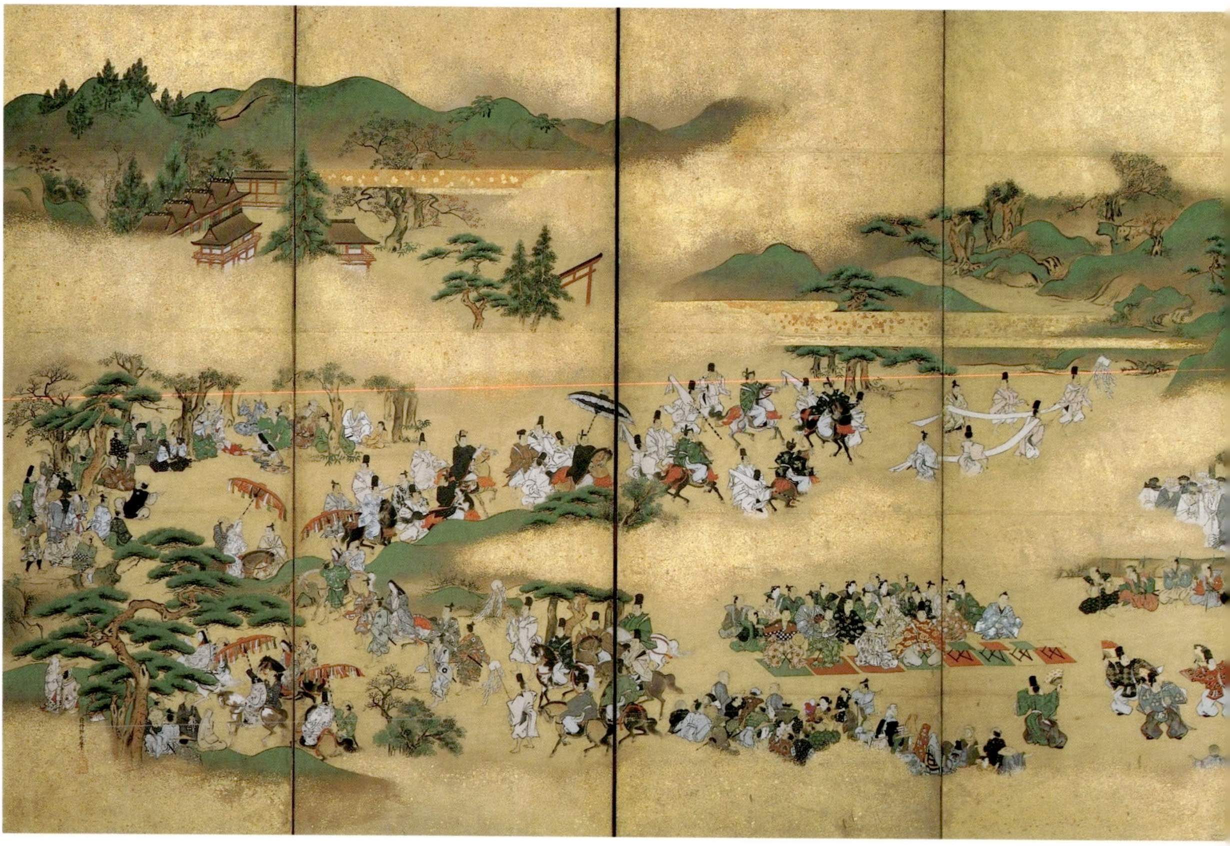

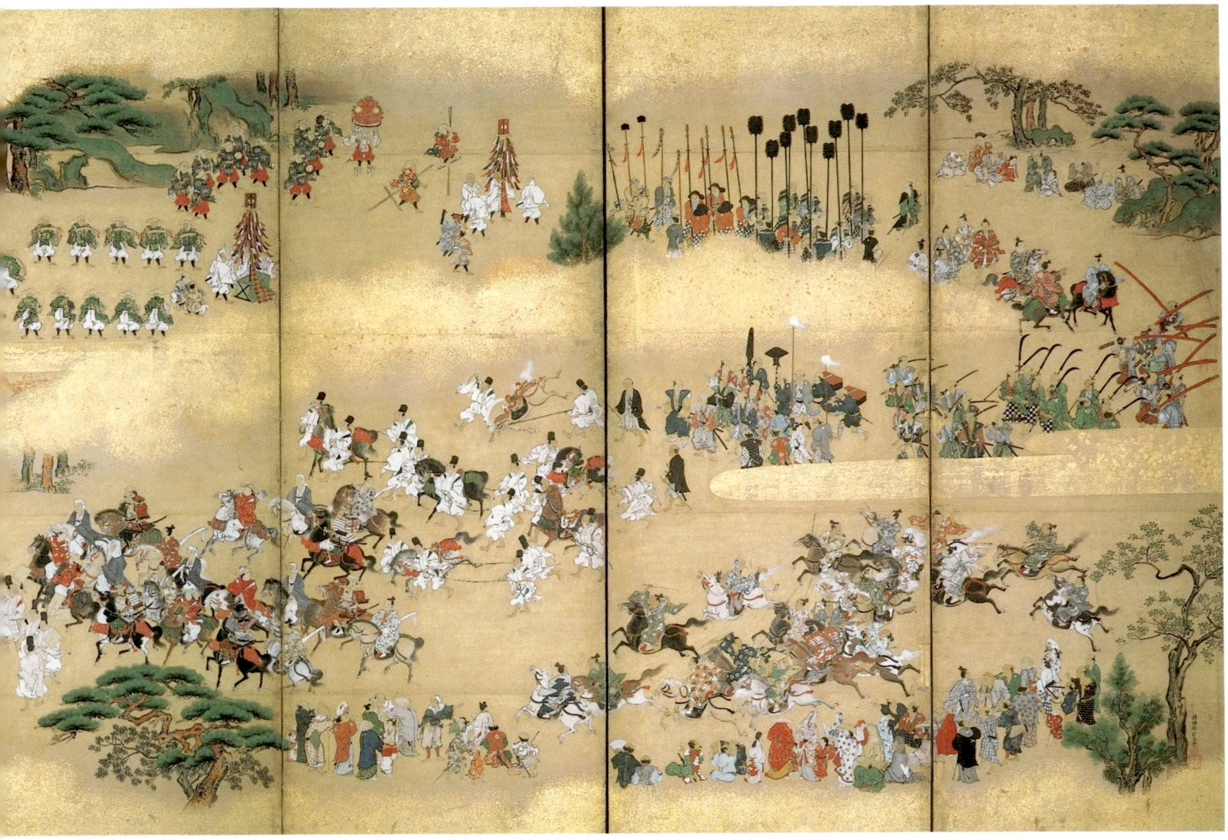

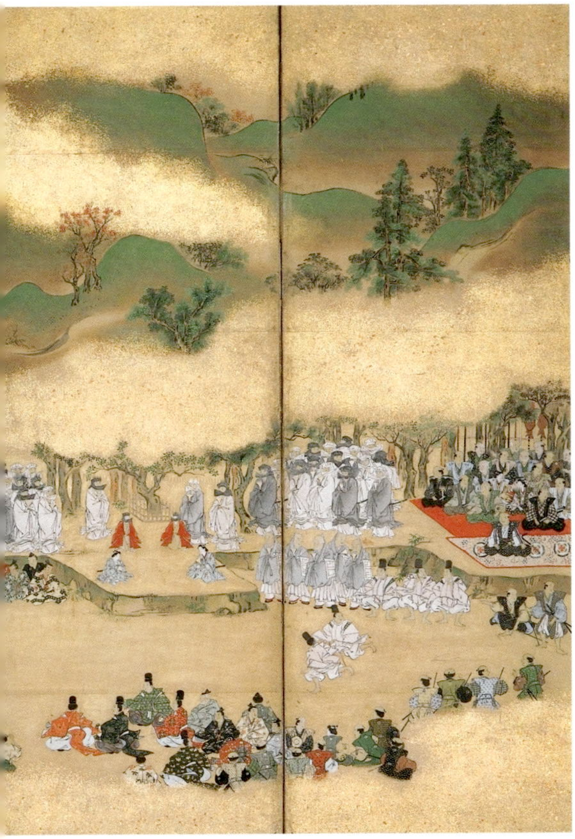

10
Kanō Ryūsetsu (1646 – 1712)
Kasuga Wakamiya Festival
Pair of six-fold screens
Color on paper
Each 161.5 x 371.0 cm
(63$\frac{9}{16}$ x 146 in.)

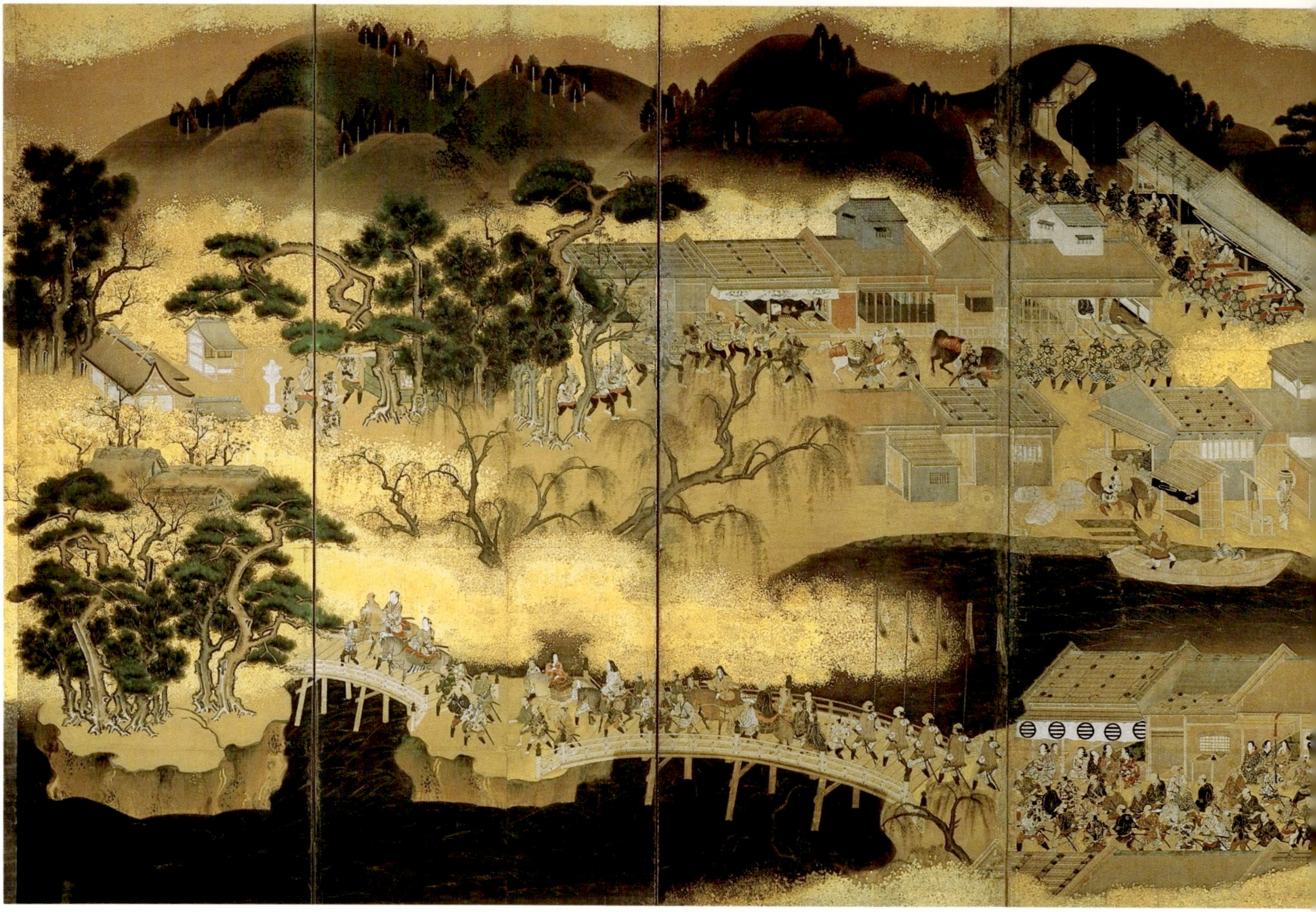

12
Matabei School
Tale of Genji:
Battle of the Carts
Seventeenth century
Six-fold screen
Color with gold ground on paper
175.9 x 270.6 cm
(69¼ x 106½ in.)

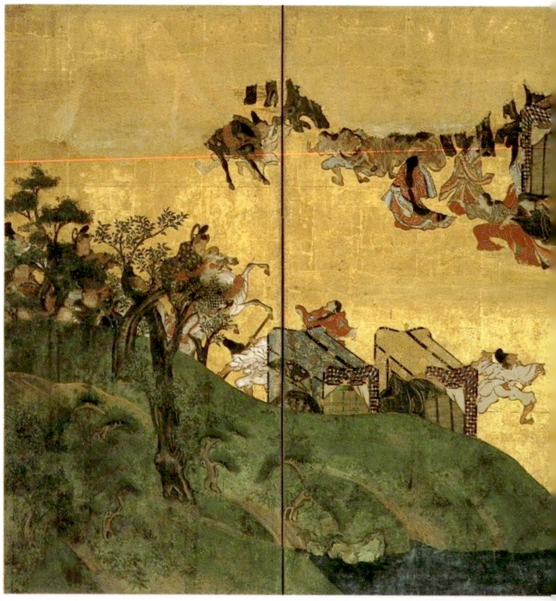

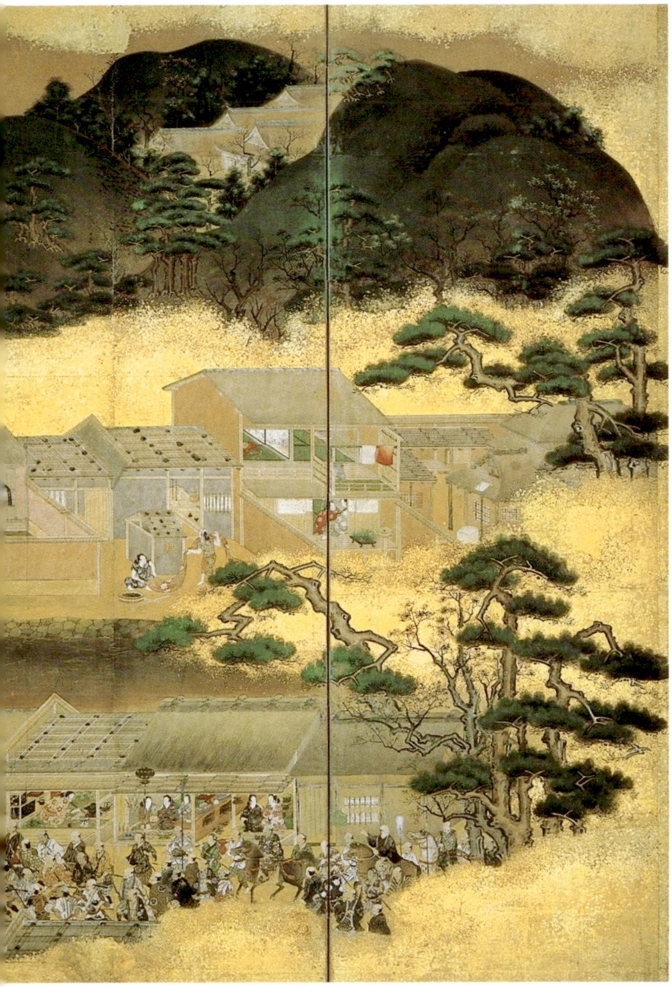

11
Anonymous
A Daimyo's Procession through Seta
Seventeenth century
Six-fold screen
Color on paper
159.8 x 363.1 cm
(62⅞ x 142$^{15}/_{16}$ in.)

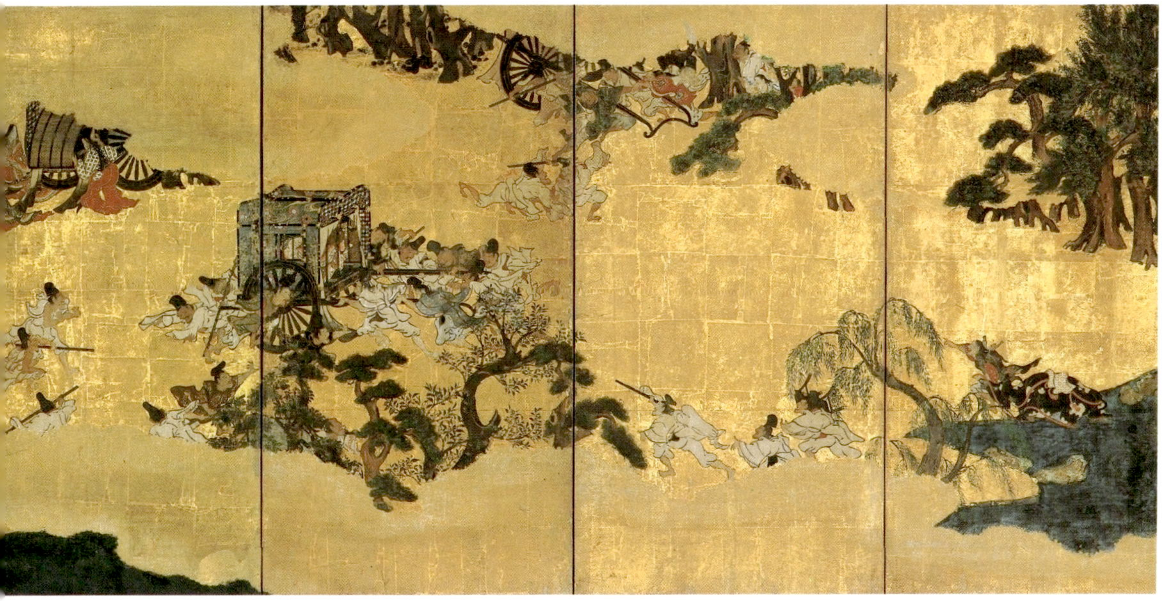

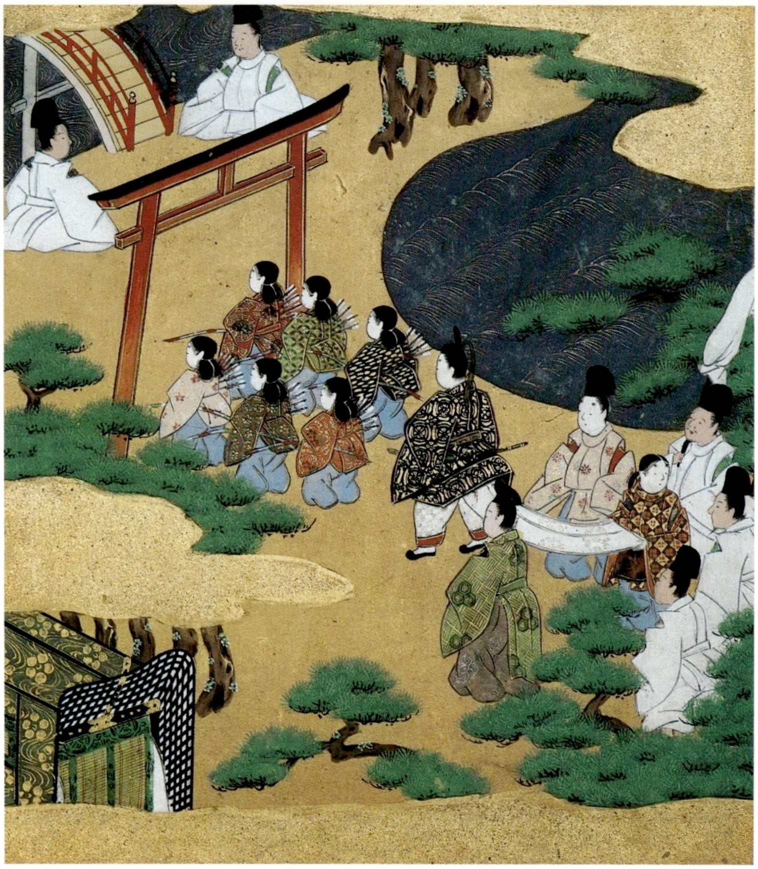

13
Anonymous
Tale of Genji
Late seventeenth-early eighteenth century
From an album with 54 leaves
Color on paper
Each leaf 19 x 16 cm
(7½ x 6⁵⁄₁₆ in.)

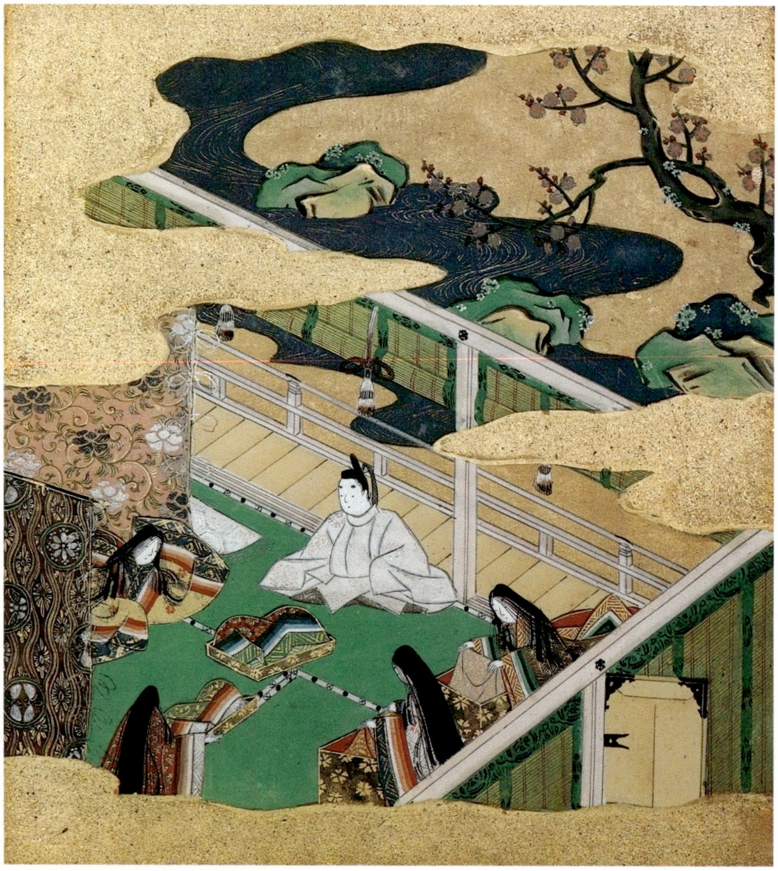

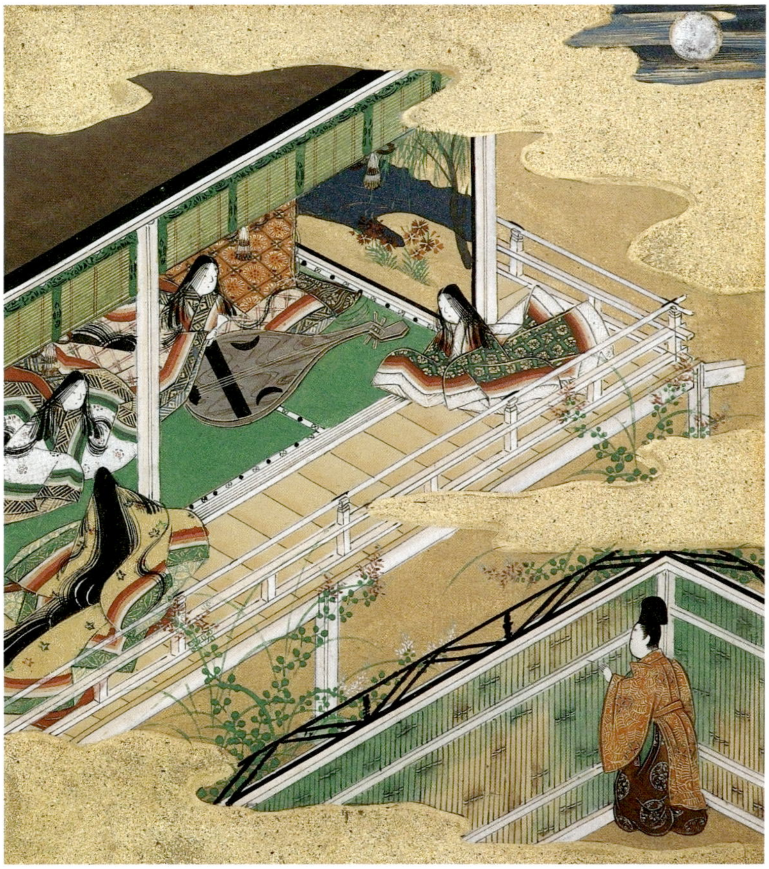

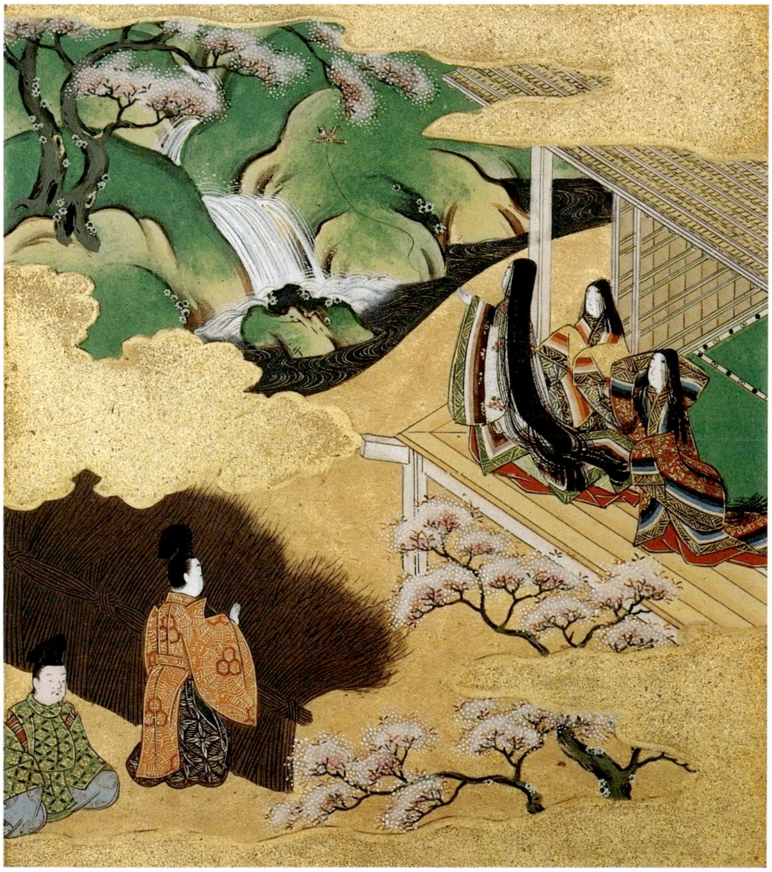

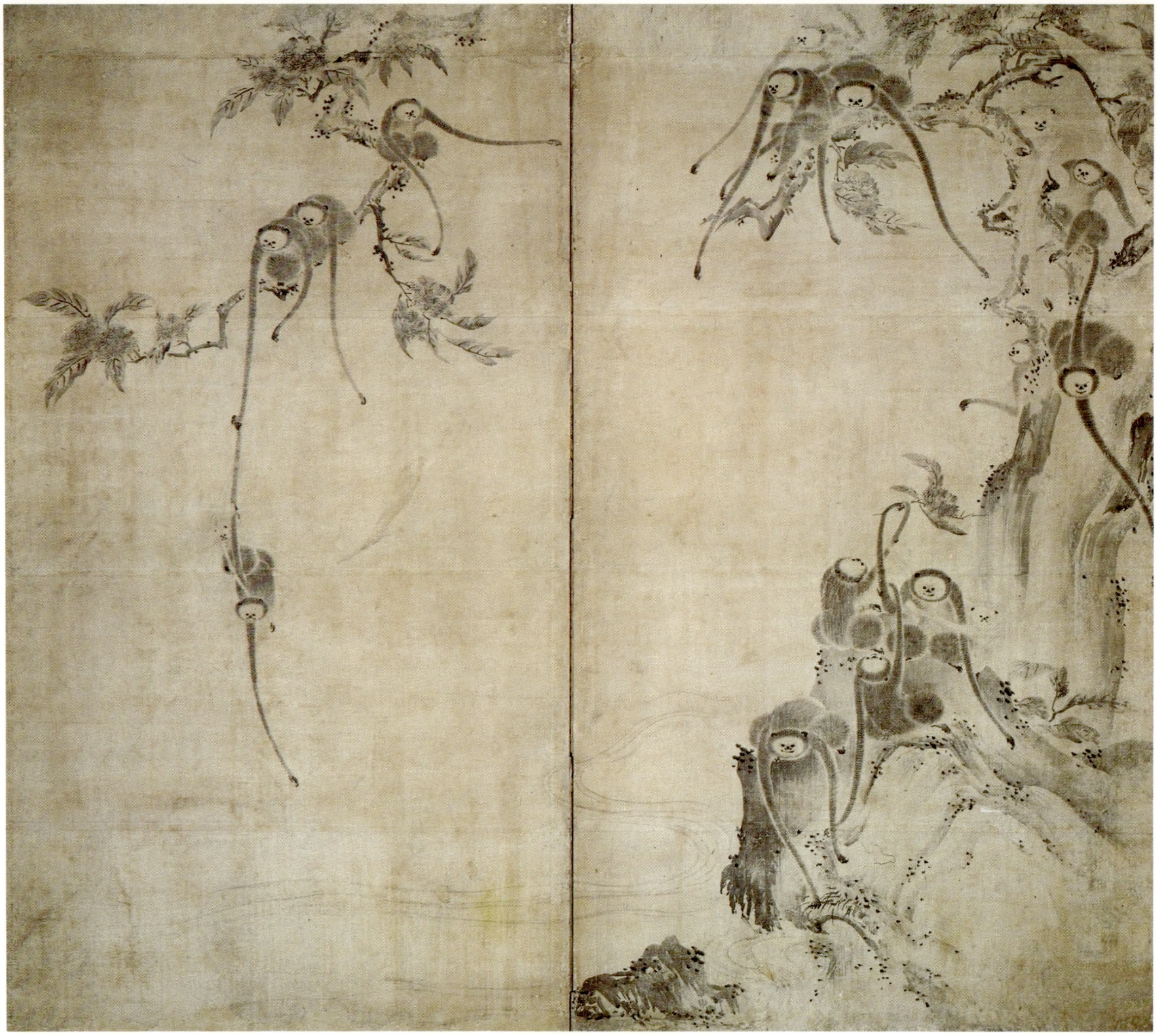

14
Anonymous
Gibbons
Seventeenth century
Two-fold screen
Ink on paper
152.4 x 175.2 cm
(60 x 69 in.)

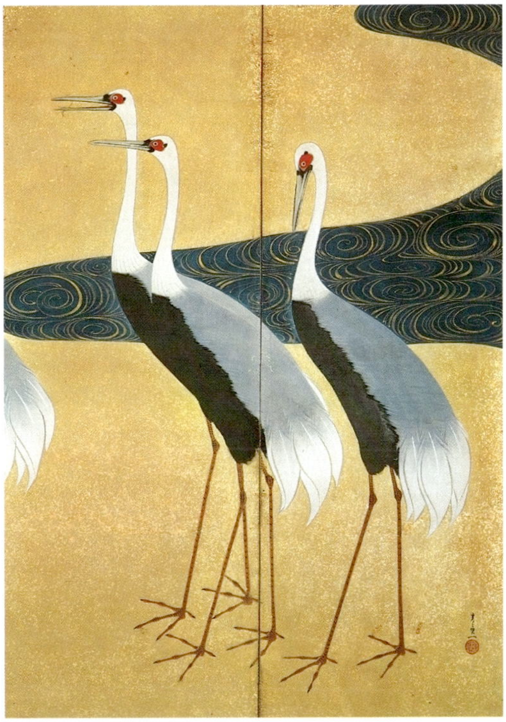

Rimpa painting is perhaps the finest expression of the Japanese genius for decorative style. Its vivid color, abstract composition, and lavish use of precious materials combine to create works that are a delight to the eye. Although Rimpa literally means "Kōrin School," today the term refers to the school of painting and other arts that was founded by Tawaraya Sōtatsu (fl. 1600–40) and his contemporary Hon'ami Kōetsu (1558–1637), revived by Ogata Kōrin (1658–1716), and further developed in Edo (present-day Tokyo) by Sakai Hōitsu (1761–1828) and his student Suzuki Kiitsu (1796–1858).

From the beginning, Rimpa School artists received patronage from the imperial court and the wealthy merchant class of Kyoto. The merchant class was largely responsible for restoring Kyoto after the near-total devastation of the city in the Ōnin War (1467–77). In the political vacuum of the time the proud Kyoto merchants became a strong economic and cultural force. As the merchant class grew more powerful, its members became interested in traditional arts and literature, and it was classical themes, such as incidents from the epic *Tale of Genji*, which provided much of the subject matter of early Rimpa painting.

Sōtatsu revived the native tradition of painting and adapted it to a larger scale by simplifying and abstracting earlier expressions of the tradition. Sōtatsu and his school also painted subjects from nature (*Poppy Flowers, Thistles, and Chinese Milk Vetches*, plate 15, and *Bush Clover, Pampas Grass, and Chrysanthemums*, plate 16) based on a keen observation of flowers and other plants. These works show a mastery of the preferred Rimpa techniques of avoiding outline and producing a soft blurring of colors by dropping ink or color onto wet surfaces (plate 15) and of delicate brushwork creating a tableau of the utmost refinement (plate 16).

Kōrin, the next great figure in the Rimpa tradition, studied the work of Sōtatsu and developed a sense of abstract design and pattern with which he produced works of stunning power. He in turn greatly influenced Nakamura Hōchū (fl. late 18th-early 19th century), whose surviving painting, mostly in the fan format, demonstrates his advancement of Rimpa techniques (*Fans*, plate 22).

The Rimpa tradition was introduced to Edo by Kōrin, but it was through Hōitsu, who spent years in an intense study of Kōrin's work, that Edo Rimpa was established. As with Kyoto Rimpa, Edo Rimpa was heavily supported by the merchant class, who sought ways to express their identity in spite of the frequent attempts by the shogunate to suppress their great economic power. The son of a daimyō, Hōitsu developed a style based on that of Kōrin but increasingly marked by a new sense of extreme elegance and refinement (*The Thirty-six Poets*, plate 17, *The Thirty-six Poets on a Field of Flowers and Grasses*, plate 18, *The Sano Crossing*, plate 19, and *Sweeping Maple Leaves*, plate 20). His colors are particularly delicate, and the atmosphere of his bird-and-flower paintings is strikingly clear, as in his masterpiece series of hanging scrolls of the twelve months (*Birds and Flowers of the Twelve Months*, plate 21).

Hōitsu's most talented pupil was Kiitsu, who lived almost to the end of the Edo period. In its best examples, Kiitsu's work possesses a clarity of line and sharpness of detail that represent the last flowering of the Rimpa tradition (*Egret and Willow*, plate 23, *Cranes*, plate 24, *Paulownia and Maple*, plate 25, *Seashells and Plums*, plate 26, *Tanabata*, plate 27, and *Dancing*, plate 28).

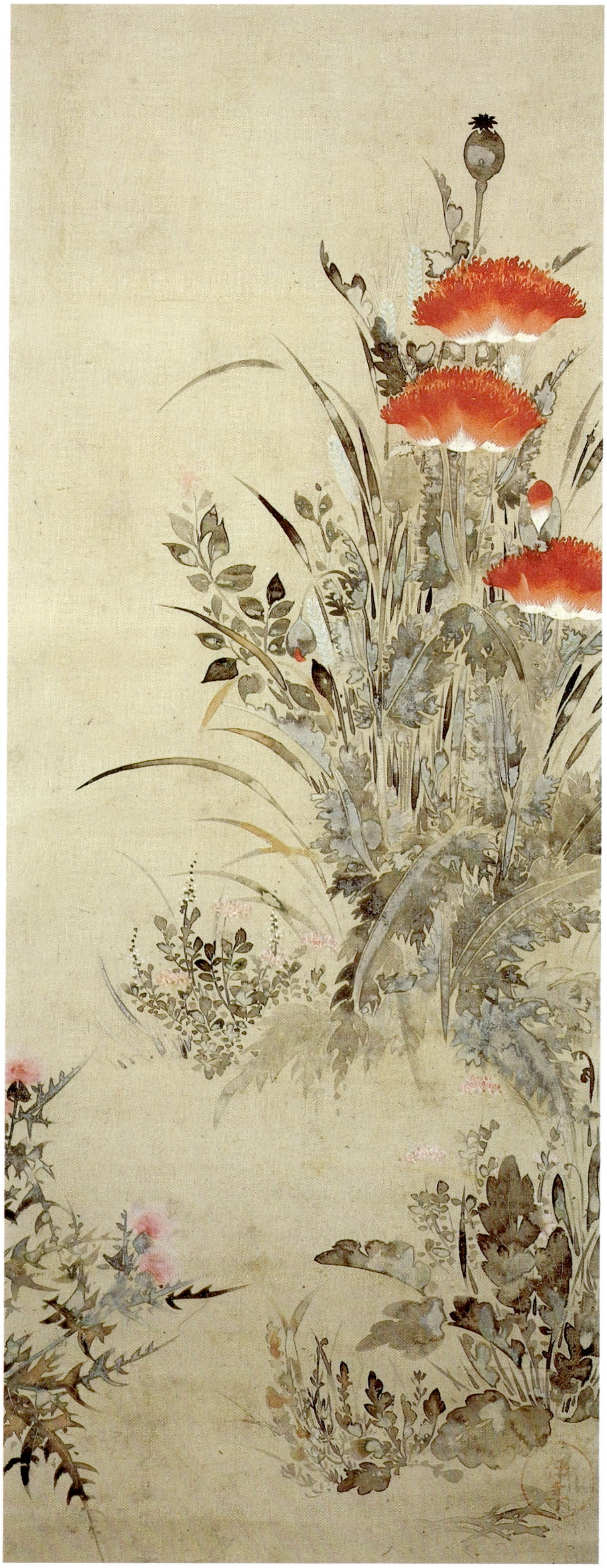

15
Kitagawa Sōsetsu (attrib.)
(fl. mid-17th century)
Poppy Flowers, Thistles, and Chinese Milk Vetches
Hanging scroll
Color on paper
121.1 x 48.1 cm
($47\frac{3}{4}$ x $18\frac{15}{16}$ in.)

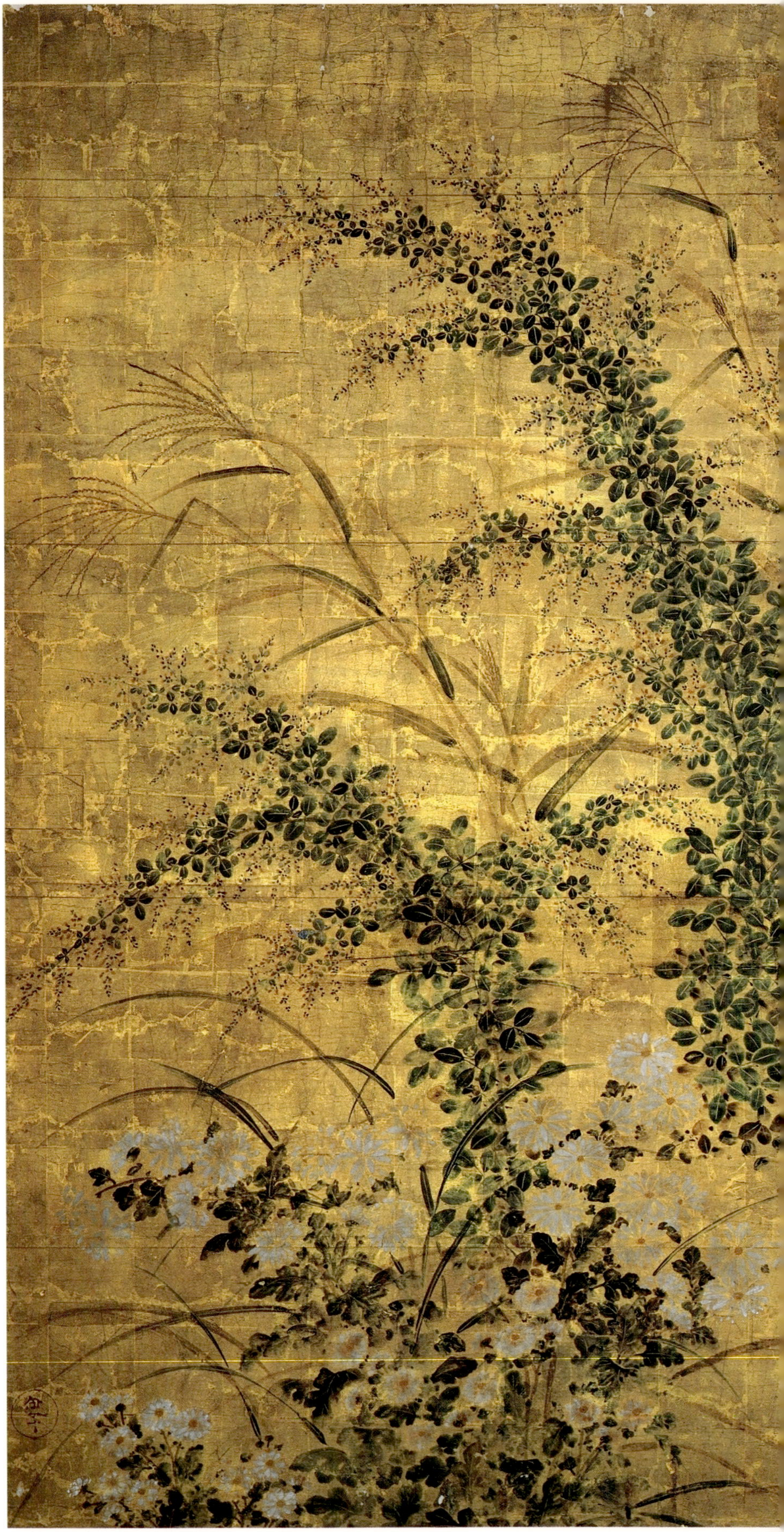

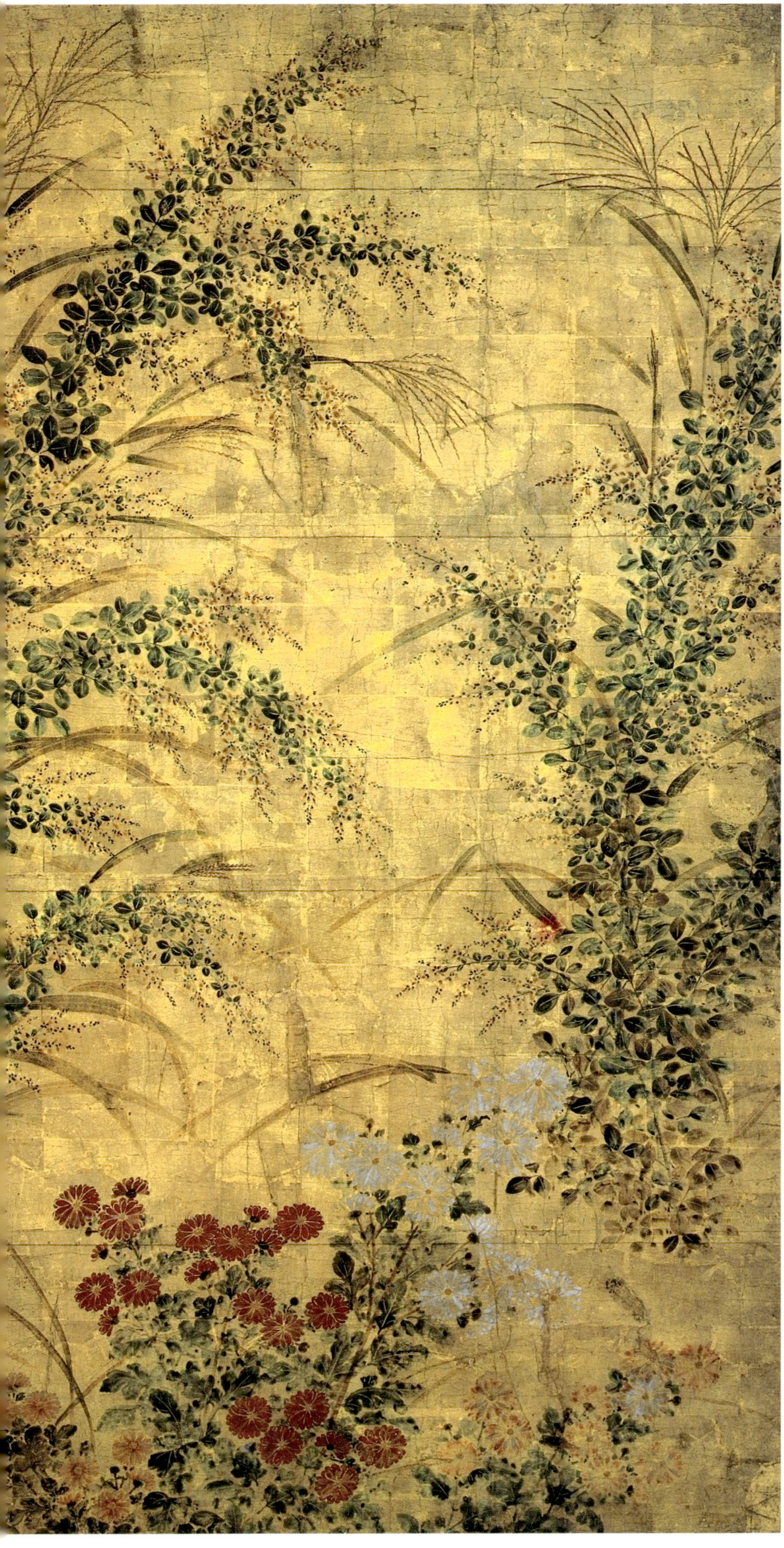

16
Inen seal
Bush Clover, Pampas Grass, and Chrysanthemums
Seventeenth century
Two-fold screen
Color with gold ground on paper
158.5 x 172.4 cm
(62⅜ x 67⅞ in.)

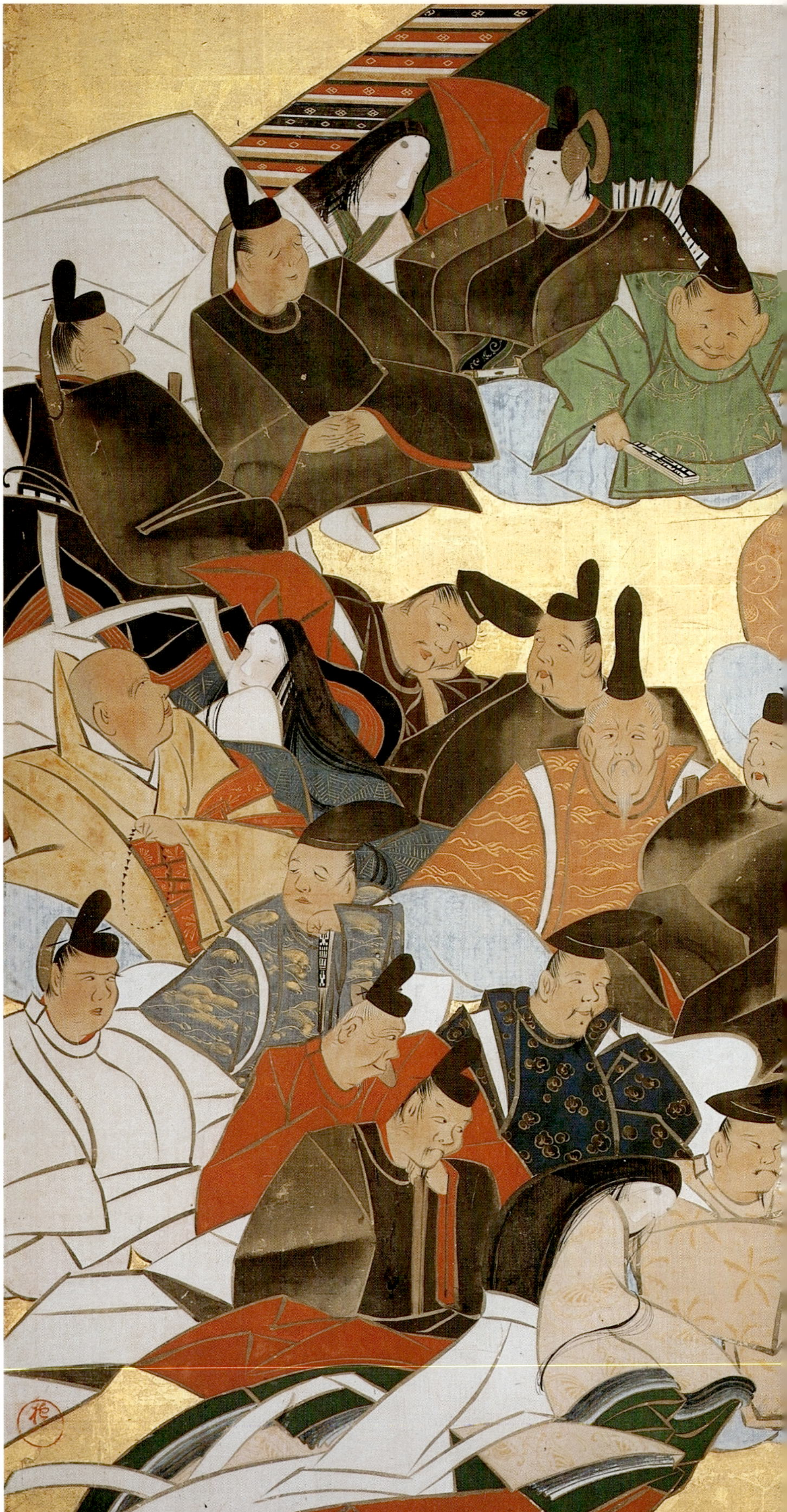

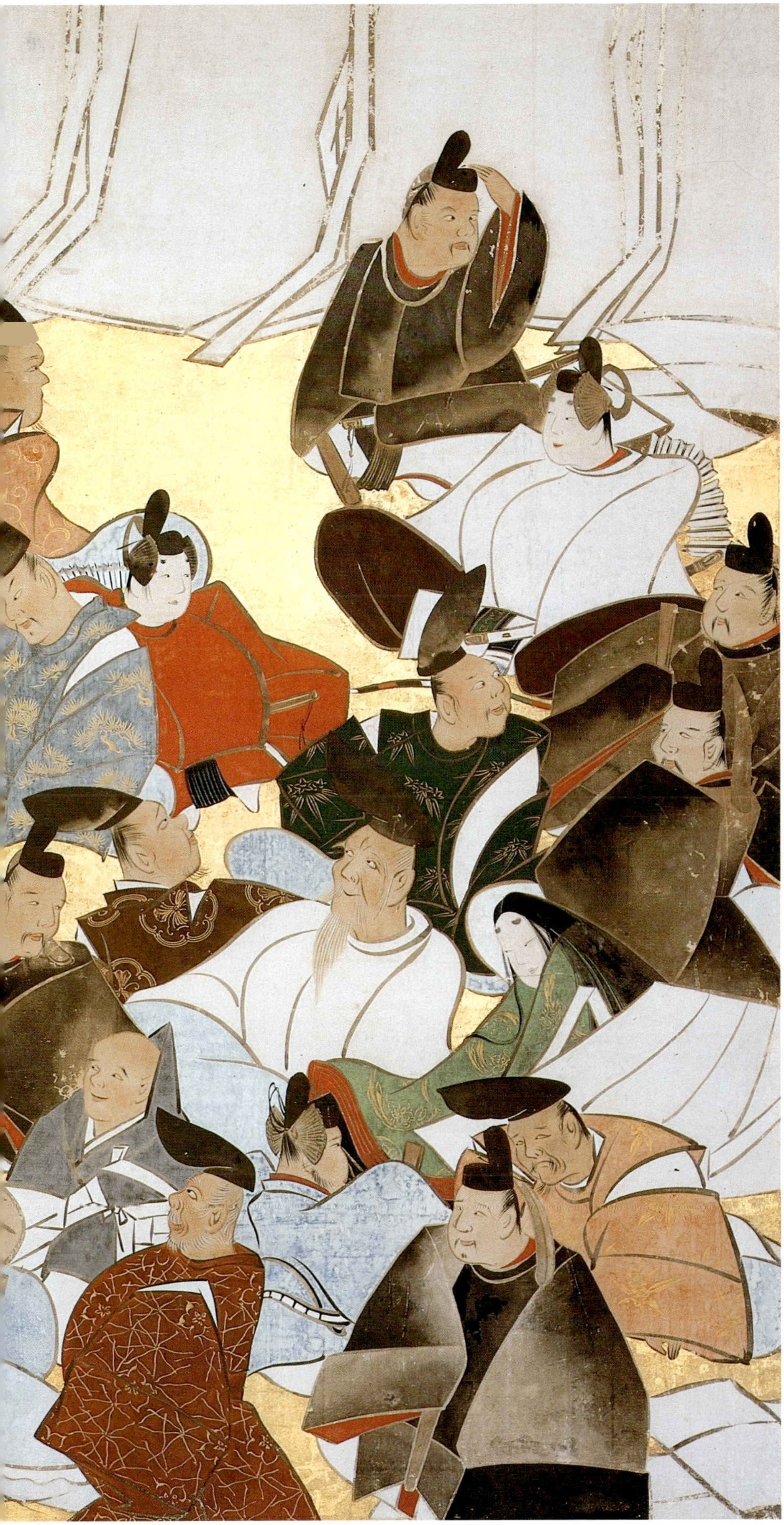

17
Sakai Hōitsu (1761 – 1828)
The Thirty-six Poets
Two-fold screen
Color with gold ground on paper
165.3 x 180.6 cm
(65⅛ x 71⅛ in.)

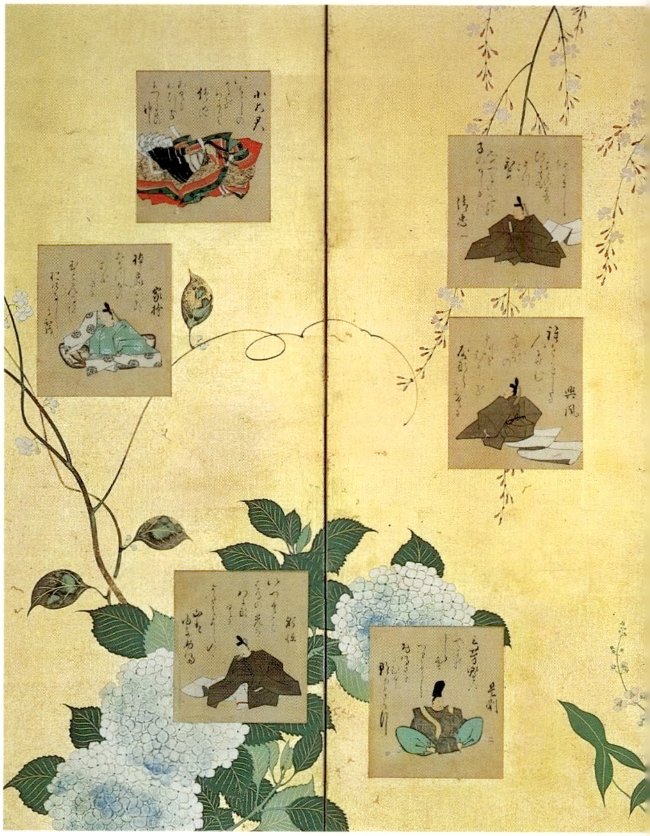

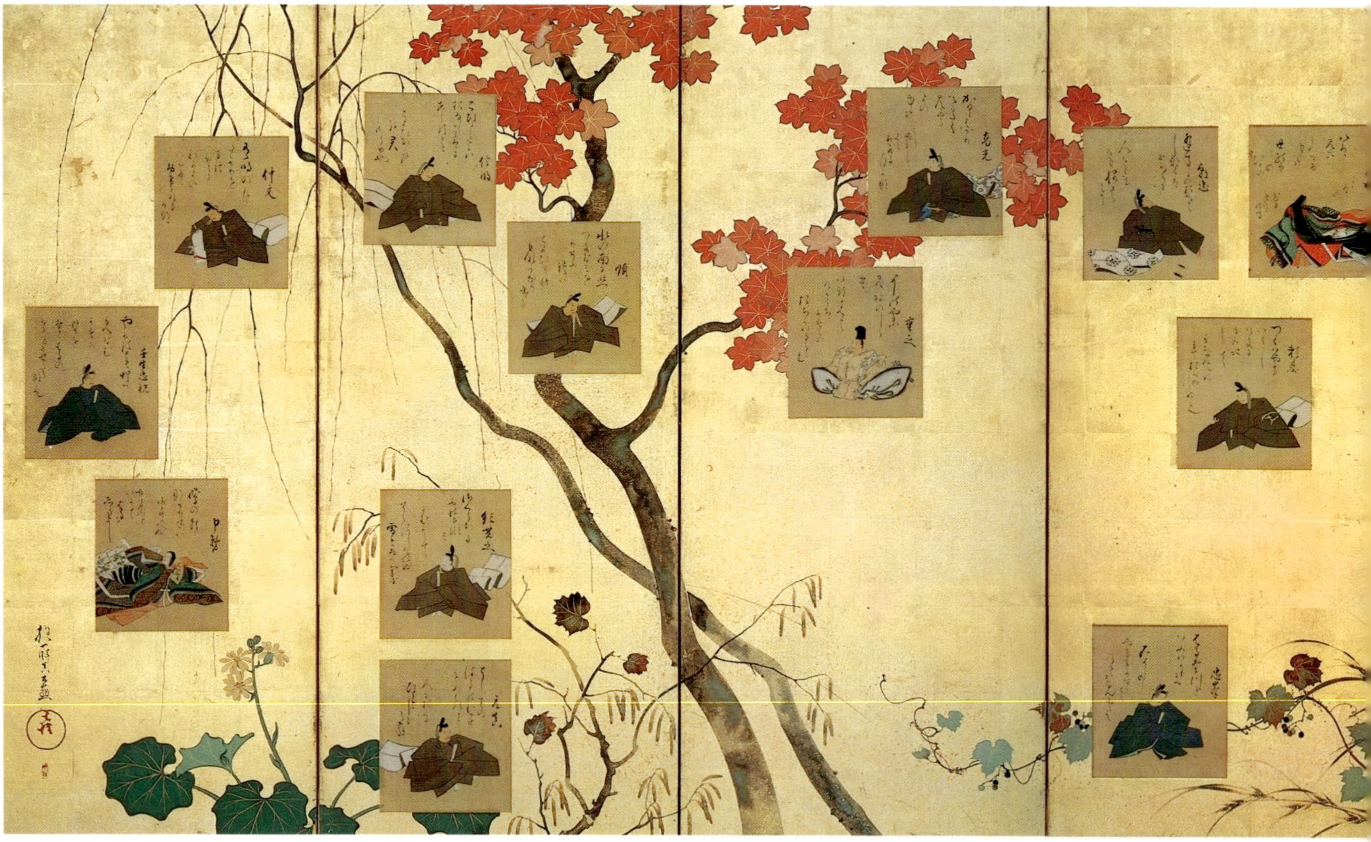

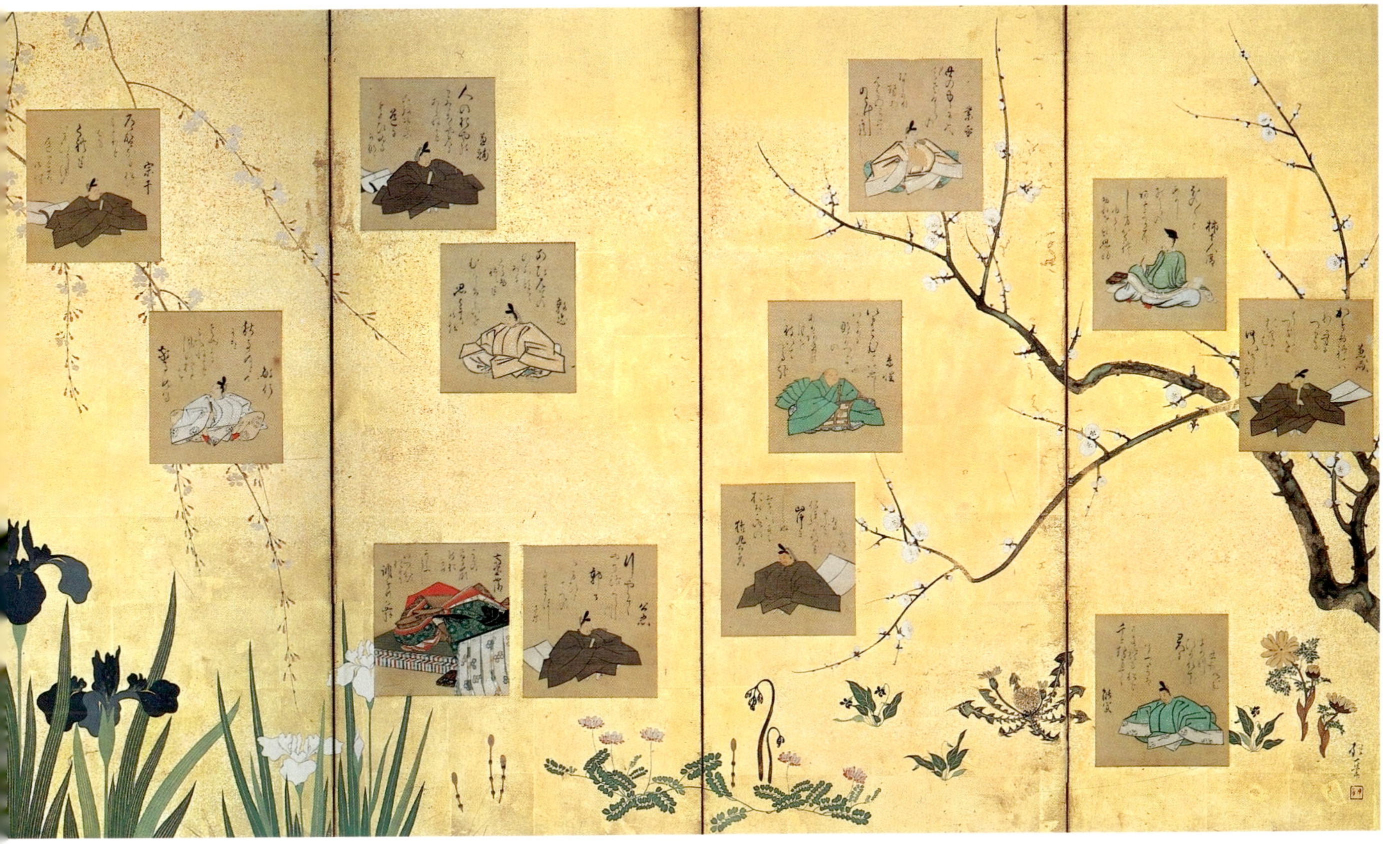

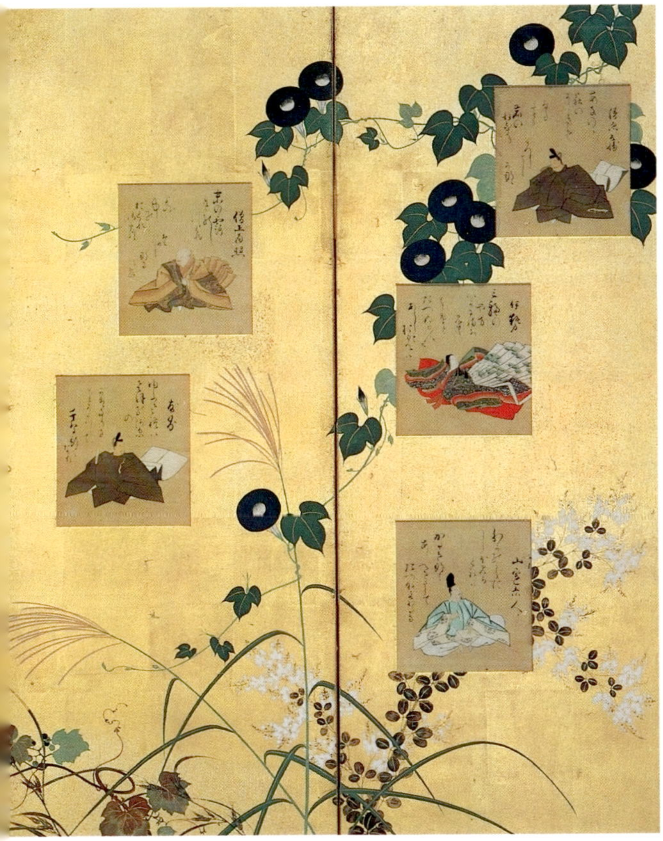

18
Sakai Hōitsu (1761 – 1828)
The Thirty-six Poets
on a Field of Flowers
and Grasses
Pair of six-fold screens
Color on silk panels
affixed to a surface of color
with gold ground on paper
Each silk panel 19.5 x 17.7 cm
($7\frac{11}{16}$ x 7 in.)

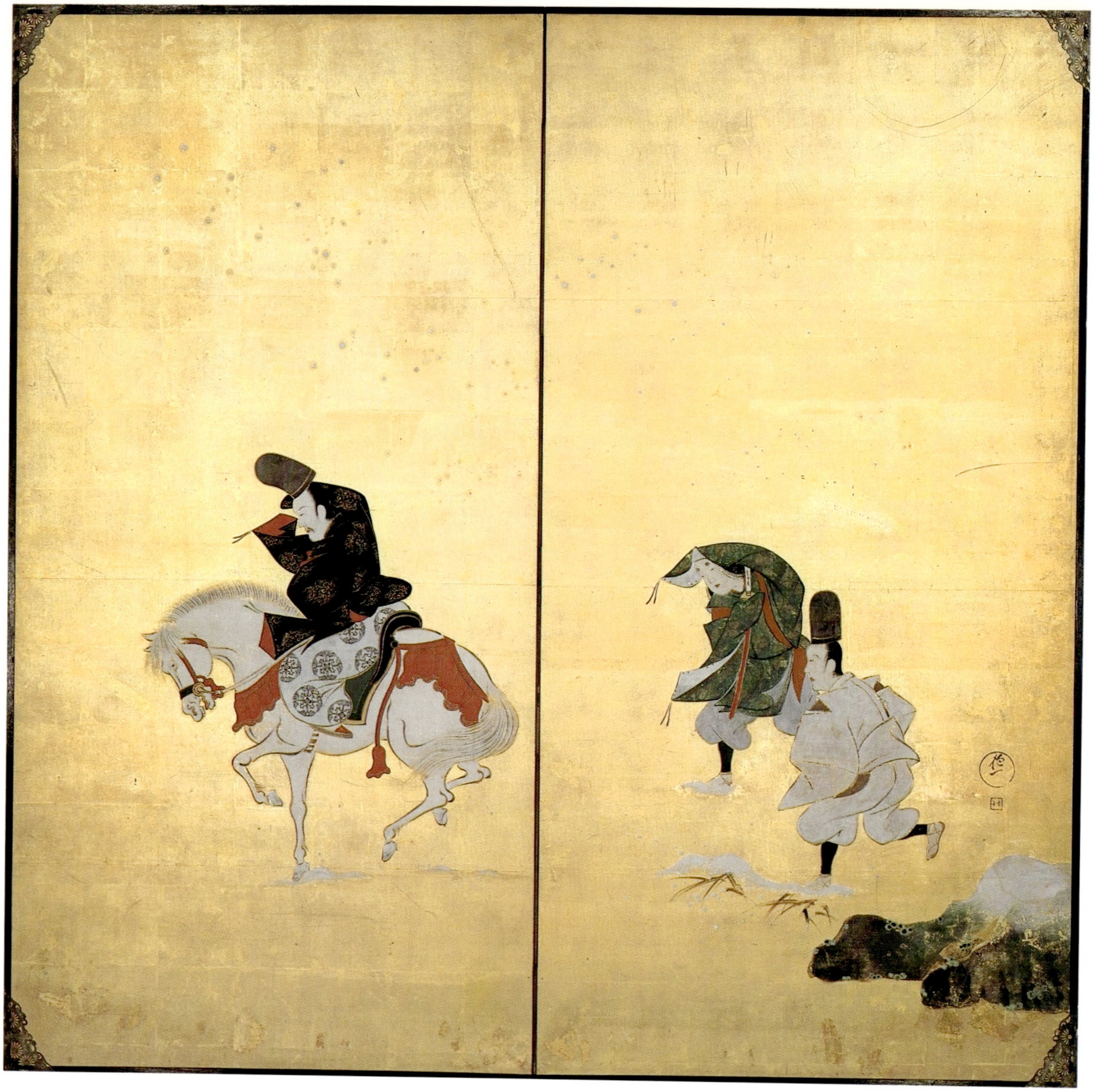

19
Sakai Hōitsu (1761 – 1828)
The Sano Crossing
Two-fold screen
Color with gold ground on paper
150.4 x 154.4 cm
(59³⁄₁₆ x 60³⁄₄ in.)

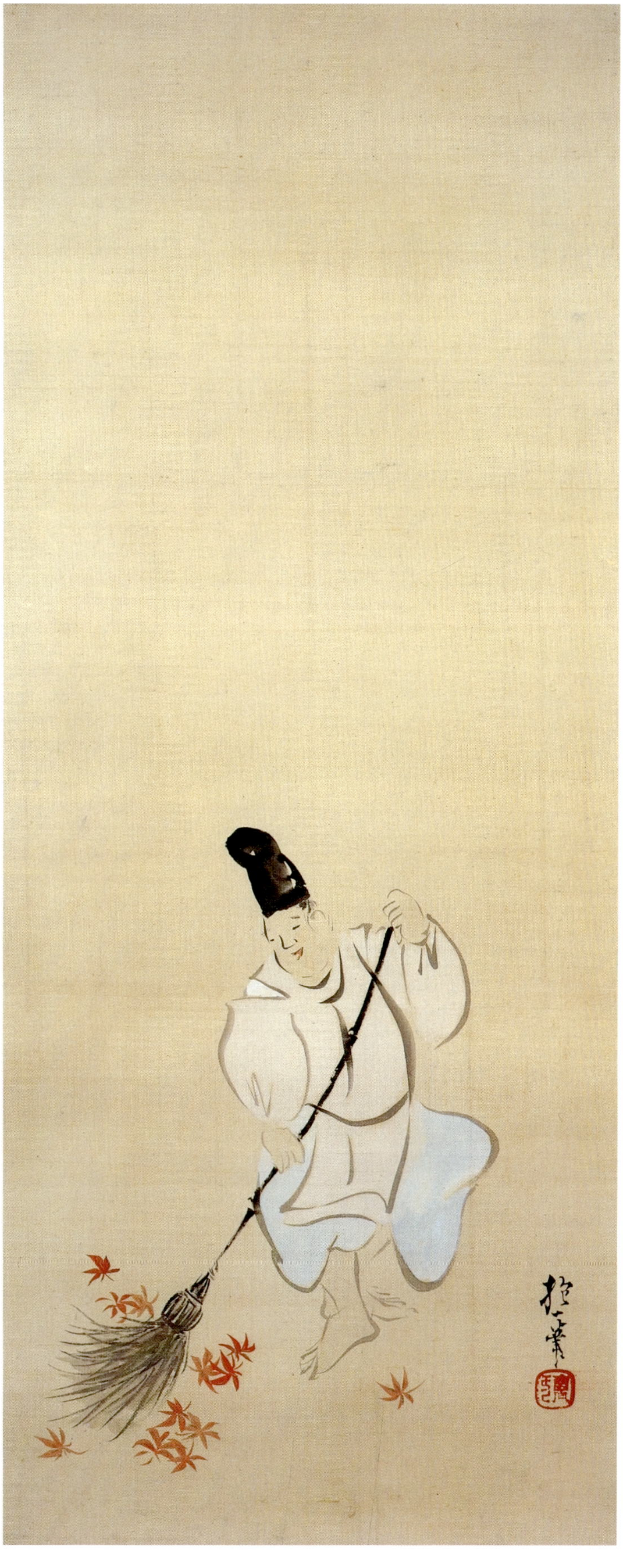

20
Sakai Hōitsu (1761 – 1828)
Sweeping Maple Leaves
Hanging scroll
Color on silk
110.5 x 46.5 cm
(43½ x 185/16 in.)

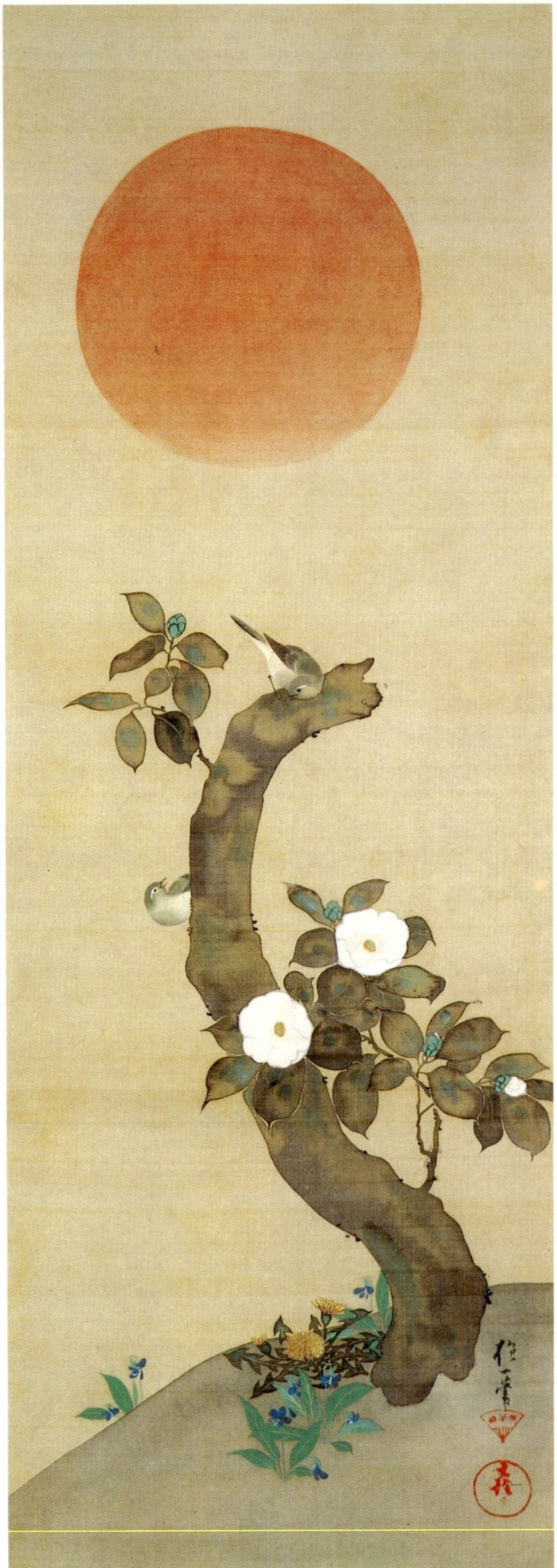

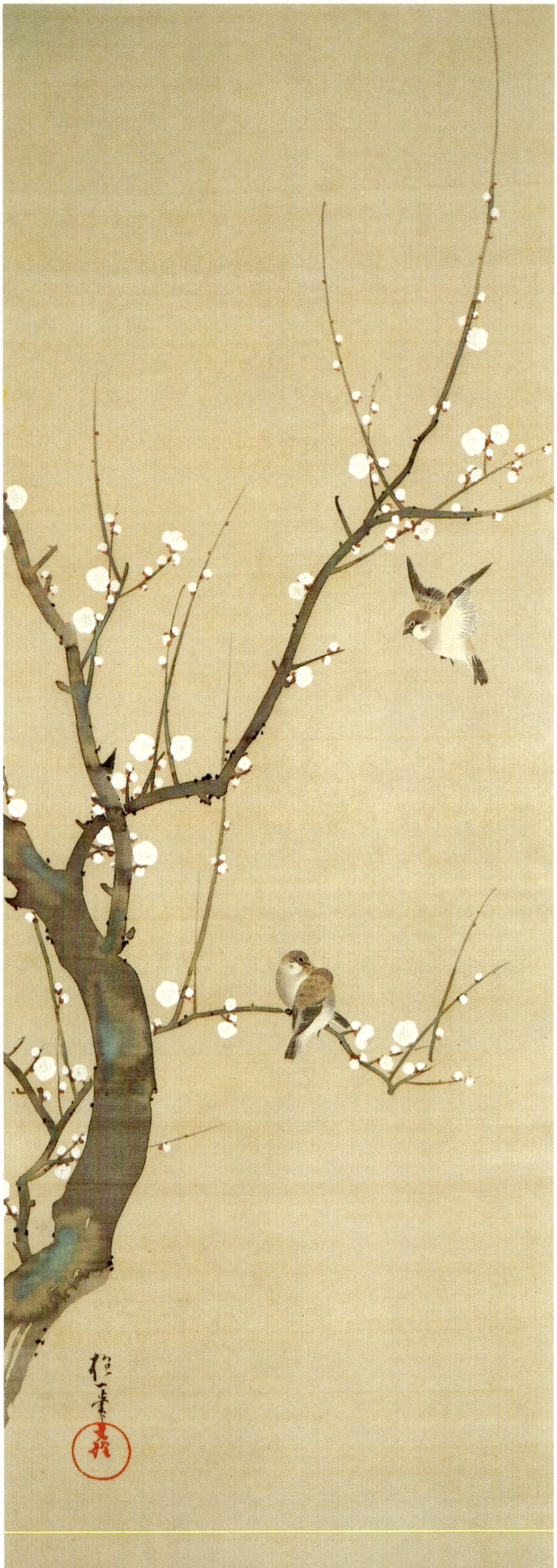

21 January

February

Sakai Hōitsu (1761 – 1828), *Birds and Flowers of the Twelve Months*

Twelve hanging scrolls; color on silk;

each 140.2 x 50.3 cm (55$\frac{3}{16}$ x 19$\frac{13}{16}$ in.)

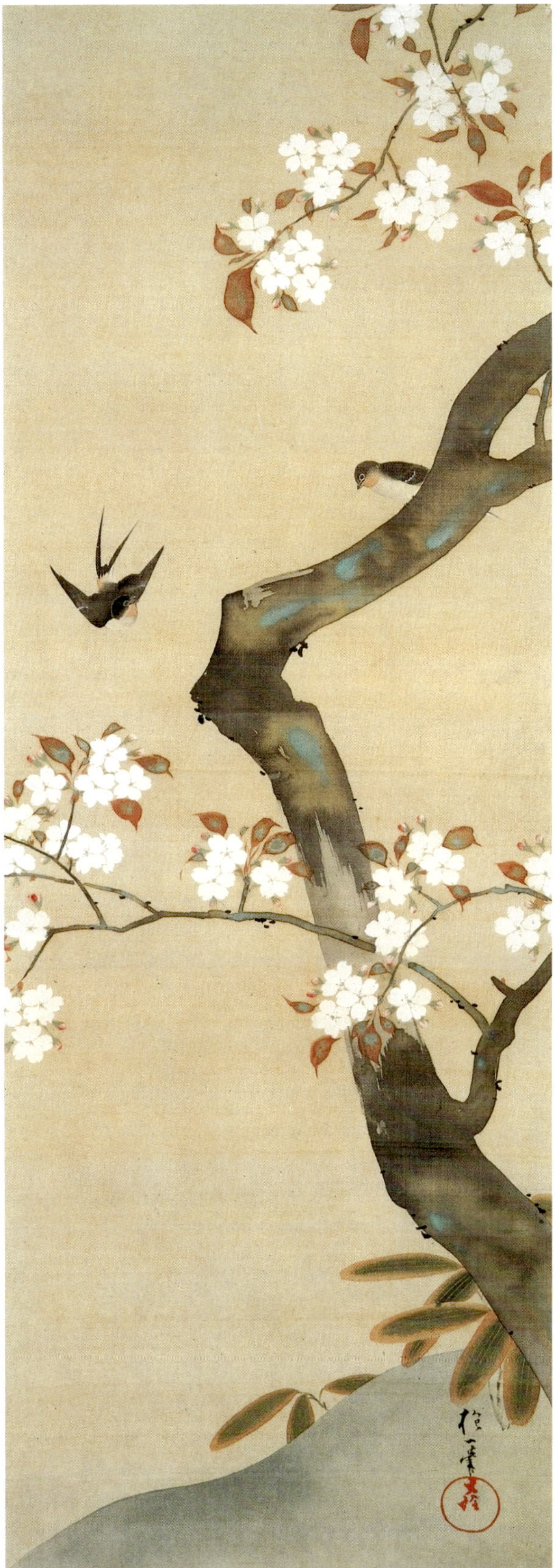

March

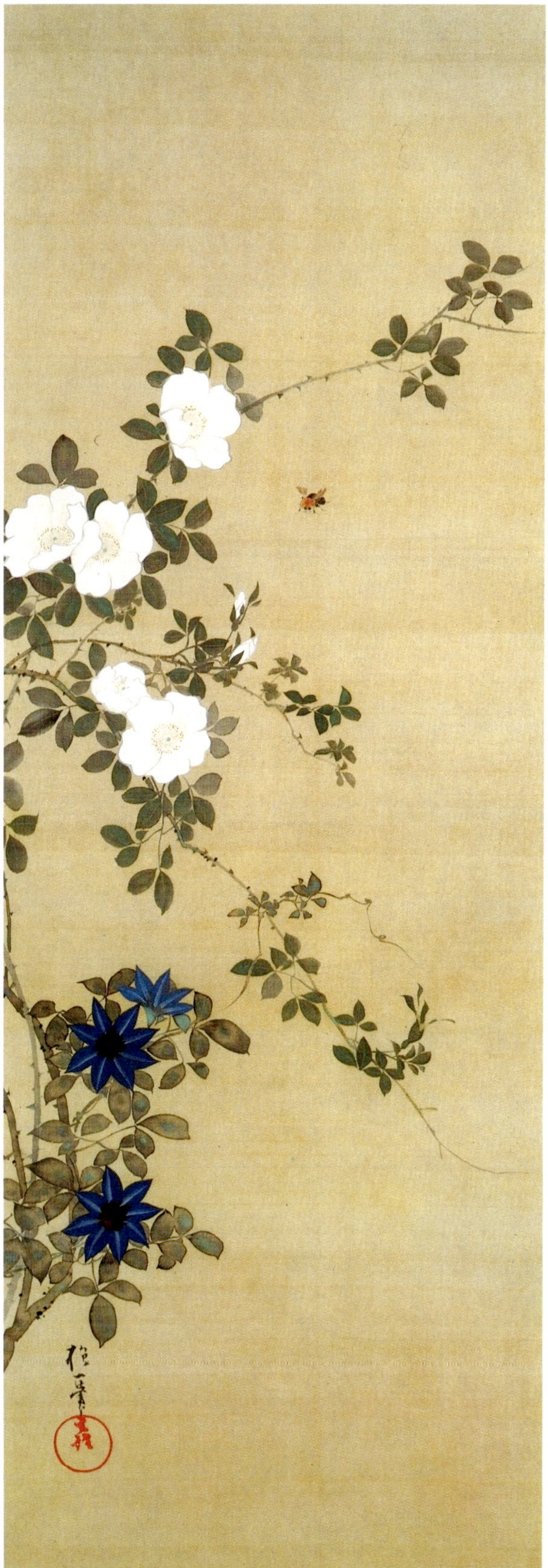

April

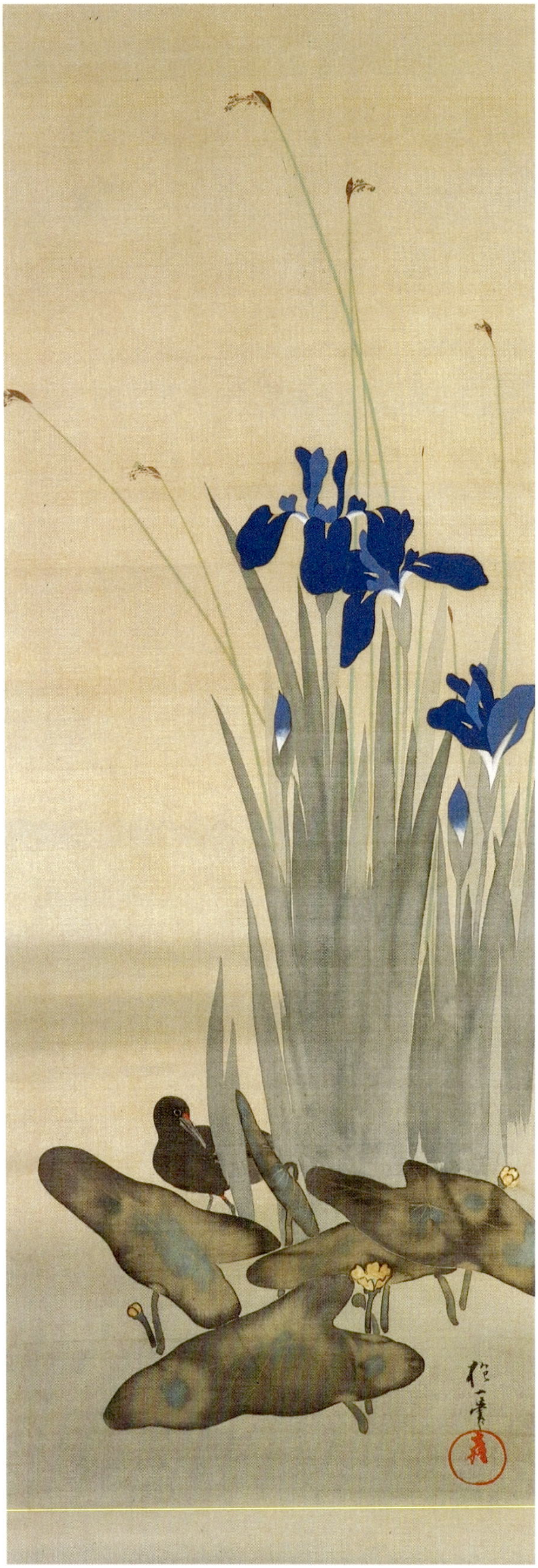

May

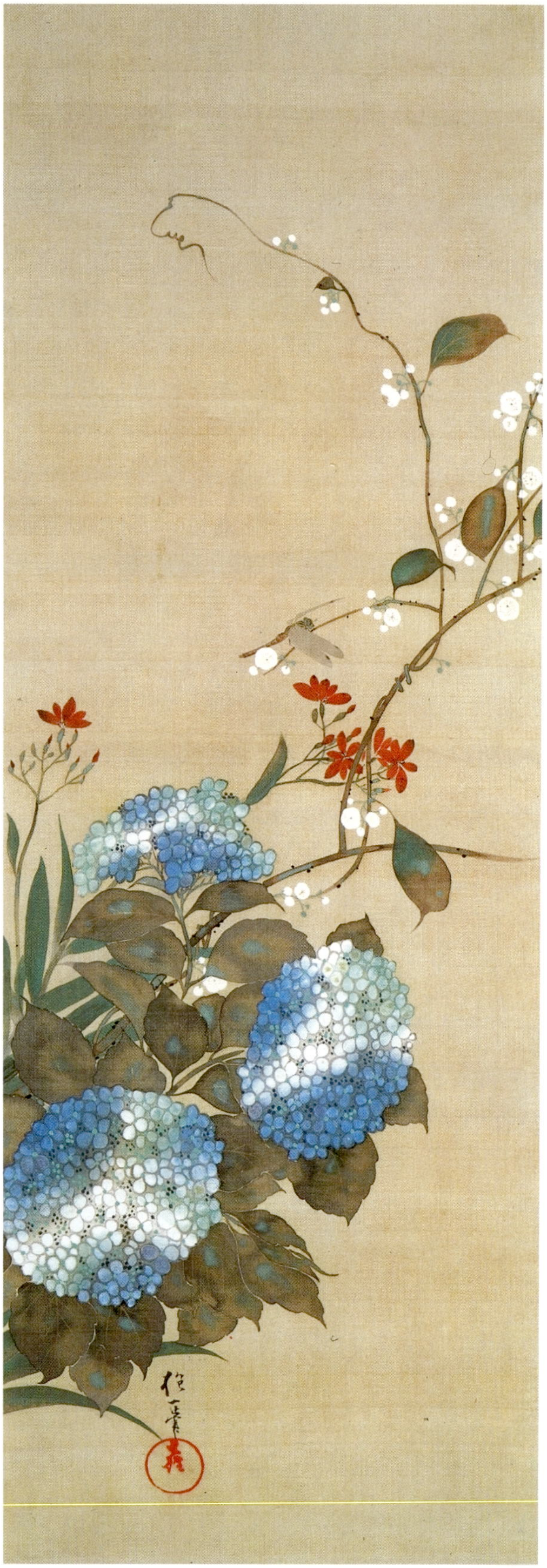

June

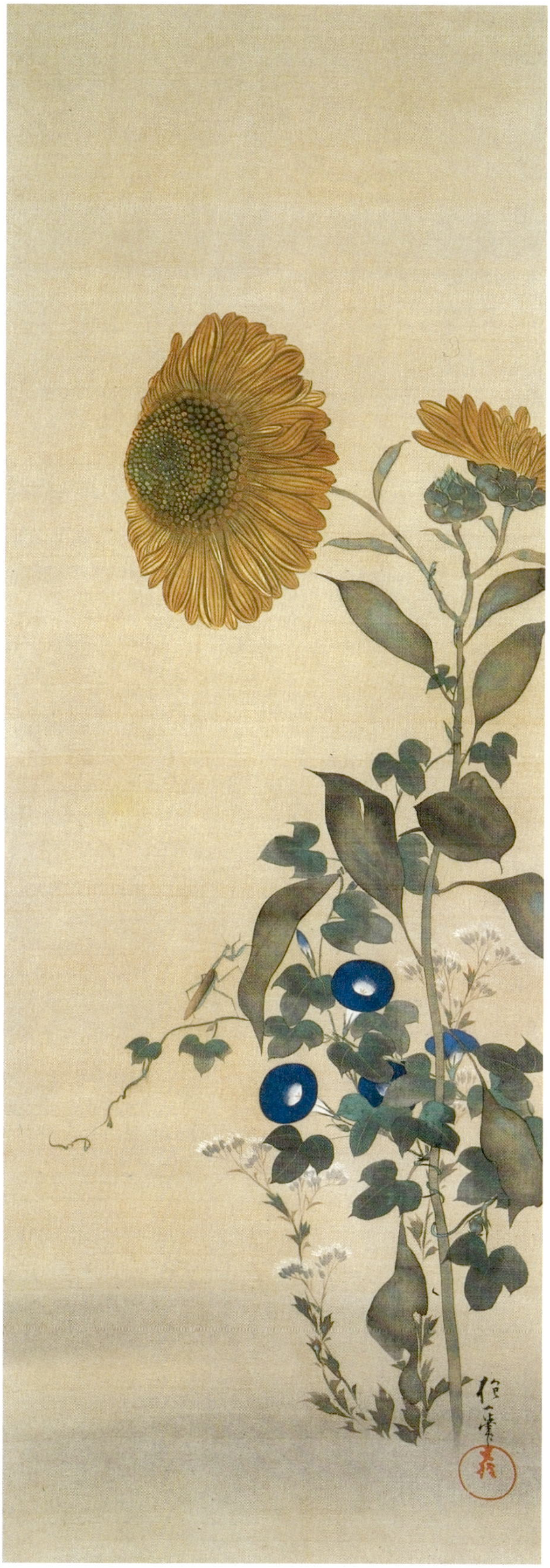

July

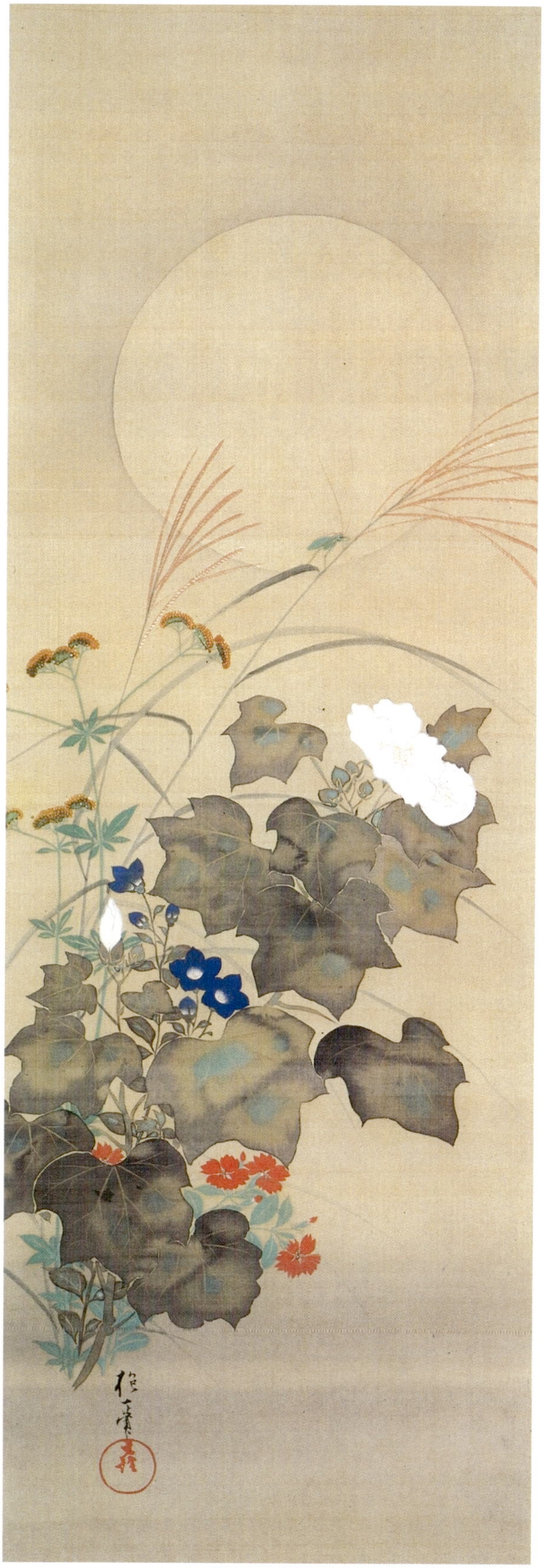

August

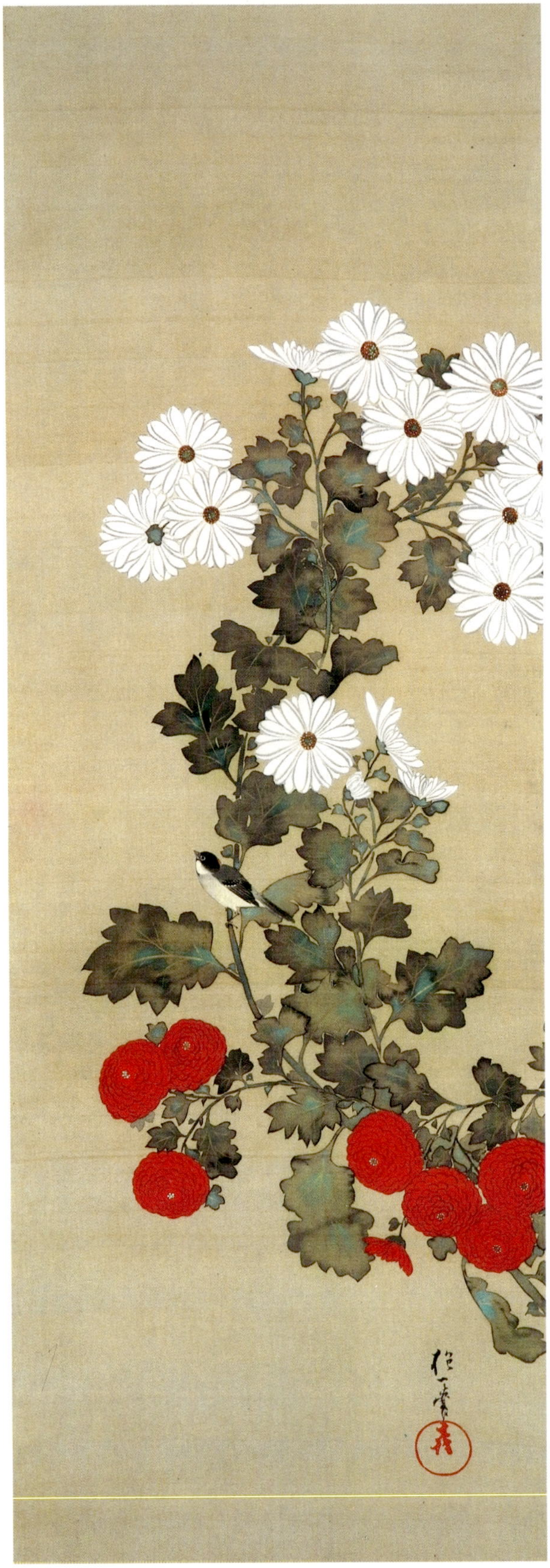

September

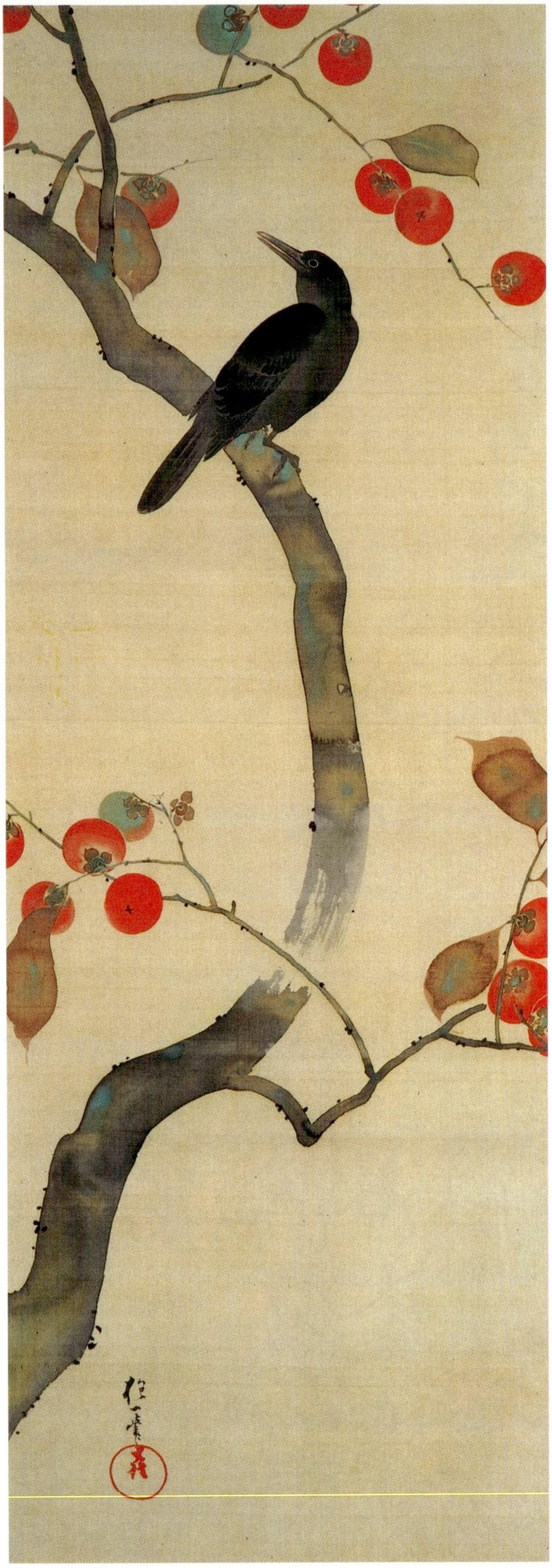

October

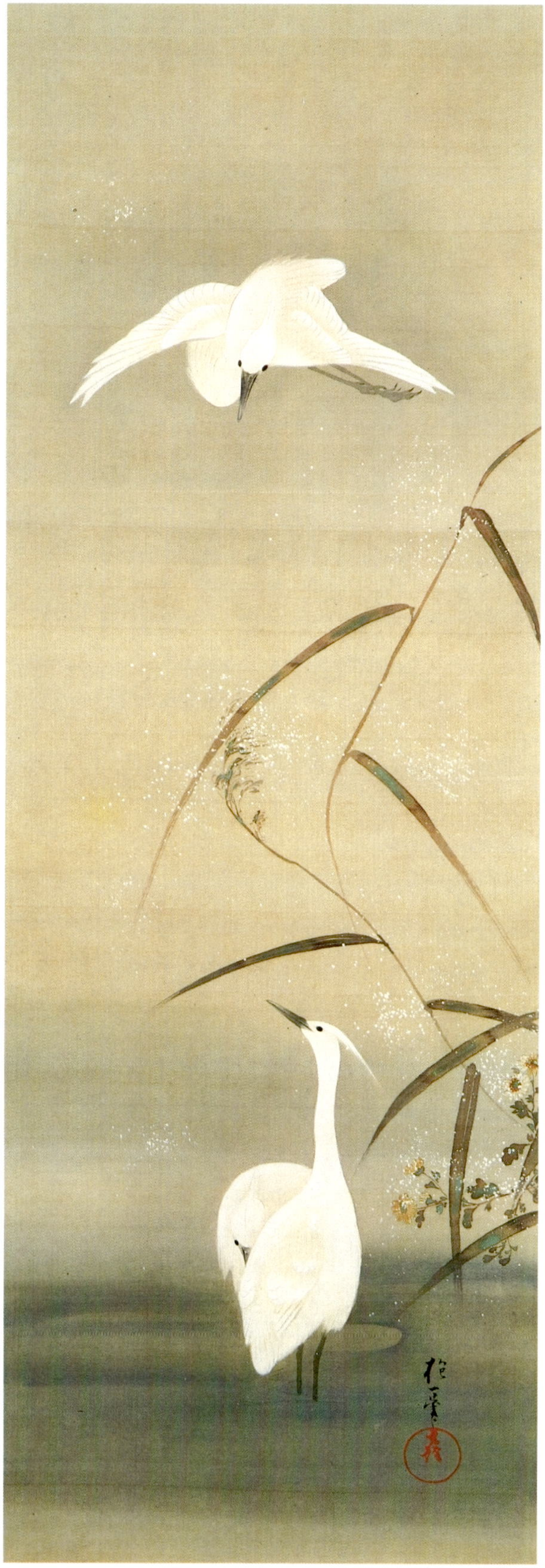

November

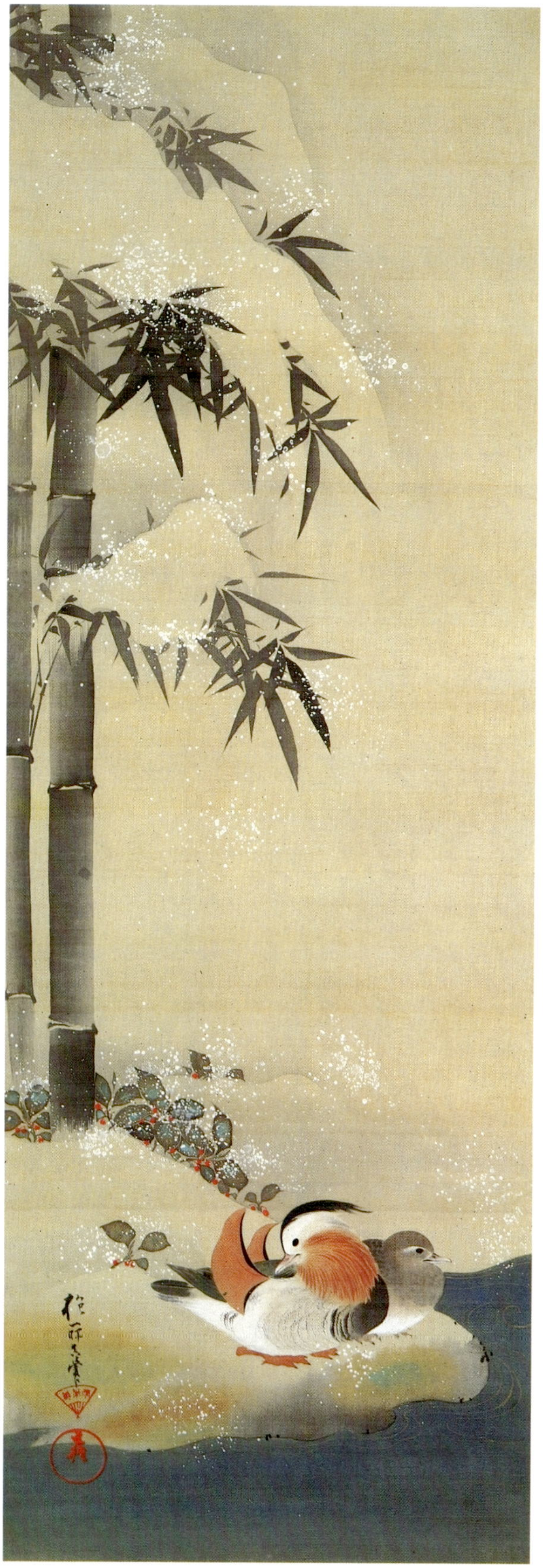

December

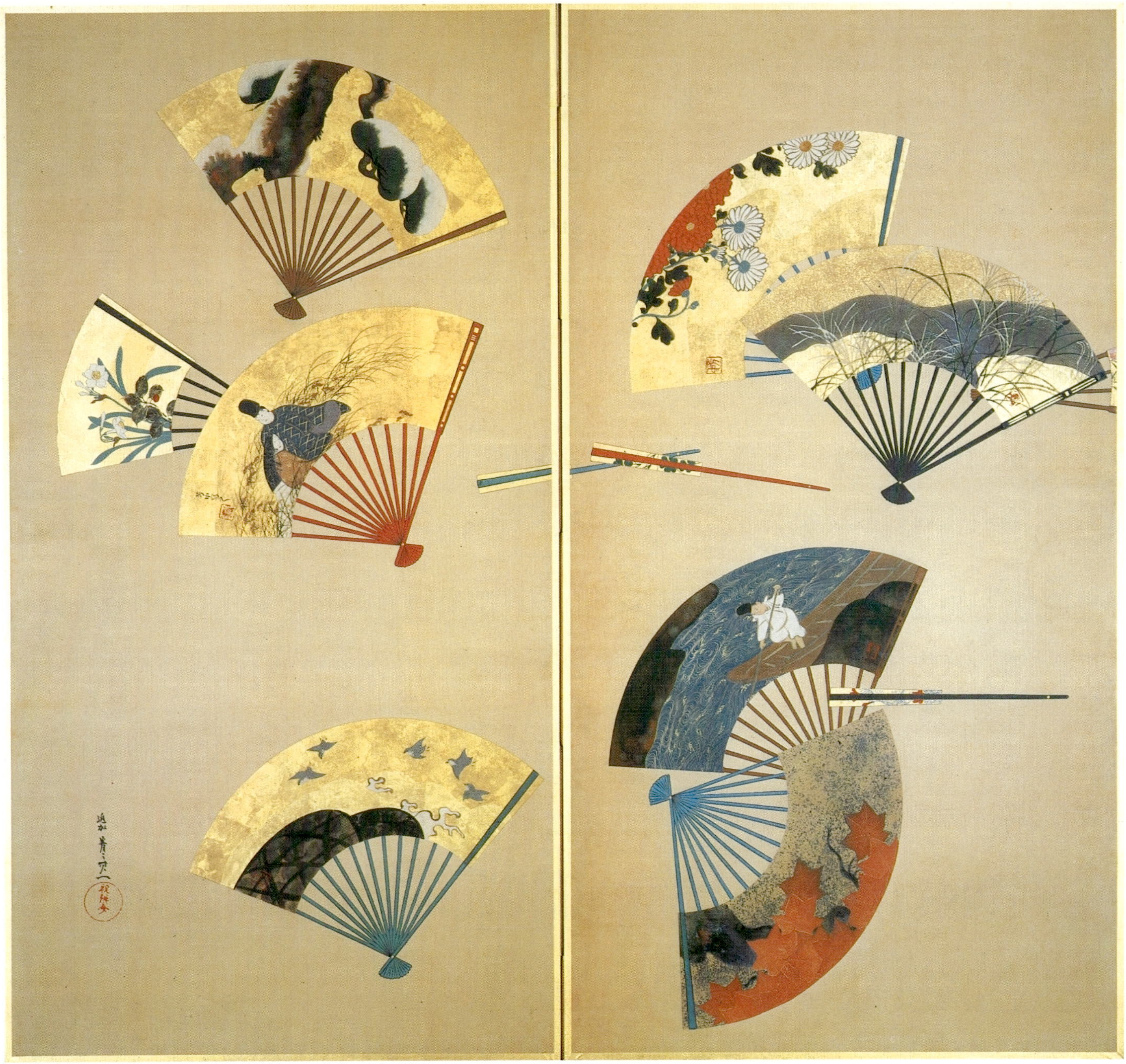

22
Nakamura Hōchū
(fl. late 18th-
early 19th century)
Suzuki Kiitsu (1796 – 1858)
Fans
Two-fold screen
Color with gold ground on paper
154.9 x 166.4 cm
(61 x 65½ in.)

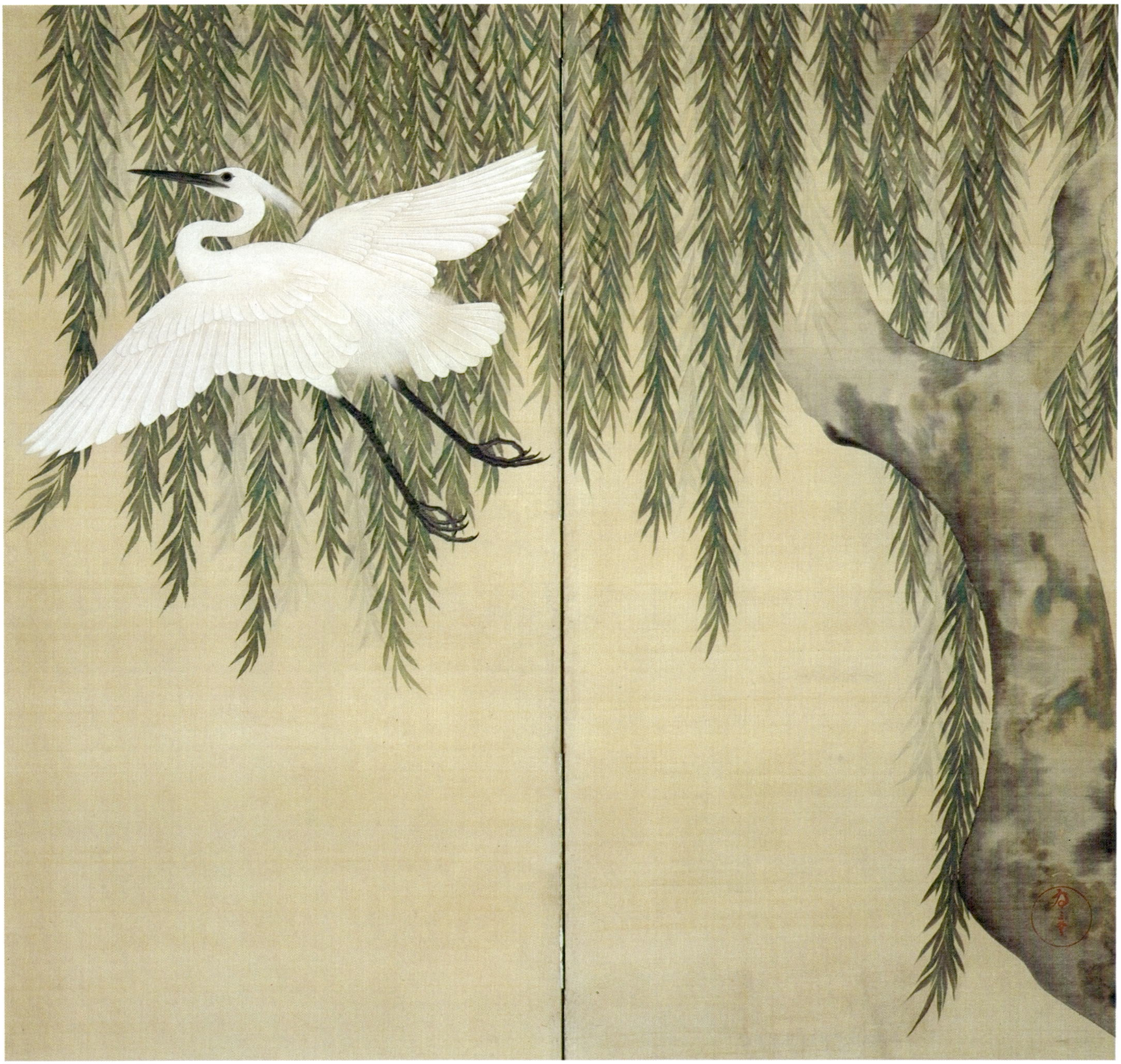

23
Suzuki Kiitsu (1796 – 1858)
Egret and Willow
Two-fold screen
Color on silk
132.3 x 141.5 cm
(52⅛ x 55 11/16 in.)

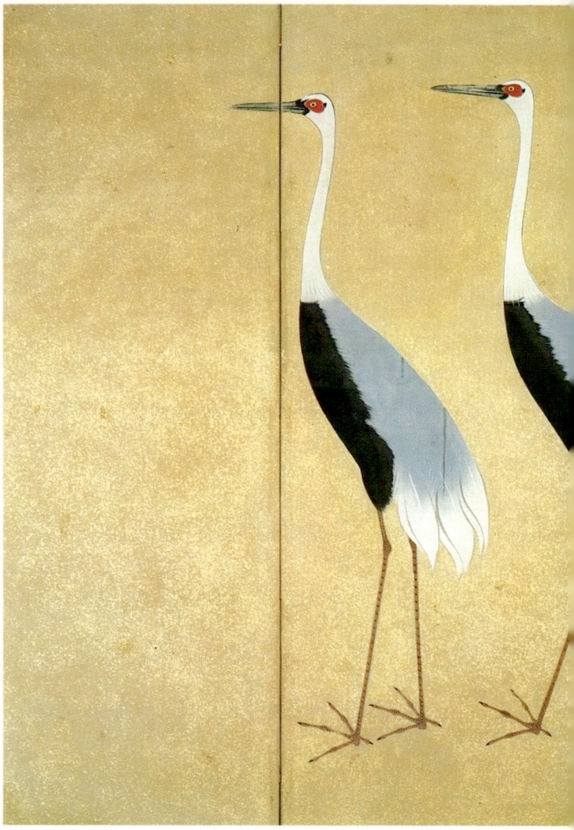

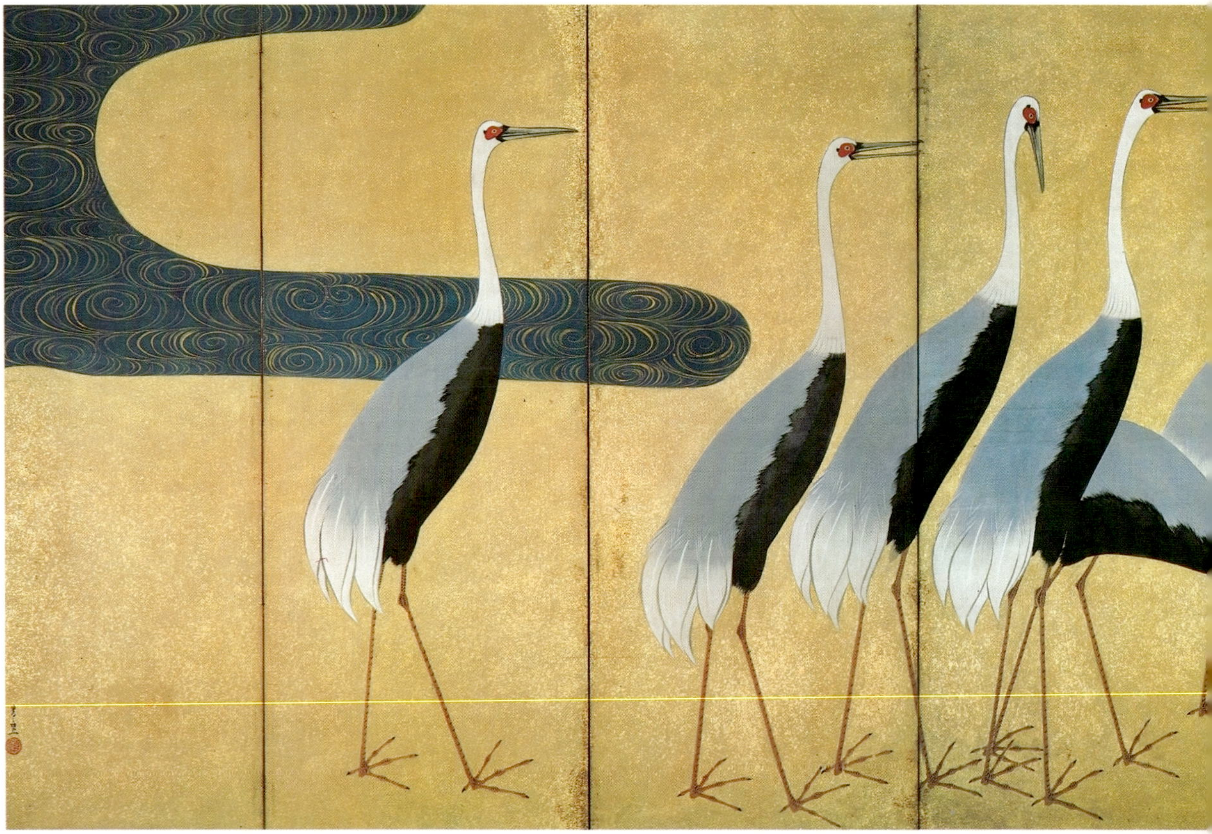

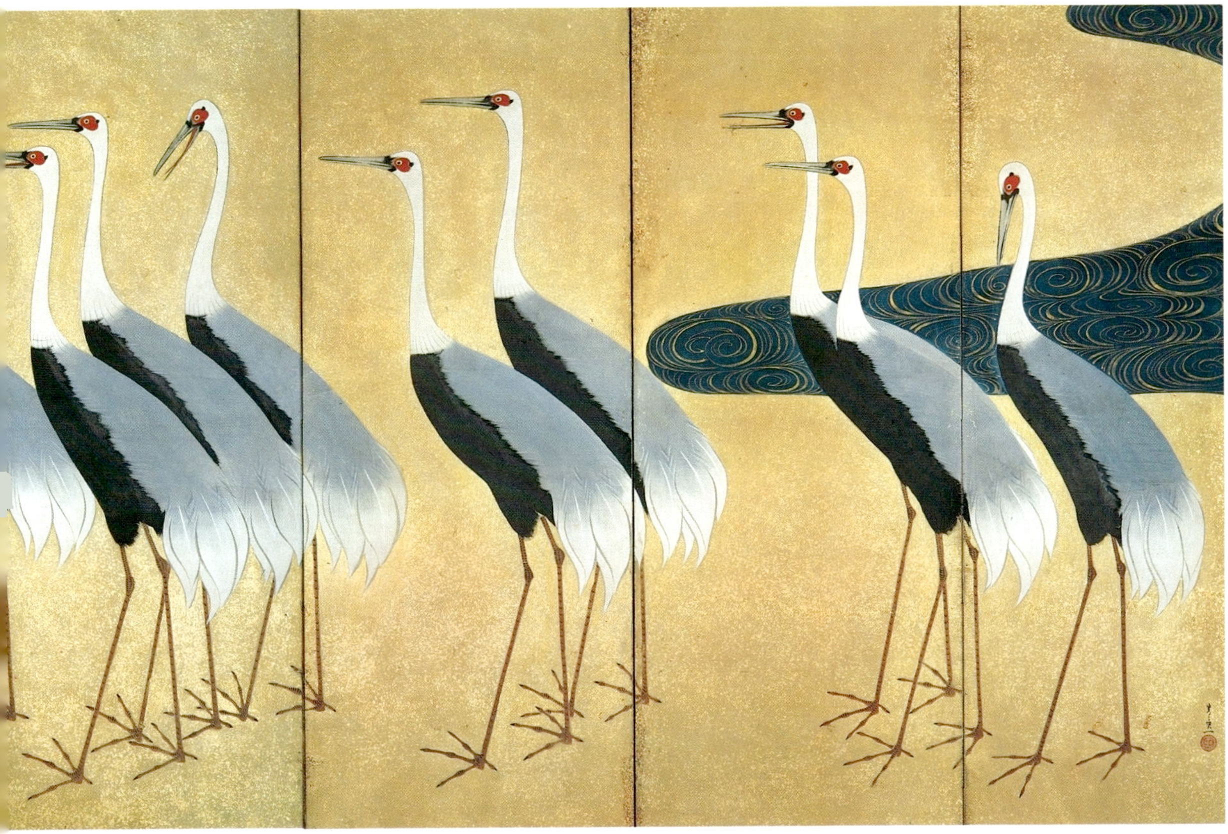

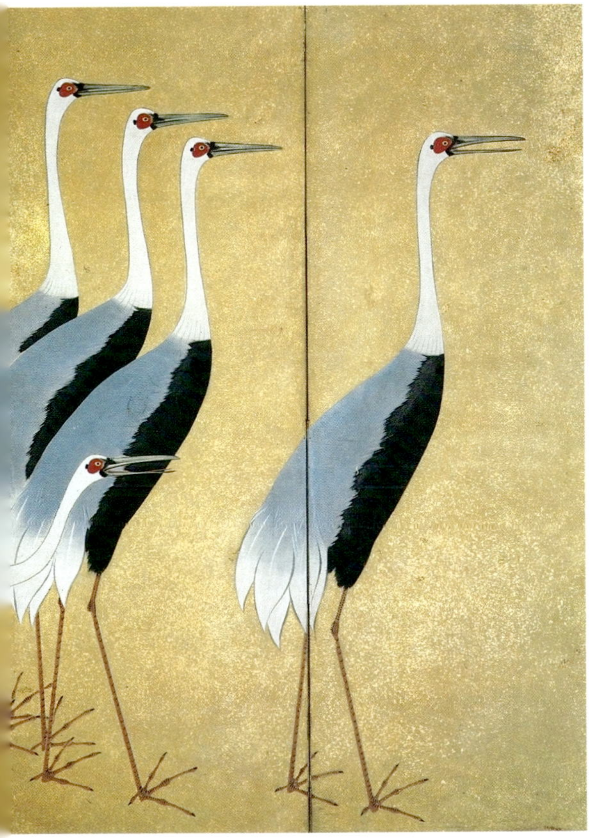

24
Suzuki Kiitsu (1796 – 1858)
Cranes
Pair of six-fold screens
Color with gold ground on paper
Each 162.7 x 372.2 cm
(64 1/16 x 146 1/2 in.)

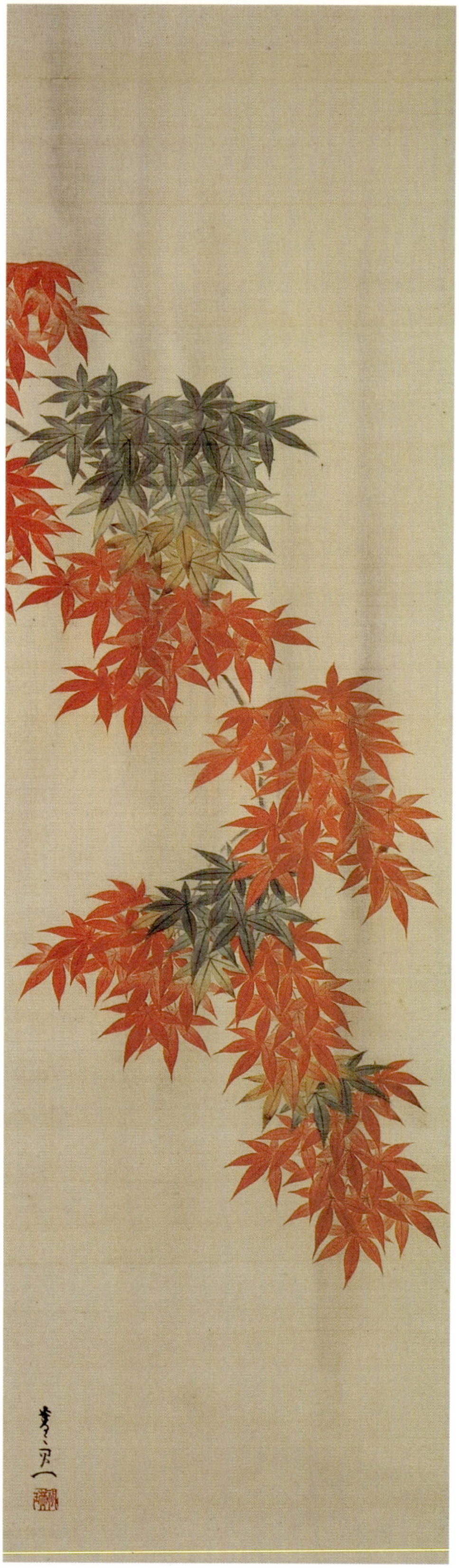

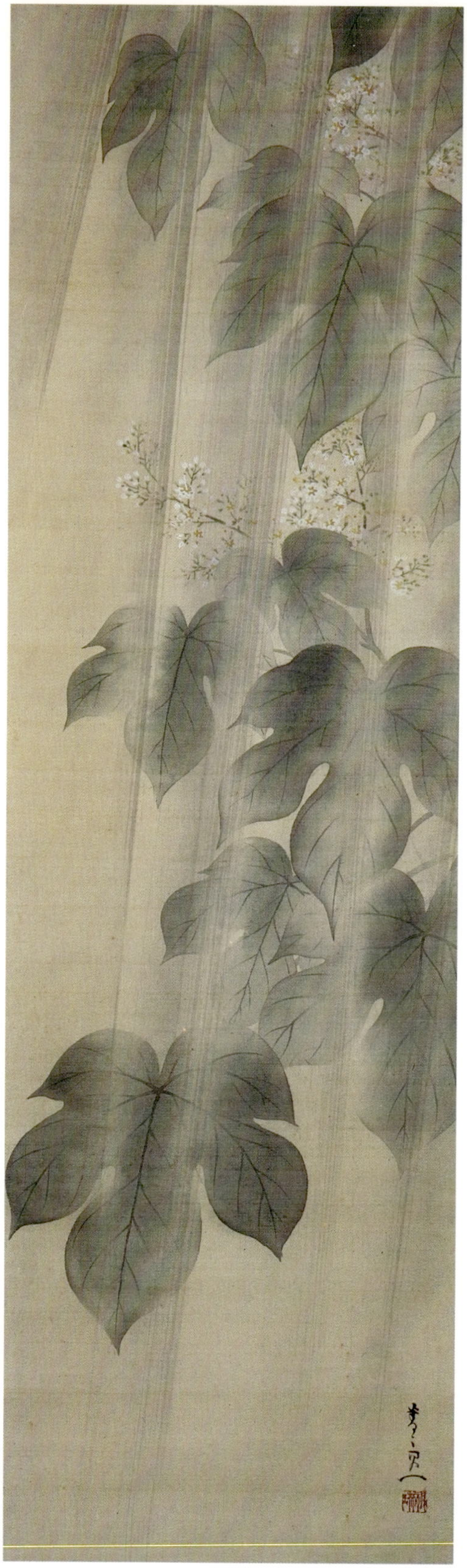

25
Suzuki Kiitsu (1796 – 1858)
Paulownia and Maple
Pair of hanging scrolls
Color on silk
Each 119.7 x 35.6 cm
(47⅛ x 14 in.)

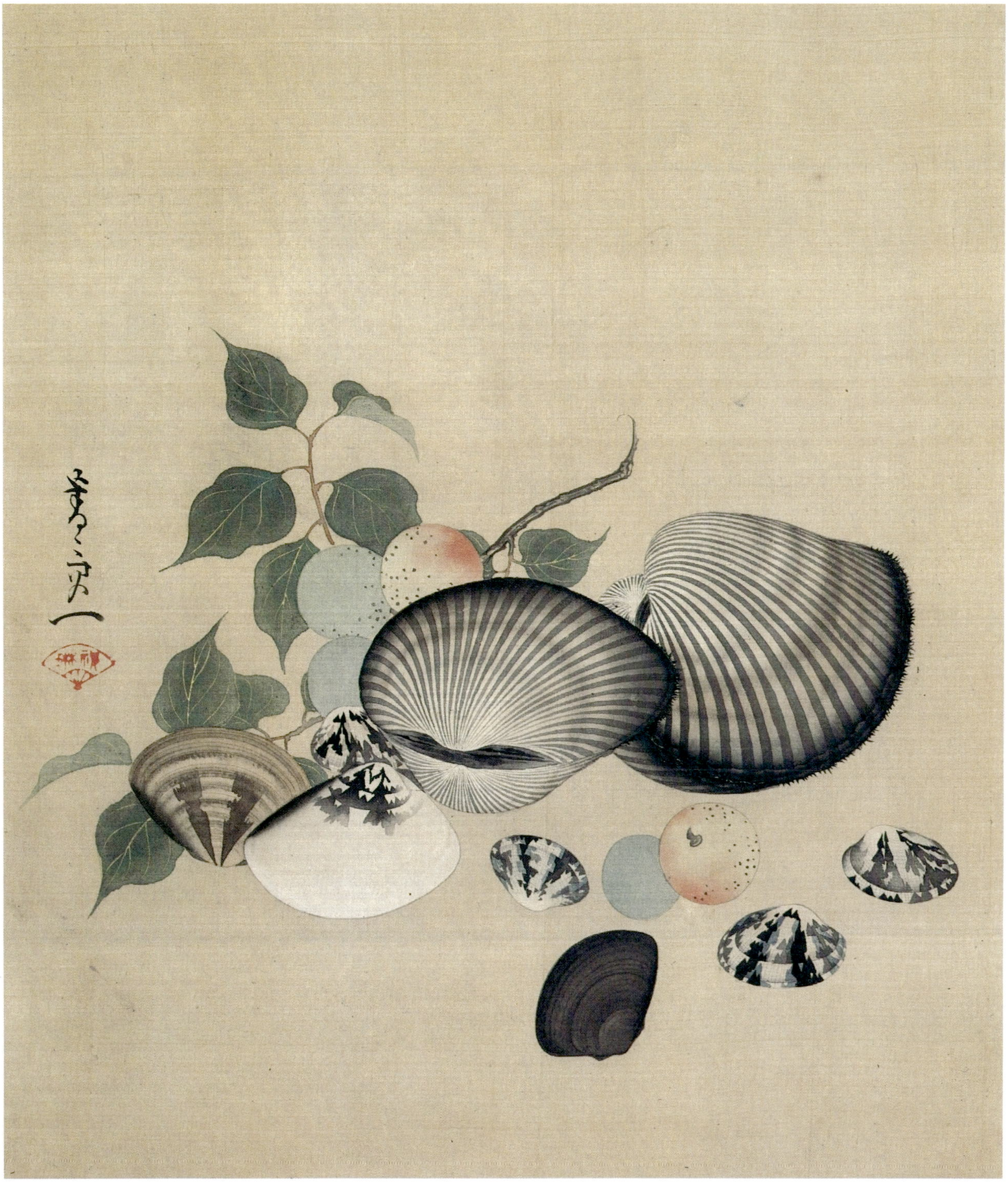

26
Suzuki Kiitsu (1796 – 1858)
Seashells and Plums
Hanging scroll
Color on silk
34.8 x 29.2 cm
($13^{11}/_{16}$ x $11^{1}/_{2}$ in.)

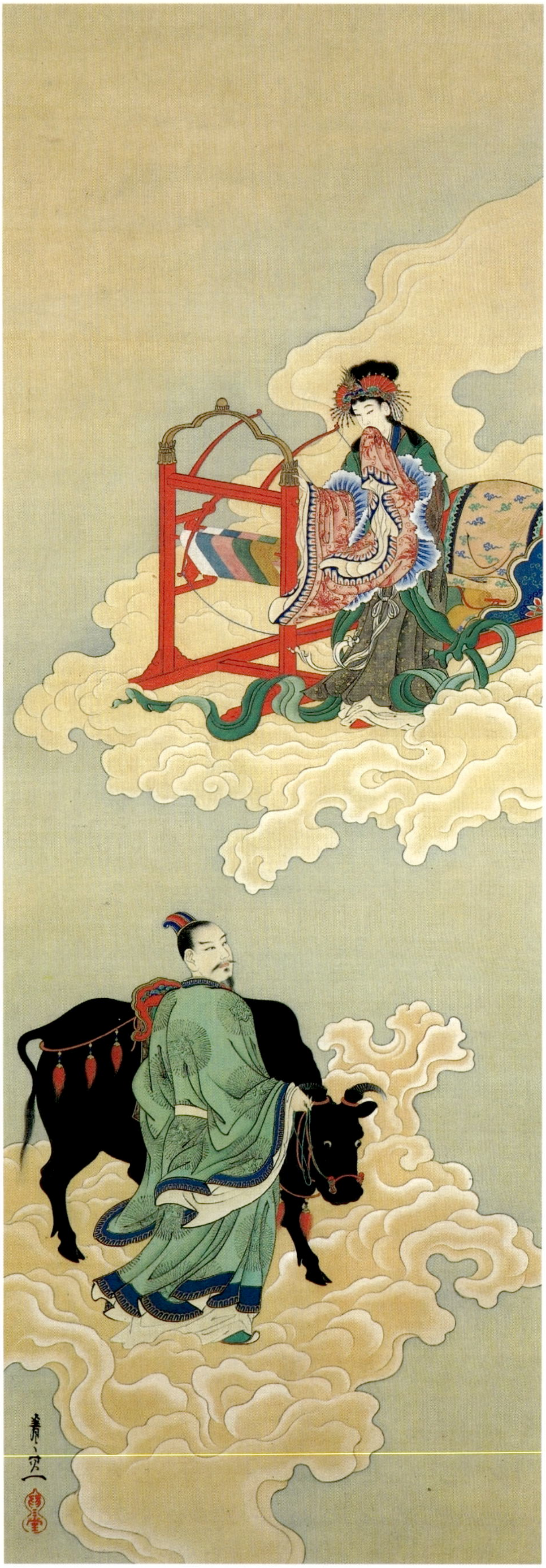

27
Suzuki Kiitsu (1796 – 1858)
Tanabata
Hanging scroll
Color on silk
110.9 x 39.3 cm
(43$\frac{11}{16}$ x 15$\frac{9}{16}$ in.)

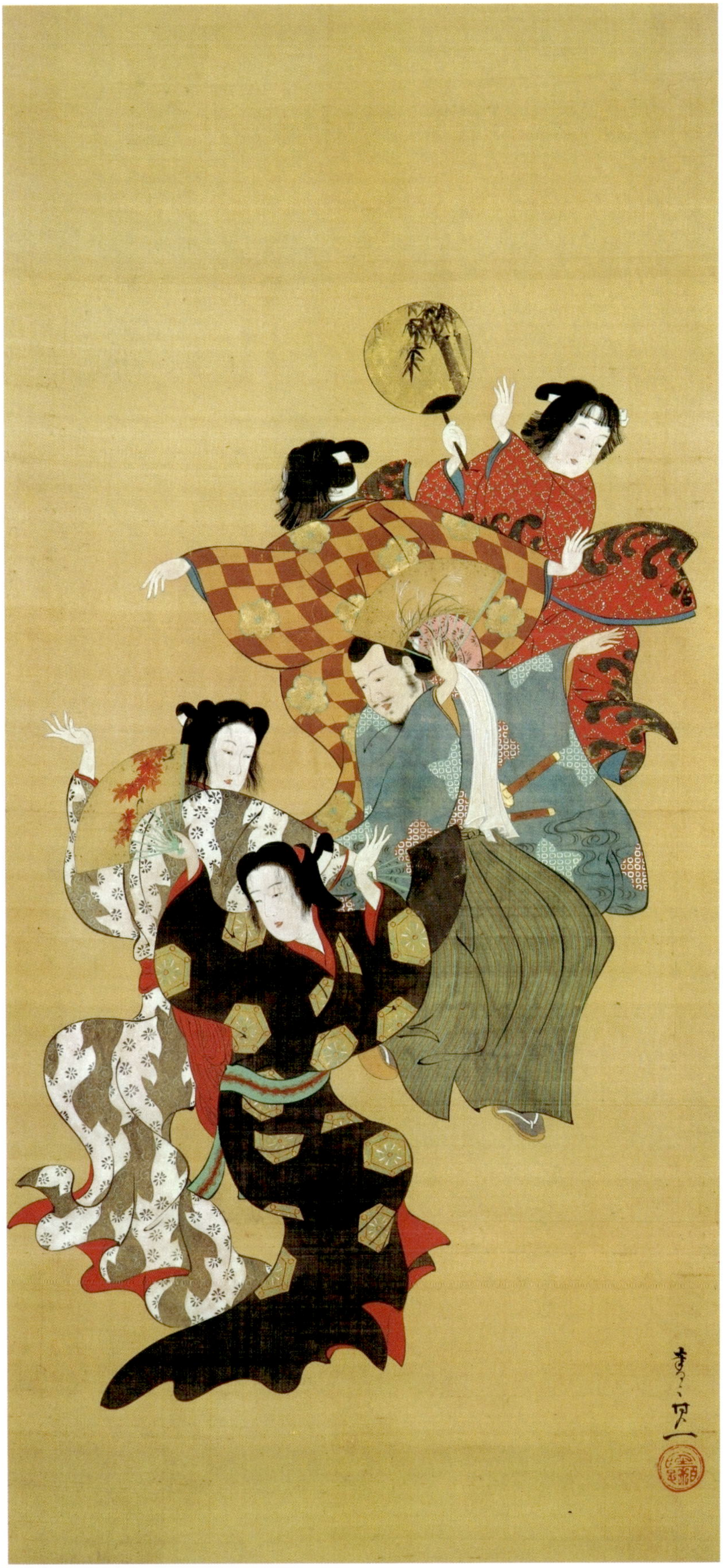

28
Suzuki Kiitsu (1796 – 1858)
Dancing
Hanging scroll
Color on silk
105.9 x 49.7 cm
(41 $^{11}/_{16}$ x 19 $^{9}/_{16}$ in.)

Ukiyo-e Paintings

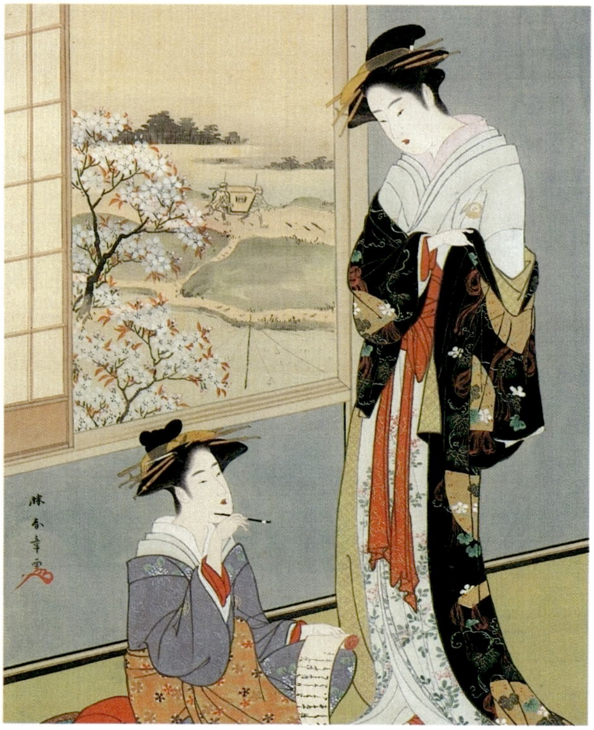

Of all the myriad forms of Japanese art, *ukiyo-e* ("pictures of the floating world") is by far the best known in the West. But the vast number of ukiyo-e woodblock prints that have come to the West have obscured the fact that many of the artists who designed prints were also, or primarily, painters. Indeed, the early history of this school can only be traced through ukiyo-e paintings.

The Edo period, in which ukiyo-e was born and flourished, was a time of unprecedented stability under the rule of fifteen generations of Tokugawa shōgun. In these two and a half centuries of peace, the government attempted to enforce a system of four classes: samurai at the top, farmers, craftsmen, and, at the bottom, merchants. In theory this class system lasted until the end of the Edo period, but in economic terms the reality was quite different. By the Genroku era (1688–1703), a great deal of economic power had passed from the hands of the samurai into those of the trader, the shopkeeper, and the moneylender. So it came to be that the samurai clung to their dignity and privileges, while the merchants had most of the money and most of the pleasures. The education and tradition of the samurai were heavily indebted to Chinese models and the classical past; the merchants were less hampered by convention and social codes and thus were free to sponsor art that was unrestrained and experimental.

The vital urban culture of the Edo period was that of a prosperous bourgeoisie devoted to the unbridled pursuit of pleasure, the "floating world" of theaters, restaurants, and brothels. The pleasure quarters of the large cities were in restricted areas—Yoshiwara in Edo, Shimabara in Kyoto, and Shinmachi in Osaka—and attracted the merchant, the samurai in disguise, government officials, and anyone else who could afford the entertainment offered there. It is not surprising that the merchants who patronized these "nightless cities" would commission paintings of the leading actors and courtesans of the day. There was a great interest too in the latest fashions in costume and hairstyle, and these were reflected in ukiyo-e paintings.

Iwasa Matabei (1578–1650) has traditionally been called the father of ukiyo-e painting, but very few of his signed works are of contemporary genre subjects. It is rather in unsigned paintings in his style (*Lady with Tethered Bird*, plate 29), that the seeds of ukiyo-e may be found. Delicate depictions of celebrated courtesans reached their height in the Kambun era (1661–73); these were sometimes inscribed with a poem written in the woman's own hand (*Beauty Leaning on an Armrest*, plate 30). The Kaigetsudō School of the first half of the eighteenth century specialized in standing figures whose sensuality and dramatic sweeping costumes are unmistakable (*Beauty Arranging Her Hair*, plate 31).

Ukiyo-e paintings are sometimes of humorous subjects: the sight of a bearded Zen patriarch and an elegant courtesan who have exchanged costumes (*Daruma and a Courtesan Wearing Each Other's Clothes*, plate 32) or the same Zen master disapprovingly surveying a raucous party in a pleasure house (*House of Pleasure*, plate 39). But most ukiyo-e paintings are of the real or idealized stars of the pleasure quarters in their resplendent costumes and elaborate coiffures, shown either in empty space (Kikumaro's *Two Beauties*, plate 34, *Beauty Reading a Letter*, plate 35, and *Genre Scenes*, plate 36) or in landscape or interior settings (Shunshō's *Two Beauties*, plate 33, *Two Beauties by the Sumida River in Spring*, plate 37, and *Beauties*, plate 38). Another treatment of women is not that of the floating world but of one hundred activities of one hundred women, providing a captivating catalogue of the duties and amusements of women in the Edo period (*One Hundred Women*, plate 40).

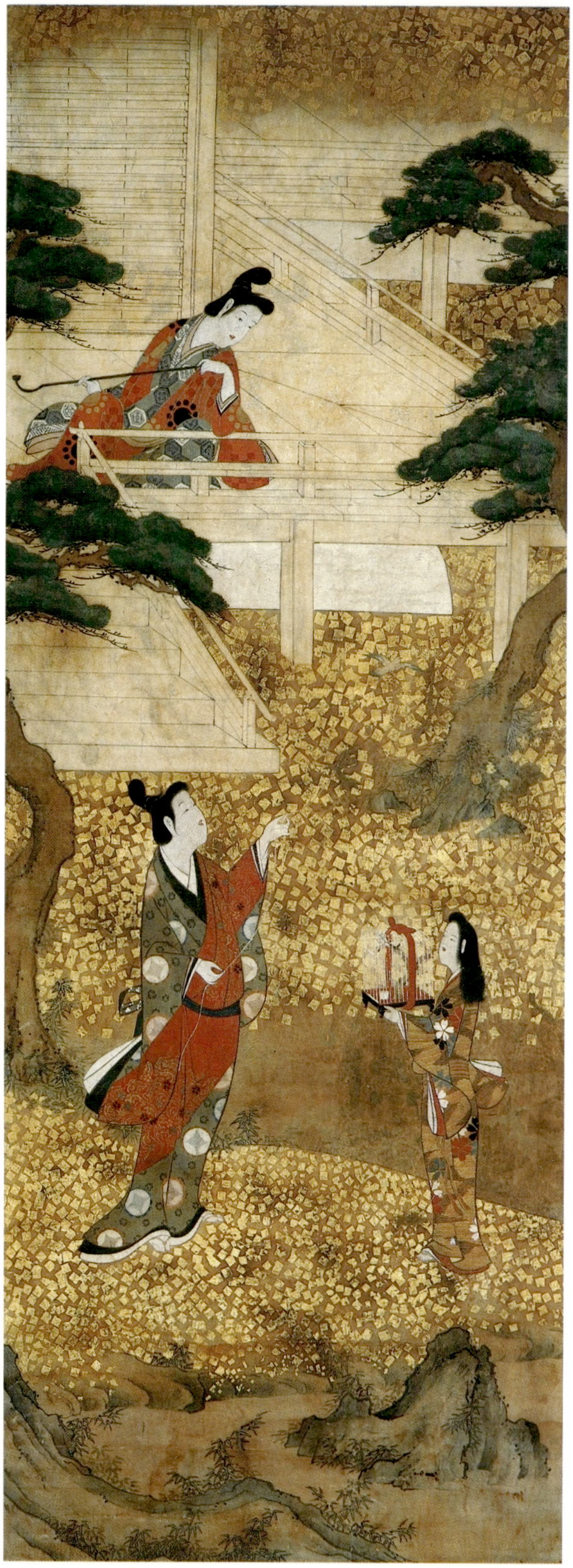

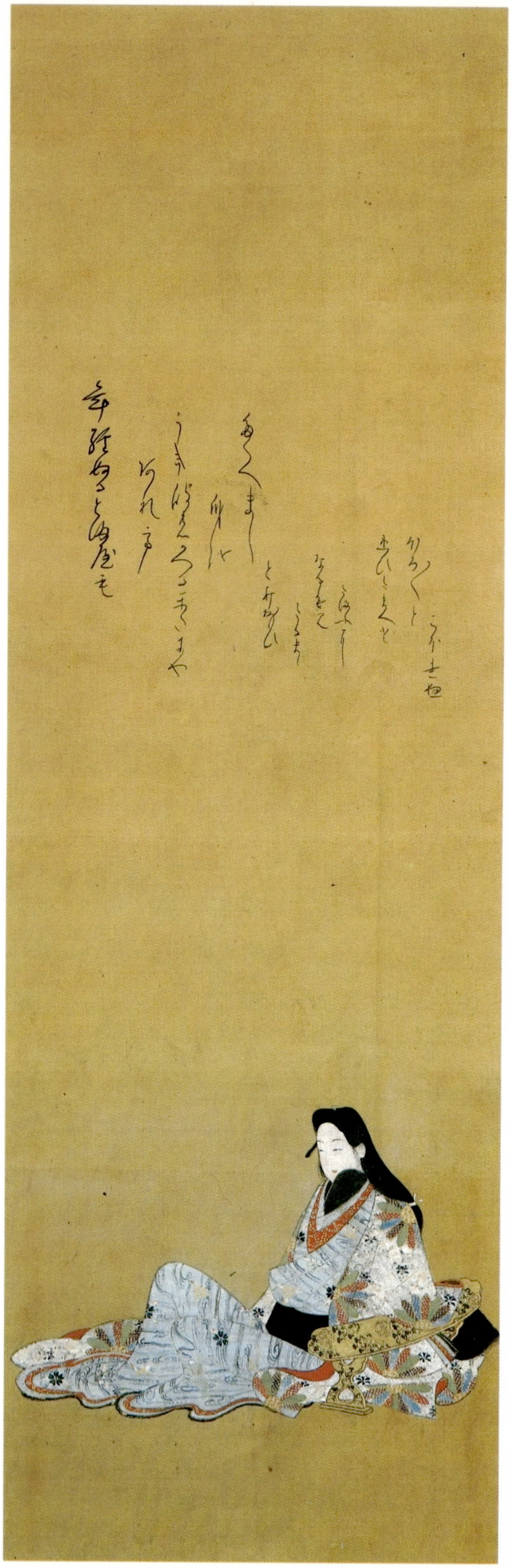

29
(far left)
Matabei School
Seventeenth century
Lady with Tethered Bird
Hanging scroll
Ink, color, and gold on paper
102.5 x 38.4 cm
($40\frac{3}{8}$ x $15\frac{1}{8}$ in.)

30
(left)
Anonymous
Beauty Leaning on an Armrest
Kambun period (1661 – 73)
Hanging scroll
Color on silk
93.2 x 30.3 cm
($36\frac{11}{16}$ x $11\frac{15}{16}$ in.)

31
(right)
Kaigetsudō Doshin
(fl. 1700 – 1716)
Beauty Arranging Her Hair
Hanging scroll
Color on paper
97.8 x 41.8 cm
($38\frac{1}{2}$ x $16\frac{9}{16}$ in.)

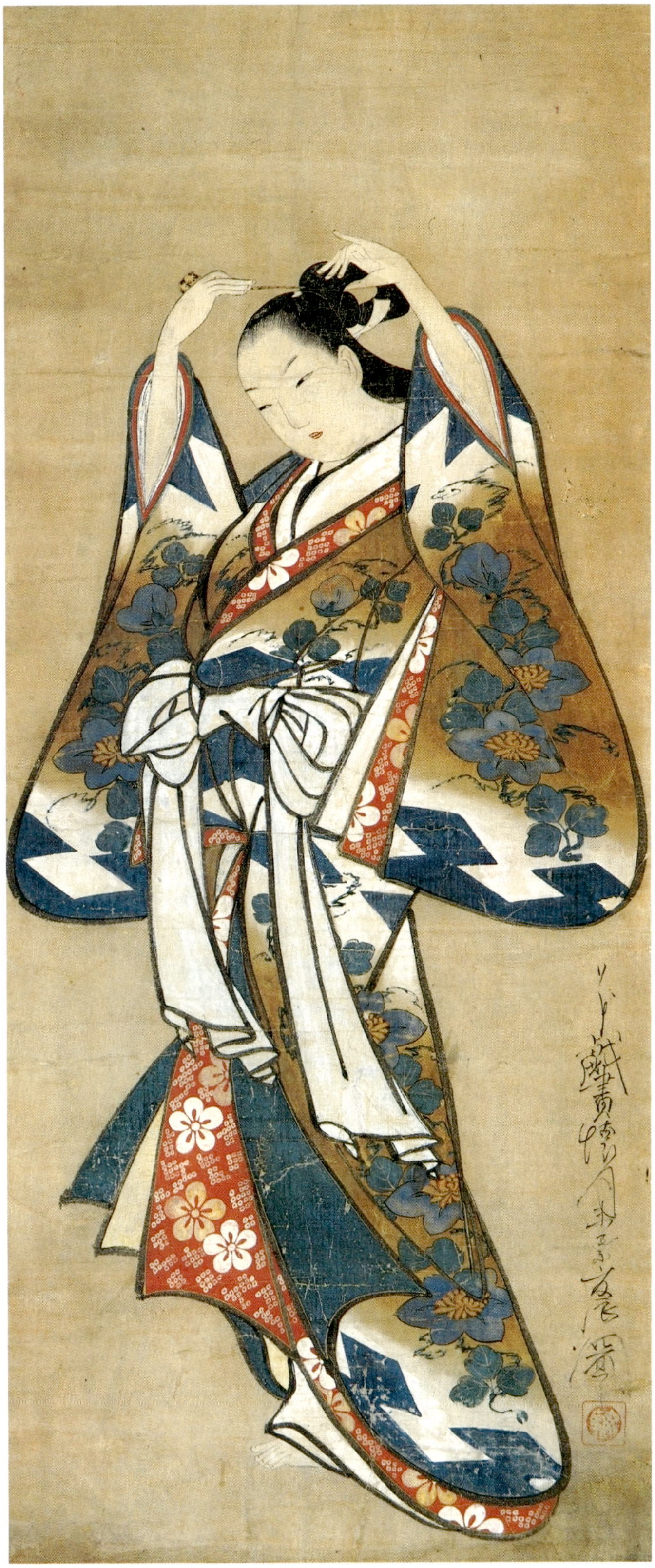

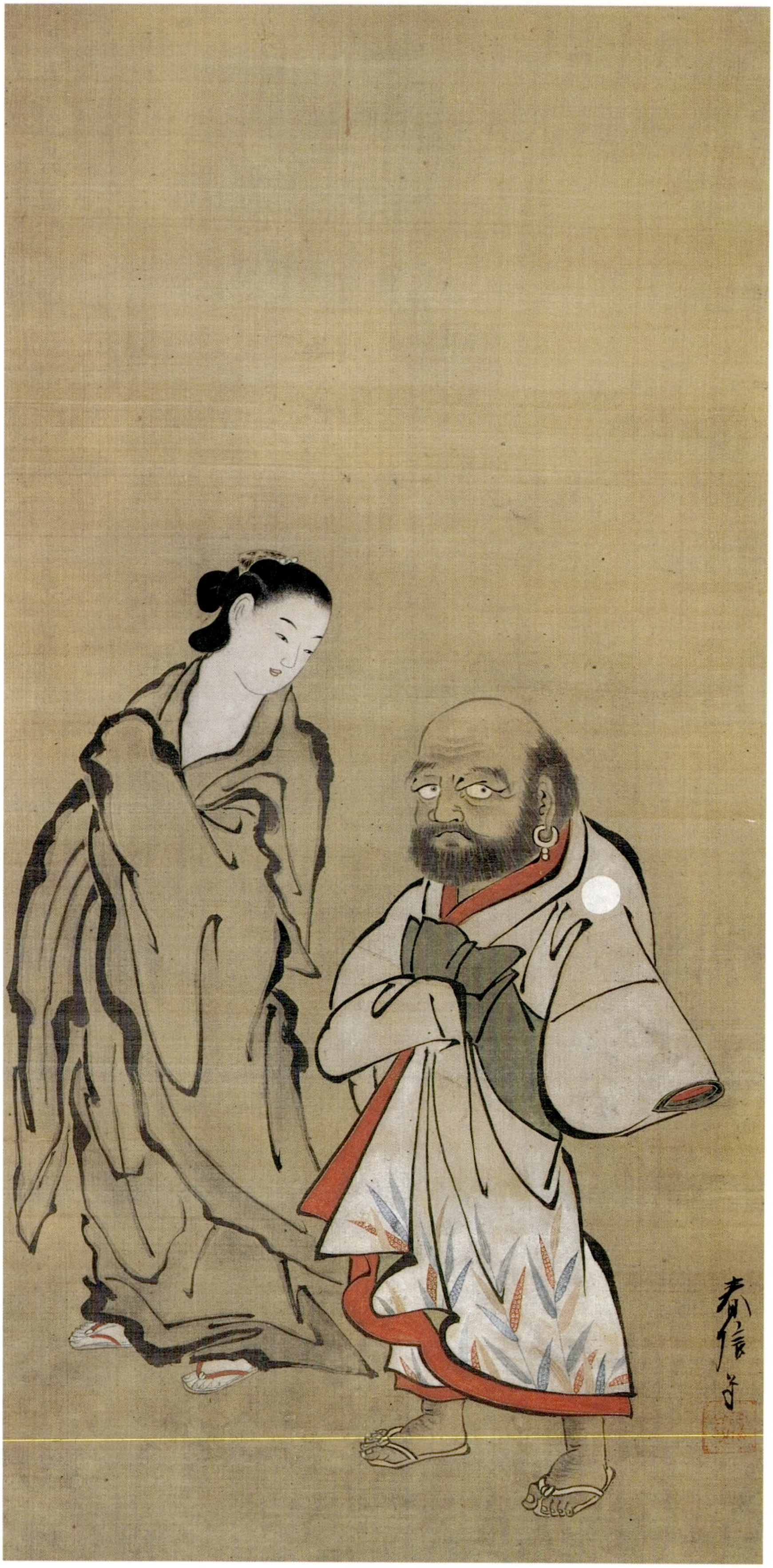

32
Takeda Harunobu
(fl. first half 18th century?)
Daruma and a Courtesan Wearing Each Other's Clothes
Hanging scroll
Color on silk
62.5 x 31.6 cm
(24$\frac{5}{8}$ x 12$\frac{7}{16}$ in.)

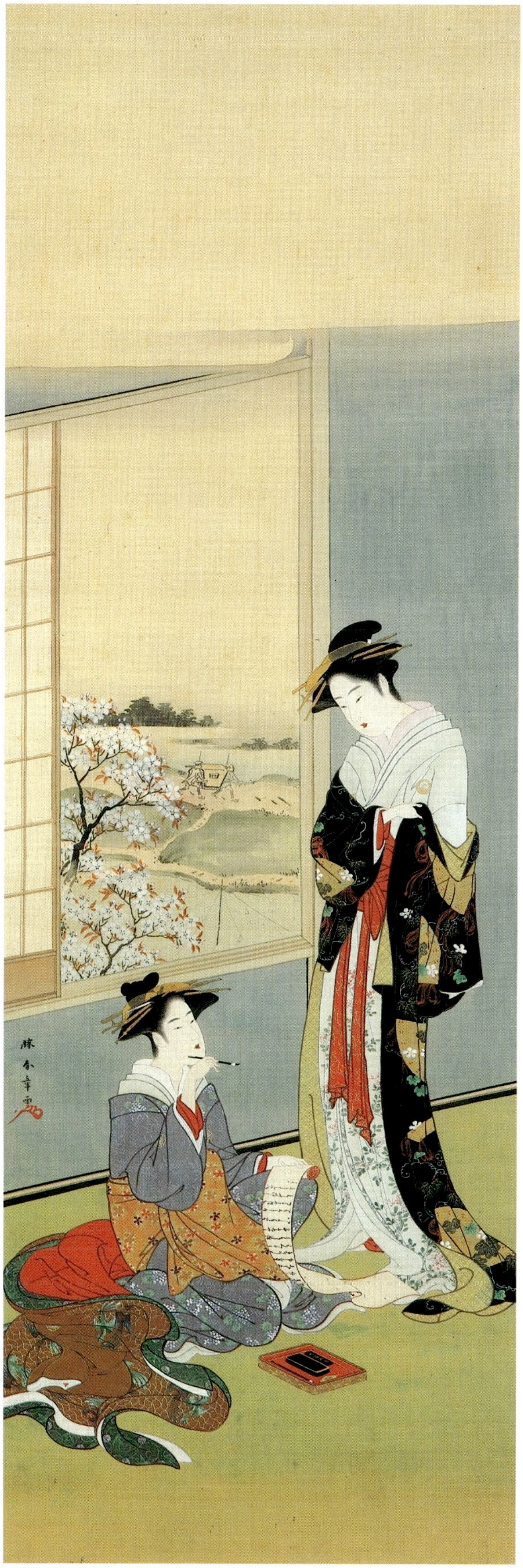

33
Katsukawa Shunshō (1726 – 92)
Two Beauties
Hanging scroll
Color on silk
100.2 x 35.2 cm
(39$\frac{9}{16}$ x 13$\frac{7}{8}$ in.)

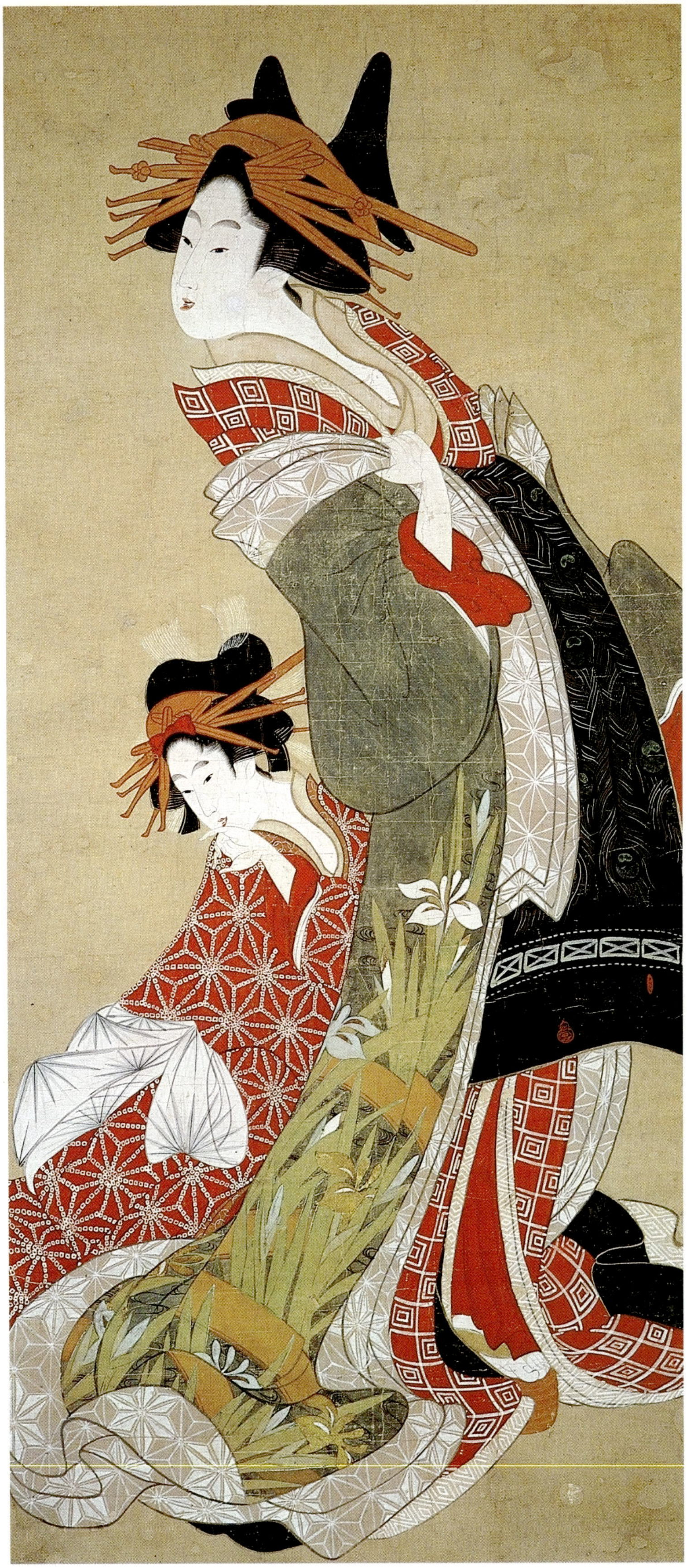

34
Kitagawa Kikumaro (d. 1830)
Two Beauties
Hanging scroll
Color on paper
124.7 x 55.8 cm
(49⅛ x 22 in.)

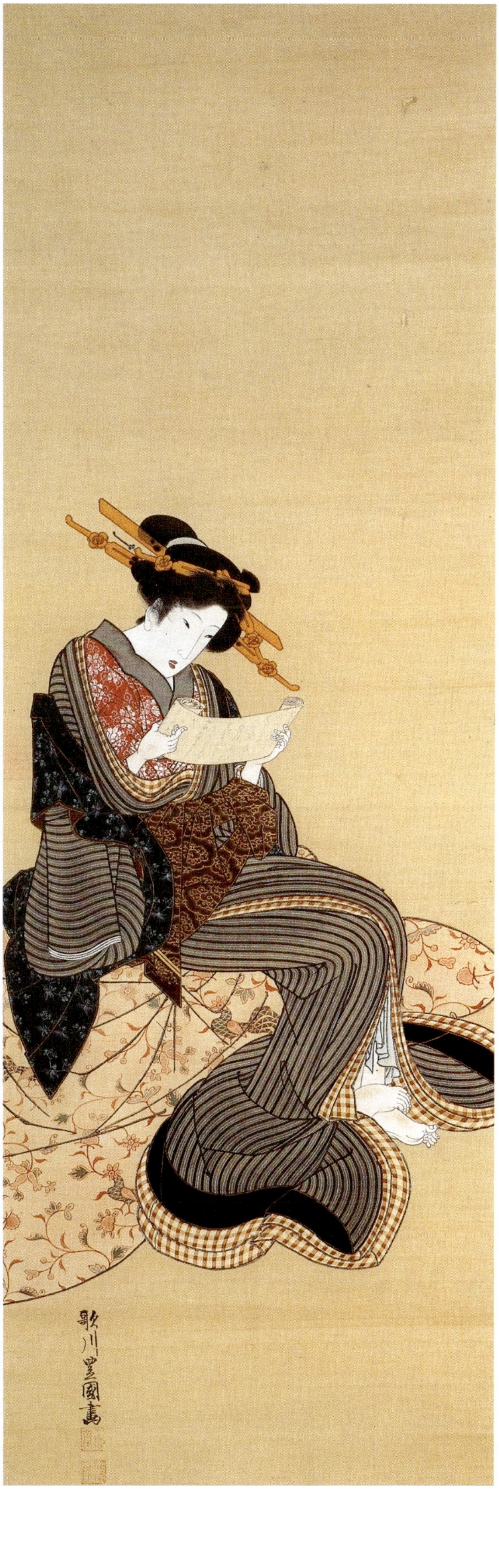

35
Utagawa Kunisada (1786 – 1864)
Beauty Reading a Letter
Hanging scroll
Color on silk
86.0 x 29.4 cm
(33 7/8 x 11 9/16 in.)

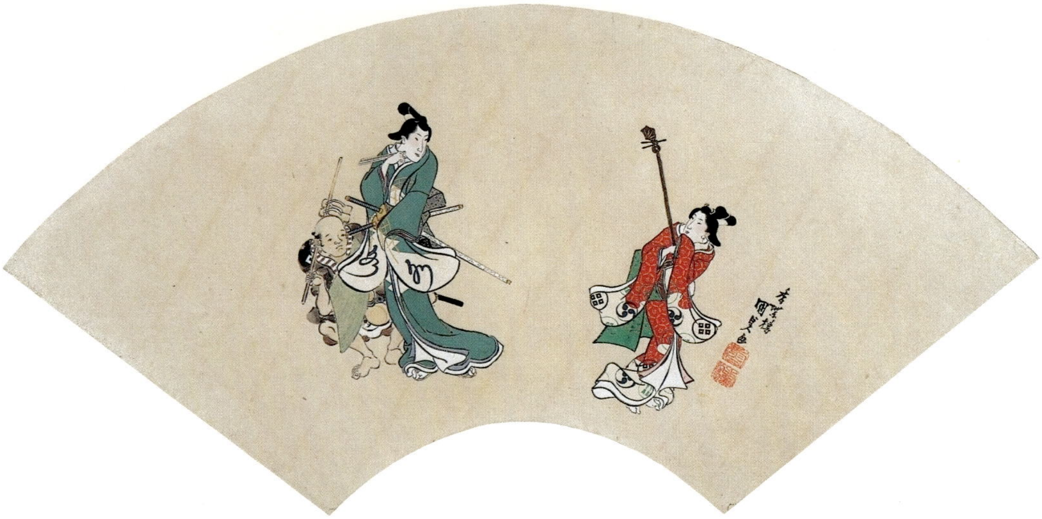

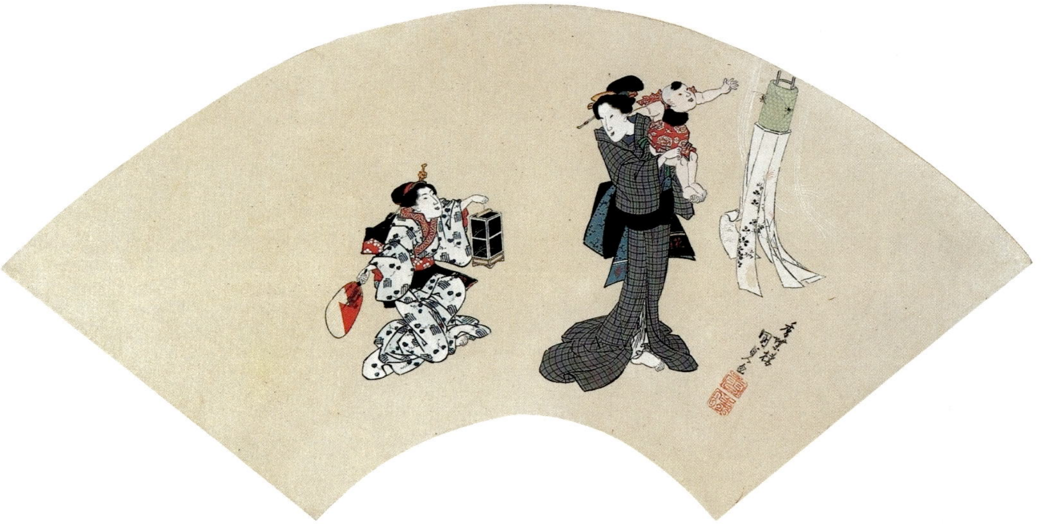

36
Hanabusa Ikkei (1749 – 1844)
Utagawa Kunisada (1786 – 1864)
Genre Scenes
From an album with 12 leaves
Color on paper
Each fan 53.5 cm across
(21$\frac{1}{16}$ in.)

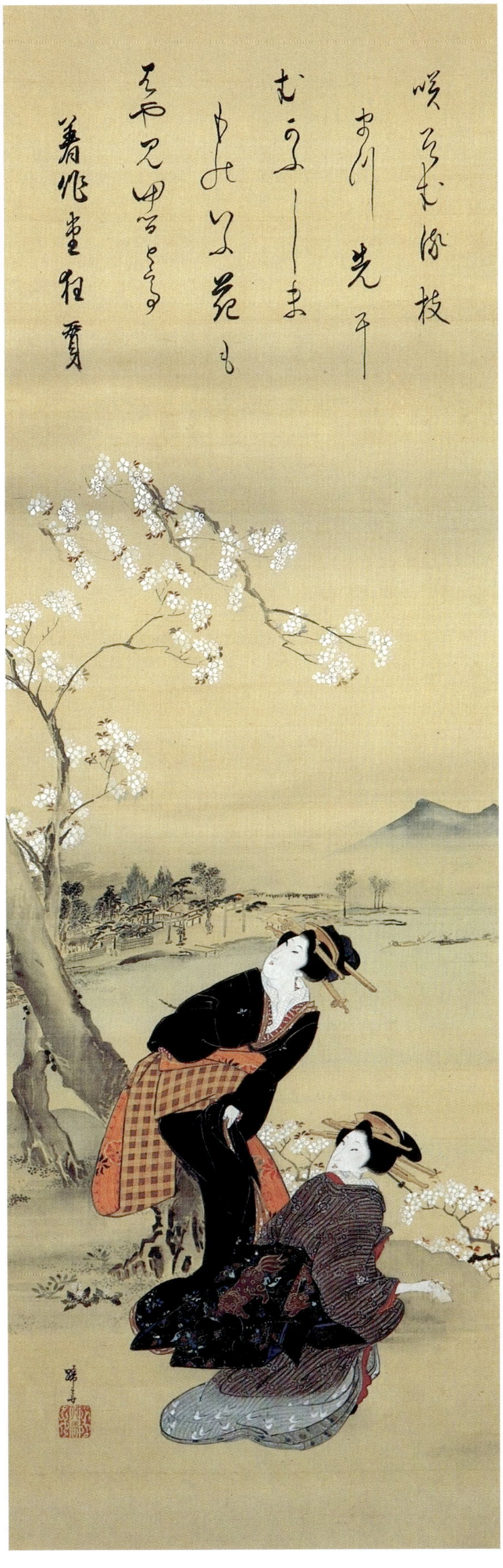

37
Teisai Hokuba (1771 – 1844)
Two Beauties by the Sumida River in Spring
Hanging scroll
Color on silk
103.1 x 33.7 cm
(40⅝ x 13¼ in.)

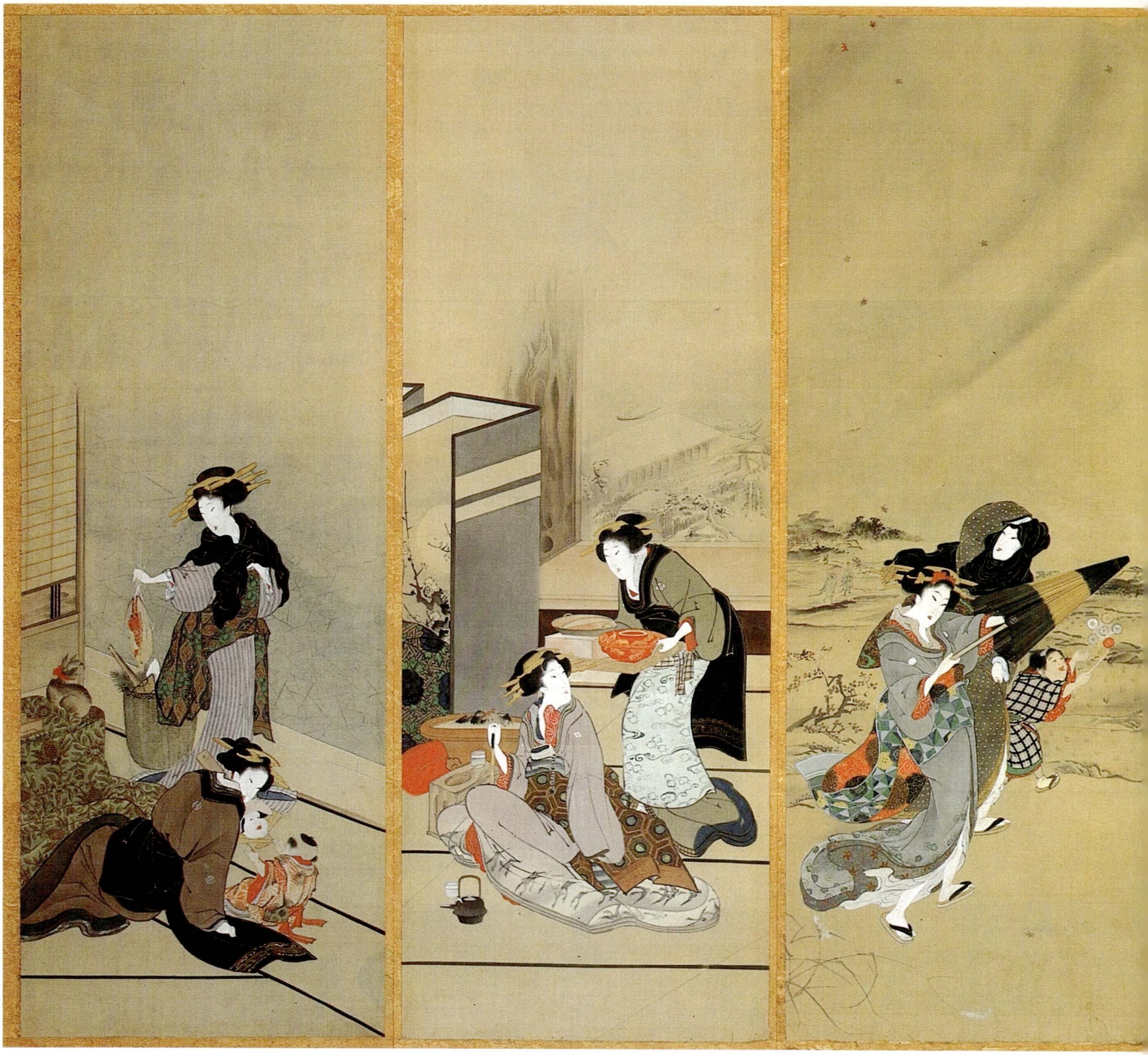

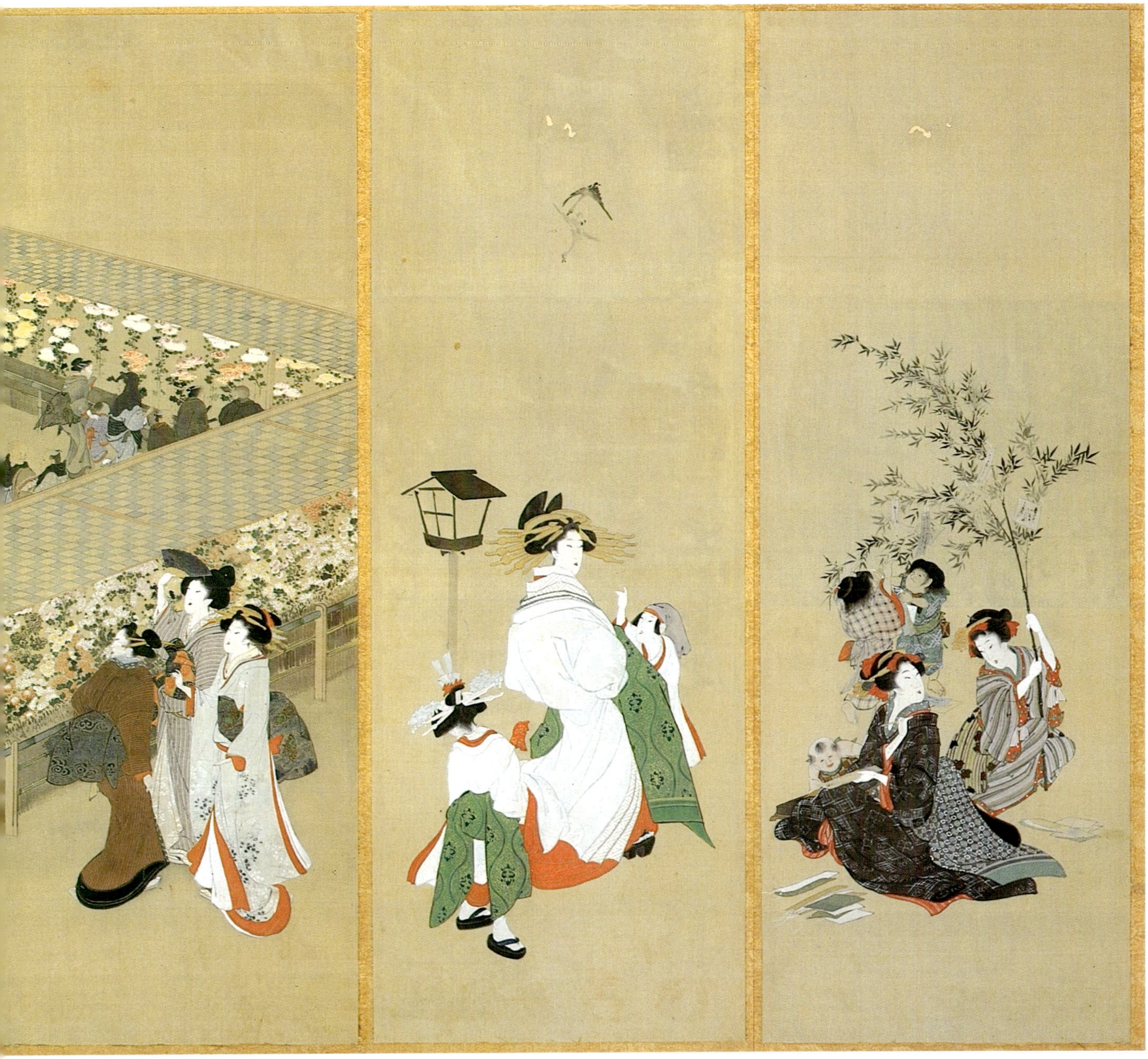

38
Teisai Hokuba (attrib.)
(1771 – 1844)
Beauties
Six-fold screen
Color on silk
91.5 x 33.8 cm
(36 x 13⁵⁄₁₆ in.)

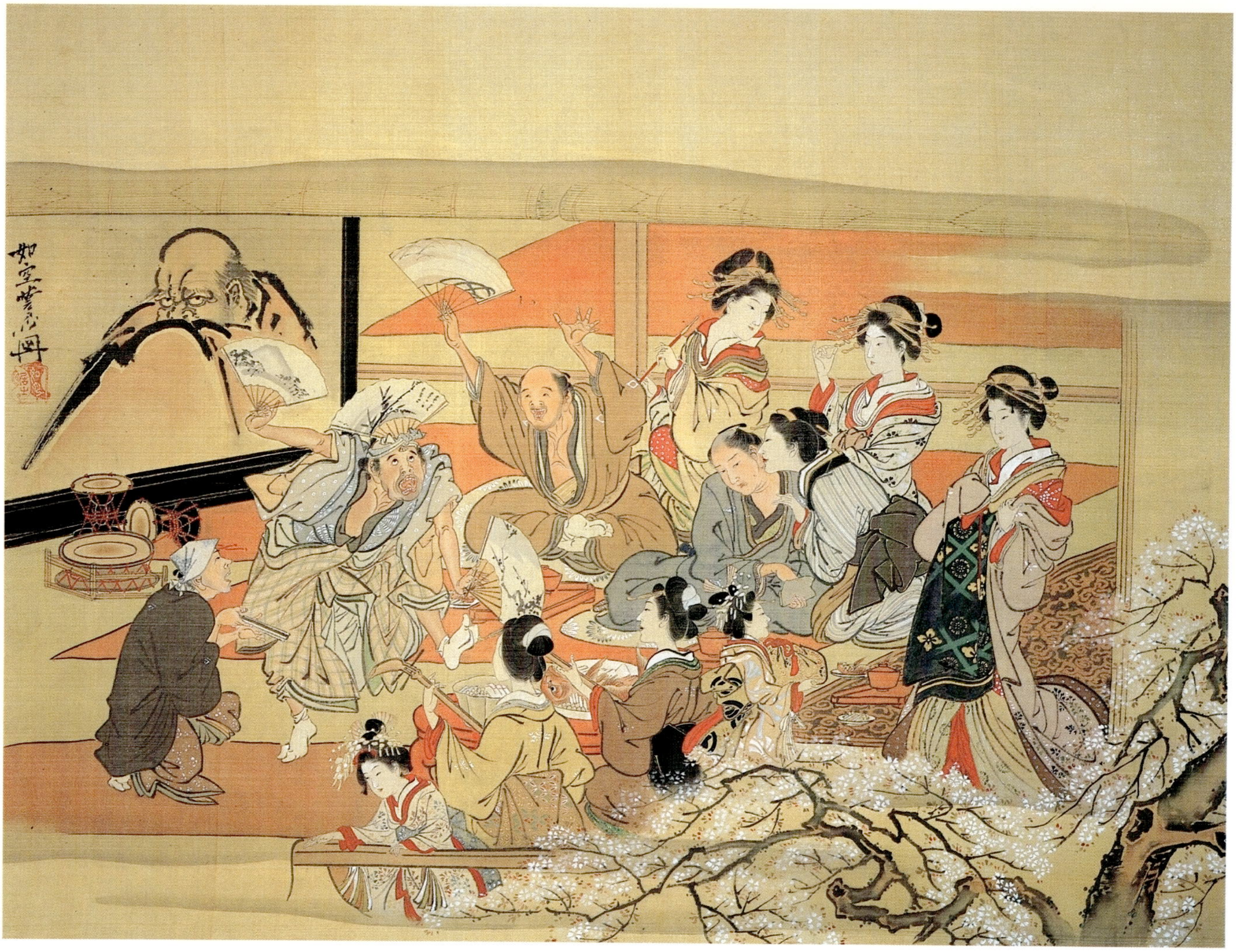

39
Kawanabe Gyōsai (1831 – 89)
House of Pleasure
Hanging scroll
Color on silk
52.5 x 67.4 cm
(20$\frac{13}{16}$ x 26$\frac{9}{16}$ in.)

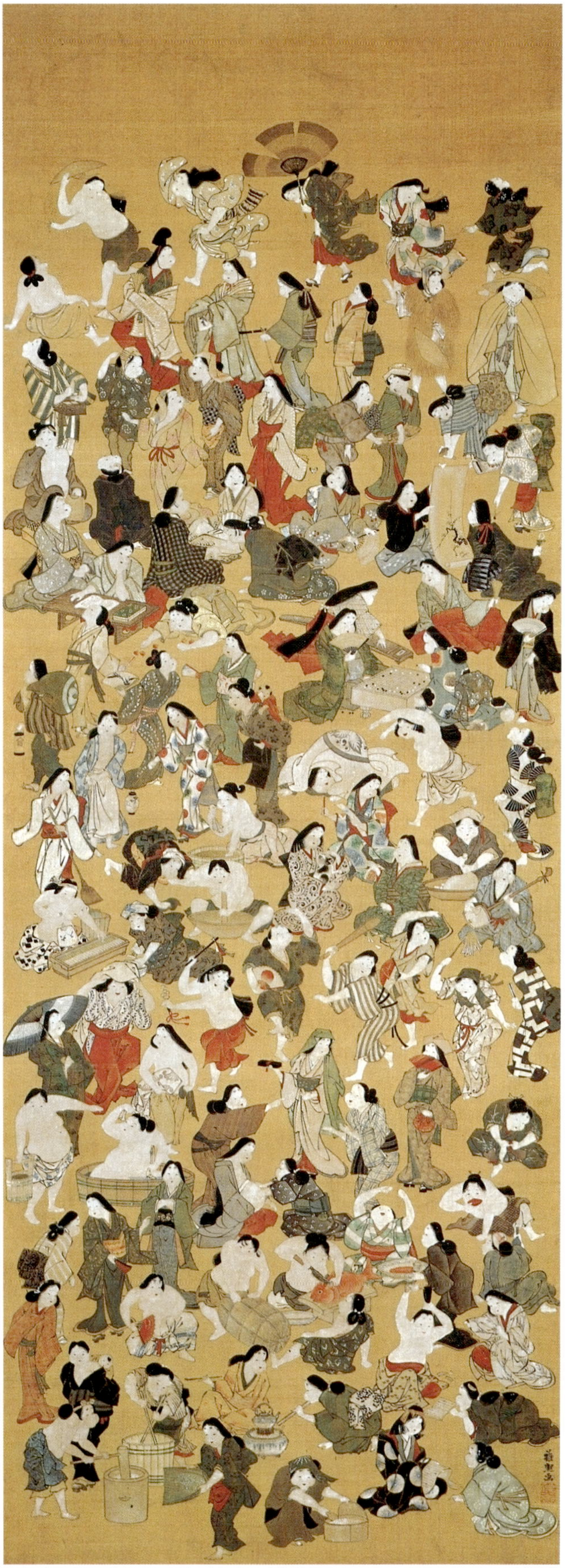

40
Masahiro (dates unknown)
One Hundred Women
Hanging scroll
Color on silk
113.6 x 42.3 cm
(44¾ x 16⅝ in.)

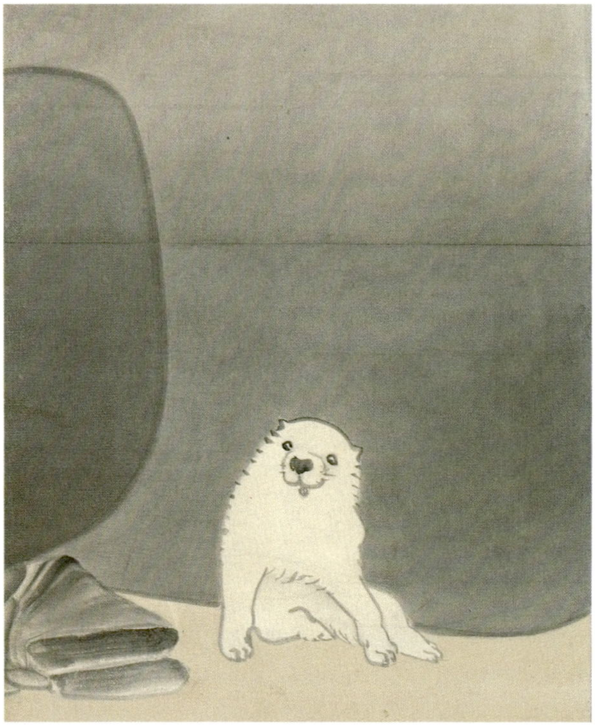

In late eighteenth-century Japan two new schools of painting developed. Since Maruyama Ōkyo (1733 – 95), the founder of one, was the teacher of Matsumura Goshun (1753 – 1811), the founder of the other (on Shijō, an avenue in Kyoto), they are known collectively as the Maruyama-Shijō School.

Ōkyo was one of the great figures in the history of Japanese painting. His training was eclectic. He absorbed ideas and techniques from several traditional schools. Equally important, he was exposed to Western-derived techniques and Chinese paintings. Ōkyo placed particular emphasis on sketching directly from nature, and it is this practice, along with his intensive study of the human figure, which gives his work and that of his followers a strongly naturalistic character in the context of Japanese painting. Even when painting a tiger, which he could have known only from seeing a tiger skin or an older painting, Ōkyo attempted to make the image as lifelike as possible (*Tiger,* plate 51). That he was successful is evident if one compares his work with tiger paintings by a late follower, Kunii Ōyō (*Tiger,* plate 50, and *Tiger,* plate 52).

The third generation of the Maruyama School was headed by Ōkyo's grandson Ōshin (1790–1838). Ōshin's delightful painting of two camels he saw when they were imported to Japan (*Two Camels,* plate 47) and his dynamic image of a dragon (*Dragon Emerging from the Sea,* plate 48) demonstrate his development of his grandfather's ideas. The Maruyama synthesis of realistic and decorative elements is illustrated here by Ōshin's acknowledged masterpiece, *Rice and Barley* (plate 49).

Nagasawa Rosetsu (1754–99) was a student of Ōkyo, yet he later developed his own style and became one of the most individualistic and versatile of Japanese painters. He made faithful copies of his teacher's work (*Peacock and Peonies,* plate 41), but his own style is marked by exuberant outbursts of line and wash (*Sea God and Sea Turtle,* plate 46). Rosetsu was a master of rich tonalities (*Tiger,* plate 45) and of spare and incisive brushwork (*Three Sparrows and Bamboo,* plate 42). Here his genius is most strikingly displayed in a monumental composition of a bull and an elephant, a tour de force of wit and contrast (*Bull and Elephant*, plate 44).

Mori Sosen (1747–1821) based his style on a close observation of nature and is therefore placed in the Maruyama-Shijō tradition. He specialized in animal paintings and is the best-known Japanese painter of monkeys. His paintings may utilize the most delicate line and color to evoke the exact feel of monkey fur or the appearance of a monkey's face (*Monkeys and Plum Tree*, plate 57) or employ a rapid brush to convey the tension of a monkey single-mindedly tracking a wasp (*Monkey and Wasp*, plate 58). In a larger format he places five carefully drawn monkeys in a moonlit autumn landscape executed in dramatic tonalities and bold brushwork (*Monkeys in an Autumn Landscape*, plate 59).

Shibata Zeshin (1807–91) is best known as a lacquer artist whose mastery of the medium was enhanced by his discovery of new techniques. He was an excellent painter as well, an expert in ink and color and the foremost practitioner of the exceedingly difficult *uriushi-e* ("lacquer picture"). Zeshin could be a master of narrative, such as a depiction of felicity driving out ill fortune (*Otafuku and Demon*, plate 53) or of the terror of a monkey being carried off by a giant hawk (*Hawk Carrying off a Monkey*, plate 54). His command of lacquer and its special luster enabled him to create rich landscapes of deep space in a small format (*Landscape*, plate 56) or dramatic compositions of textured mass contrasted with empty space (plate 54).

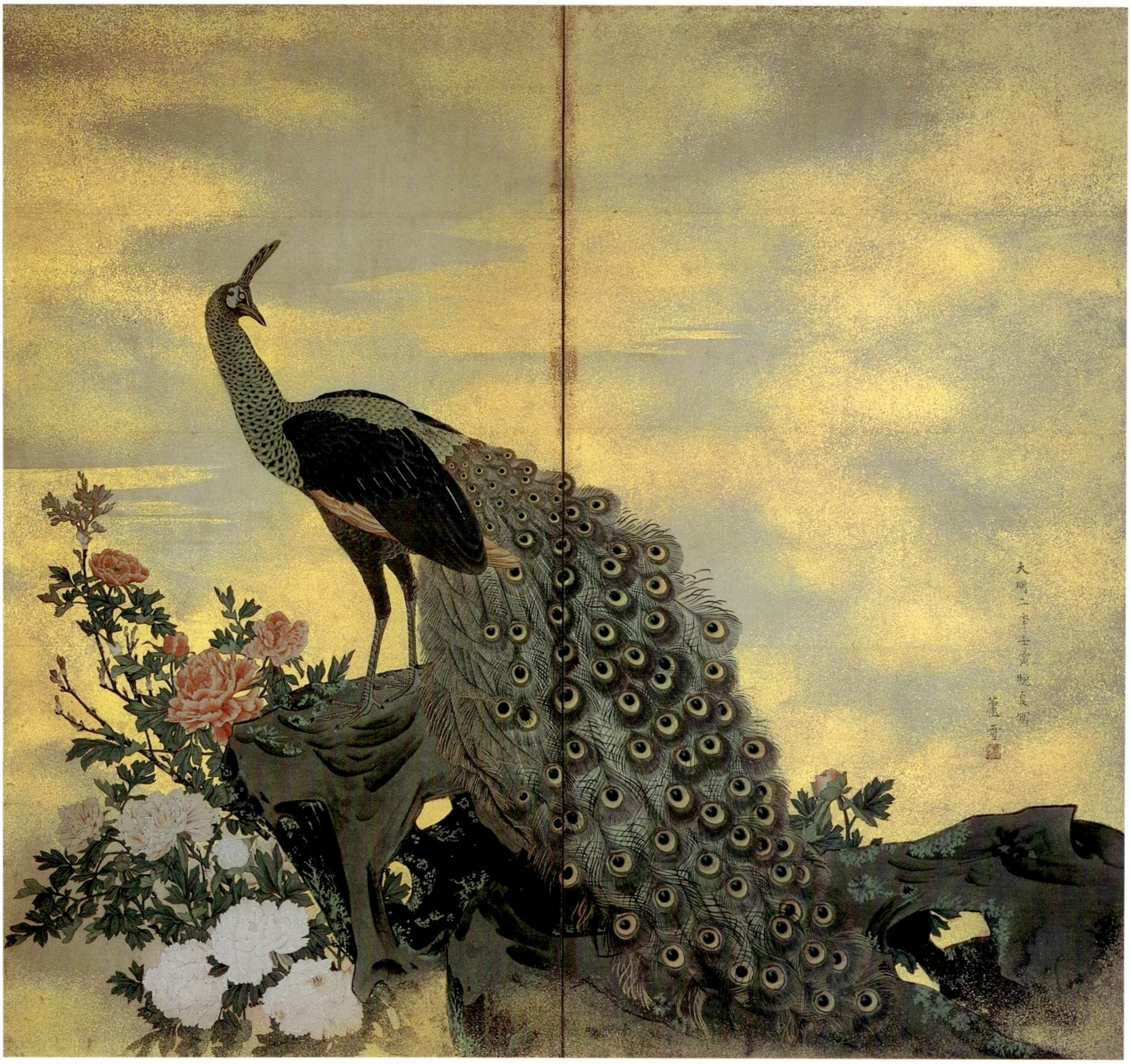

41
Nagasawa Rosetsu (1754 – 99)
Peacock and Peonies, 1781
Two-fold screen
Color on paper
165.5 x 184 cm
(65$\frac{3}{16}$ x 72$\frac{7}{16}$ in.)

42
(right)
Nagasawa Rosetsu (1754 – 99)
Three Sparrows and Bamboo
Hanging scroll
Ink and color on paper
123.2 x 28.4 cm
(48½ x 11³⁄₁₆ in.)

43
(far right)
Nagasawa Rosetsu (1754 – 99)
Rooster and Bamboo
Hanging scroll
Ink and color on paper
134.6 x 58.5 cm
(53 x 23¹⁄₁₆ in.)

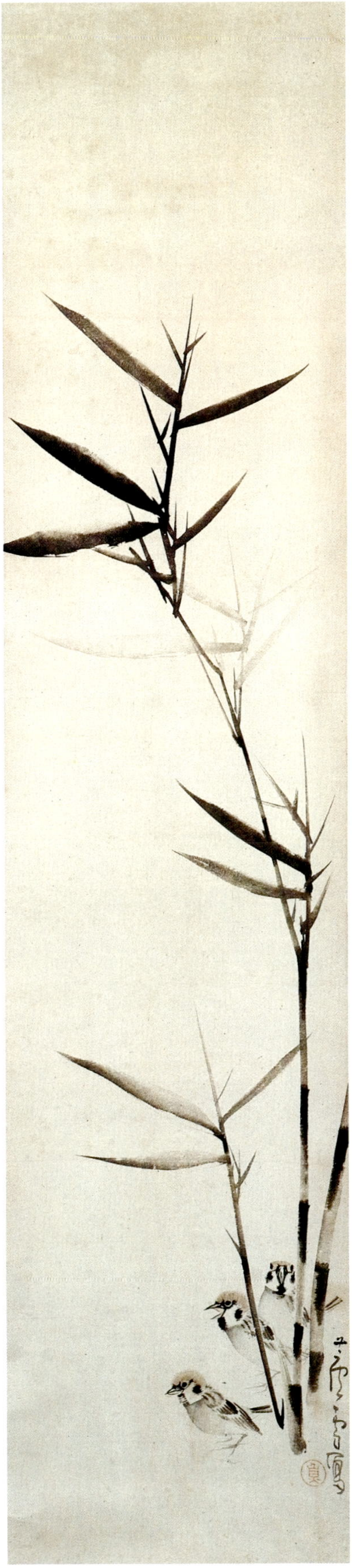

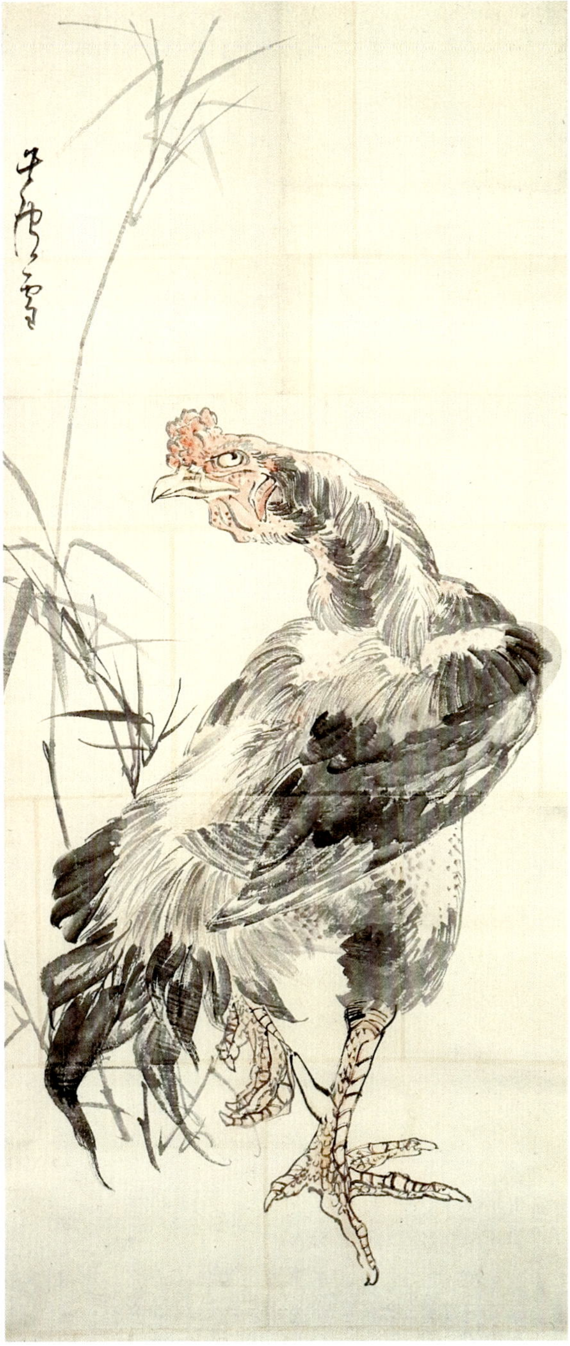

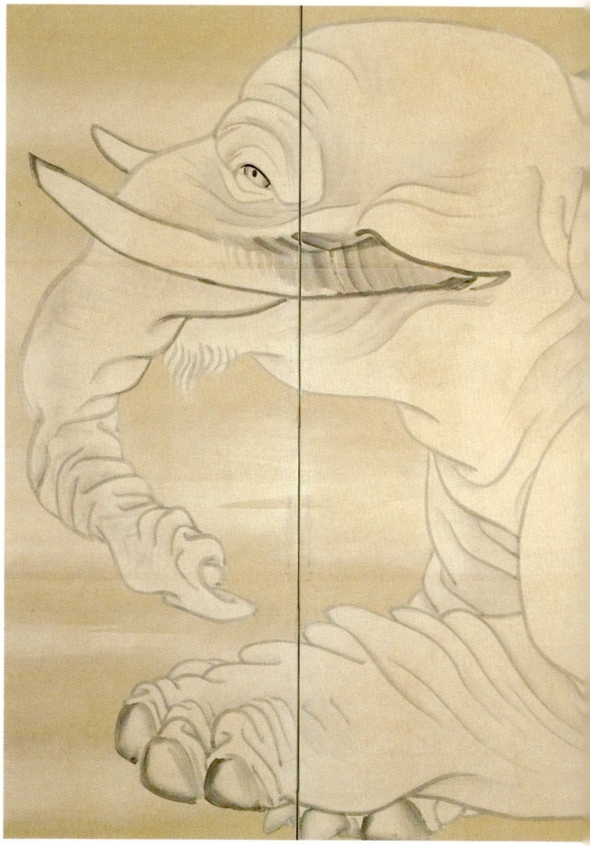

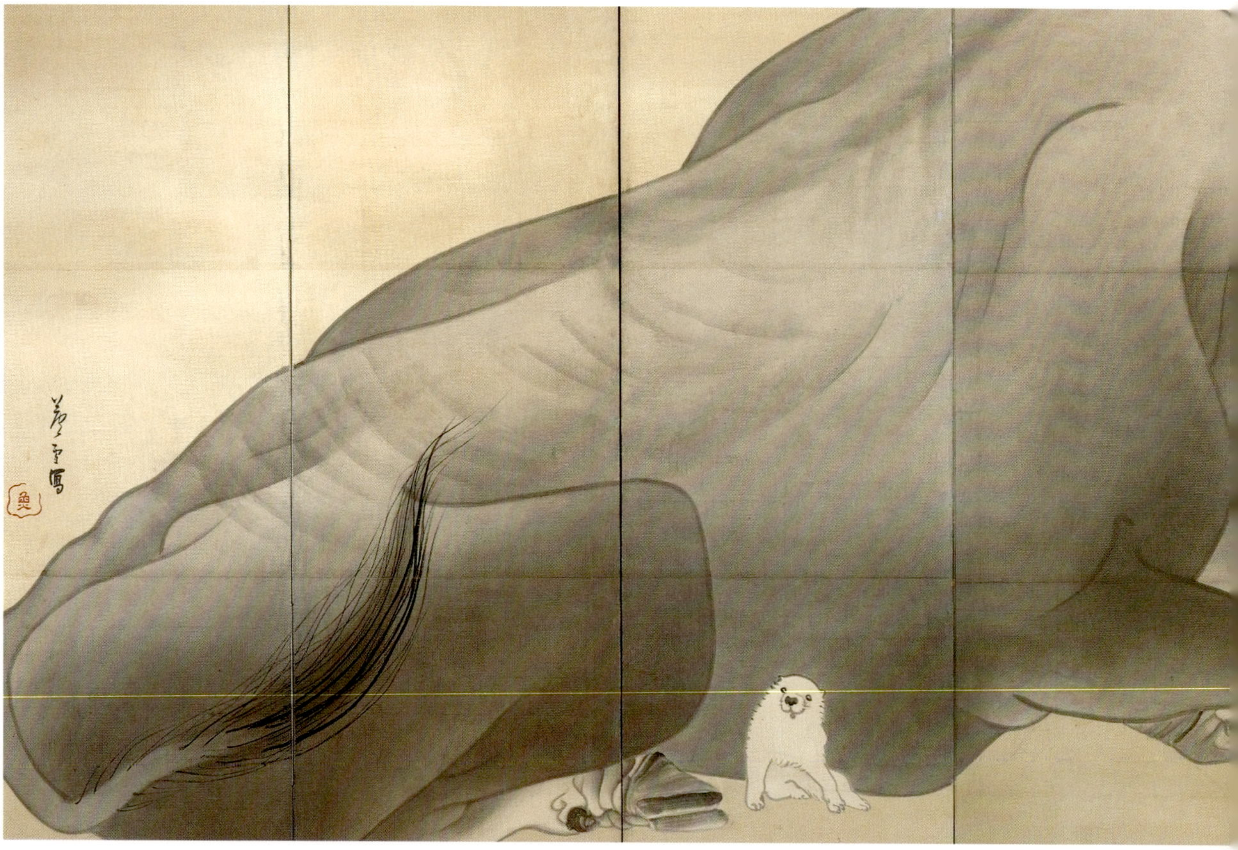

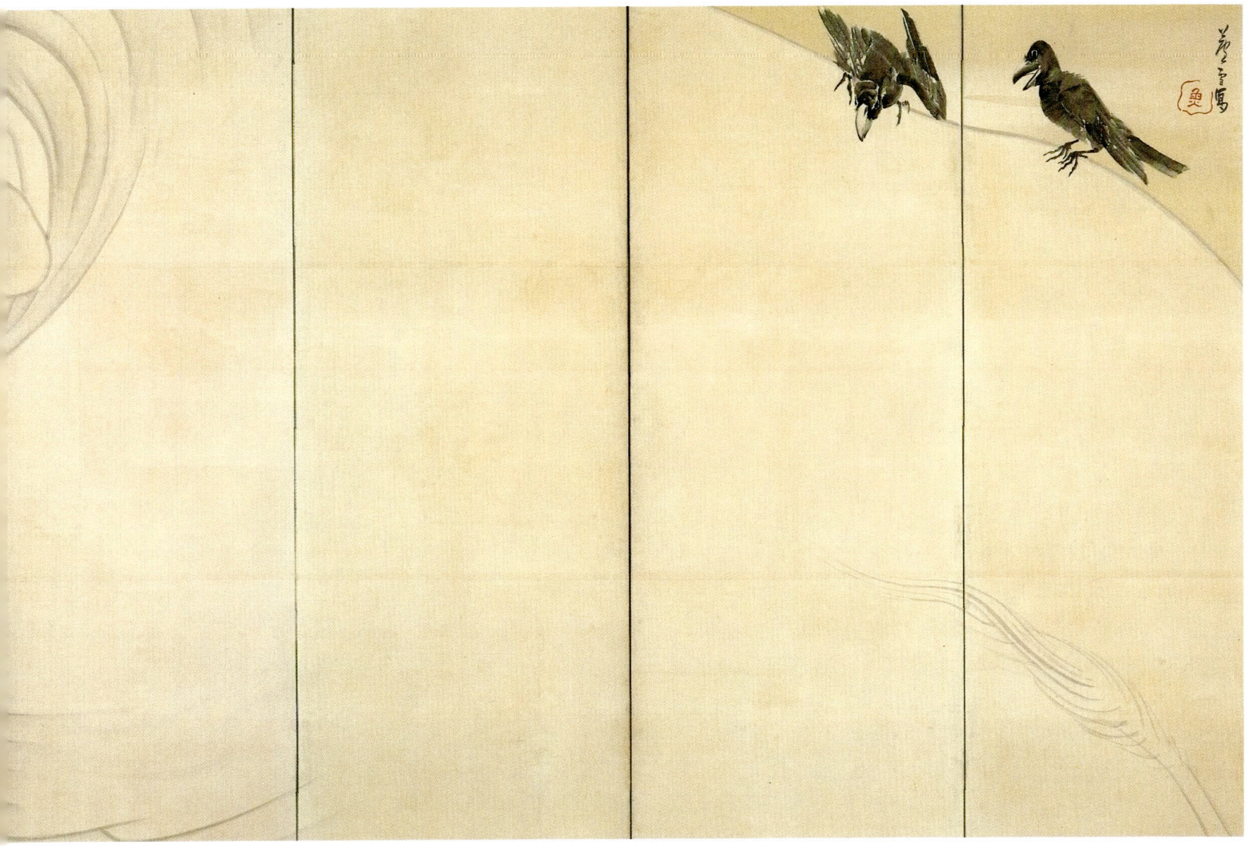

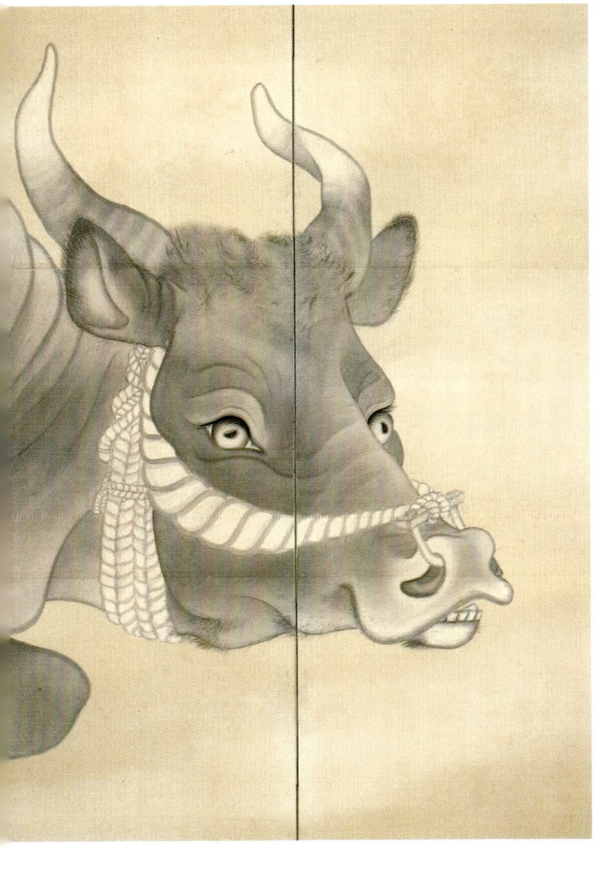

44
Nagasawa Rosetsu (1754 – 99)
Bull and Elephant
Pair of six-fold screens
Ink on paper
Each 155.5 x 360.4 cm
(61¼ x 141⅞ in.)

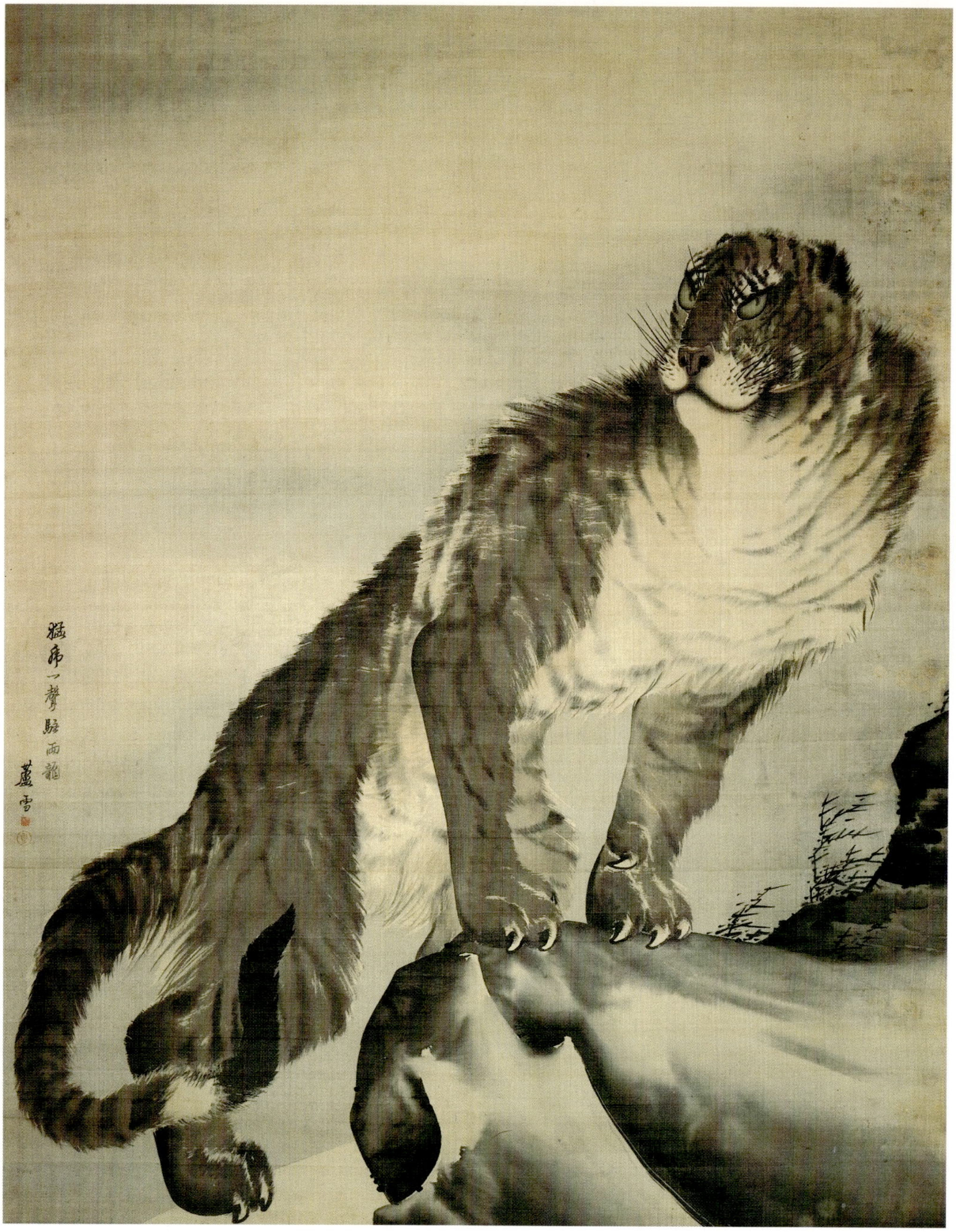

45
Nagasawa Rosetsu (1754 – 99)
Tiger
Hanging scroll
Color on silk
163.5 x 131 cm
($64\frac{3}{8}$ x $51\frac{9}{16}$ in.)

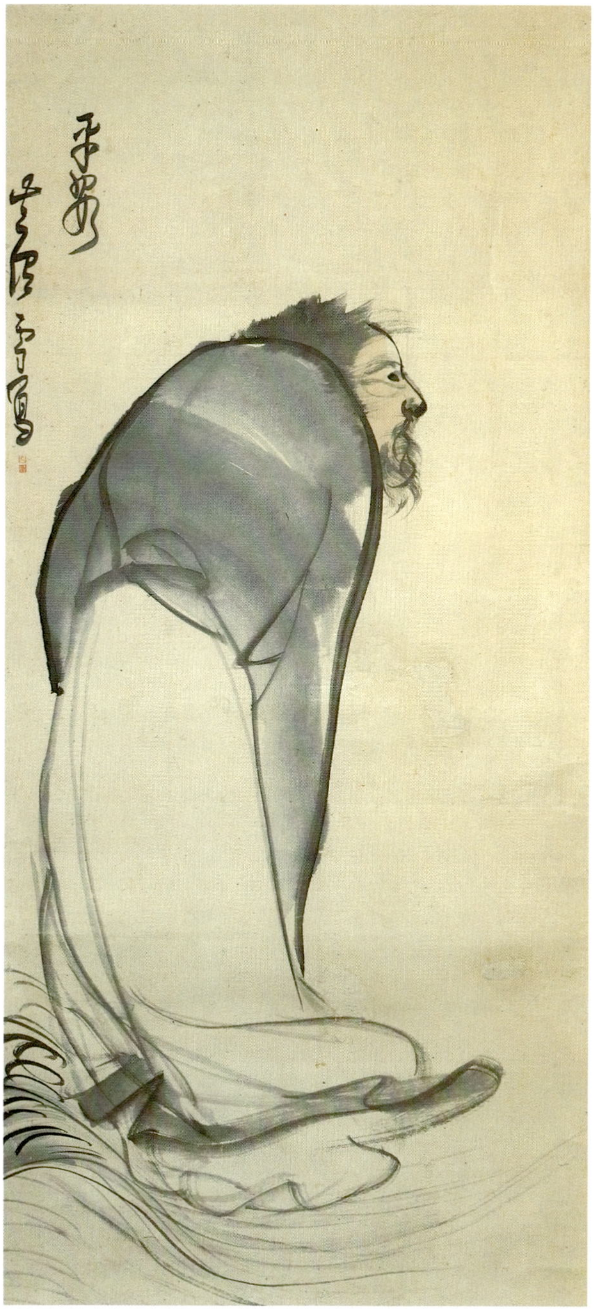

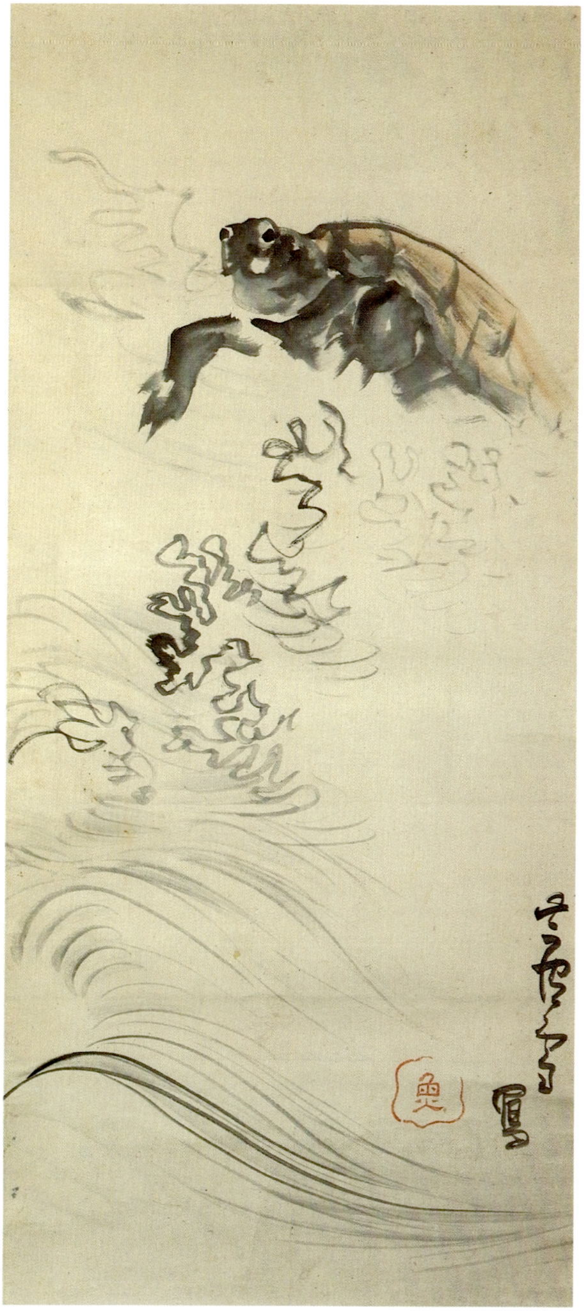

46
Nagasawa Rosetsu (1754 – 99)
Sea God and Sea Turtle
Pair of hanging scrolls
Ink and color on paper
Each 117 x 54.5 cm
(46 1/16 × 21 7/16 in.)

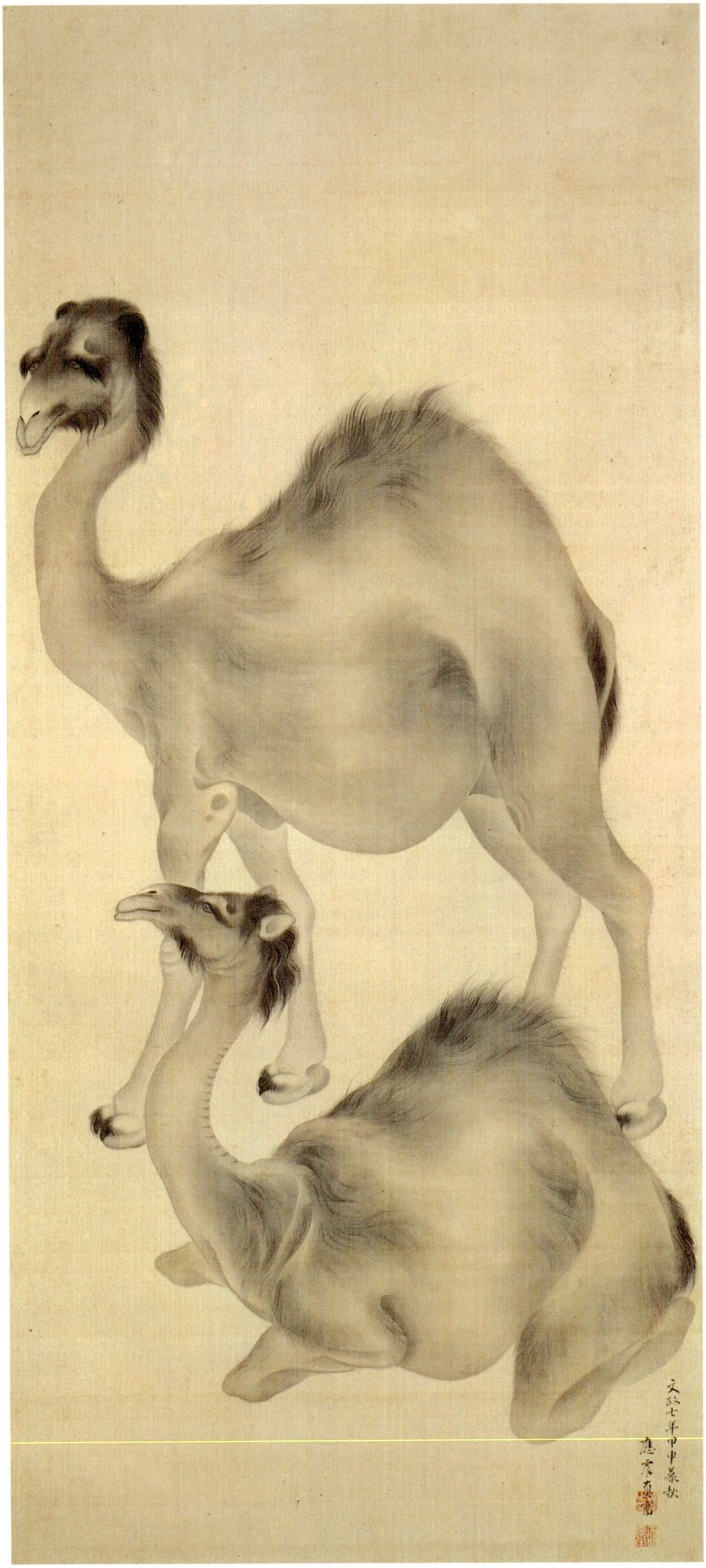

47
Maruyama Ōshin (1790 – 1838)
Two Camels, 1824
Hanging scroll
Color on silk
125.3 x 57.3 cm
(49⅜ x 22⁹⁄₁₆ in.)

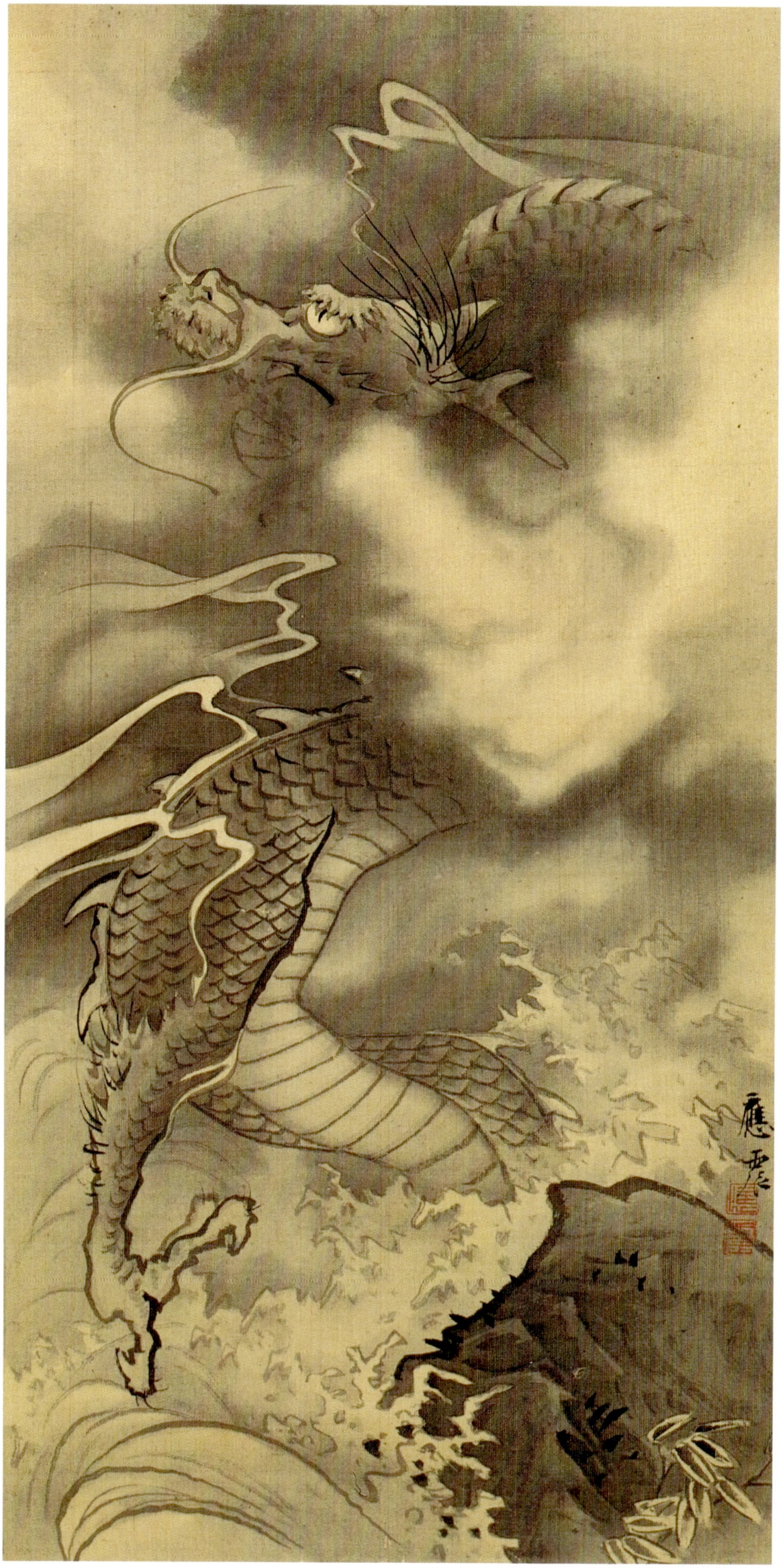

48
Maruyama Ōshin (1790 – 1838)
Dragon Emerging from the Sea
Hanging scroll
Ink on silk
30.5 x 15 cm
(12 x $5\frac{15}{16}$ in.)

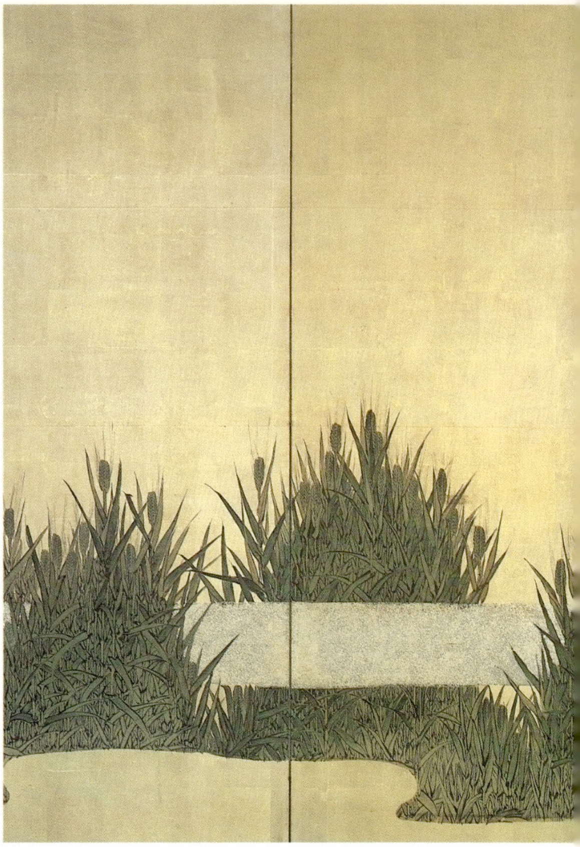

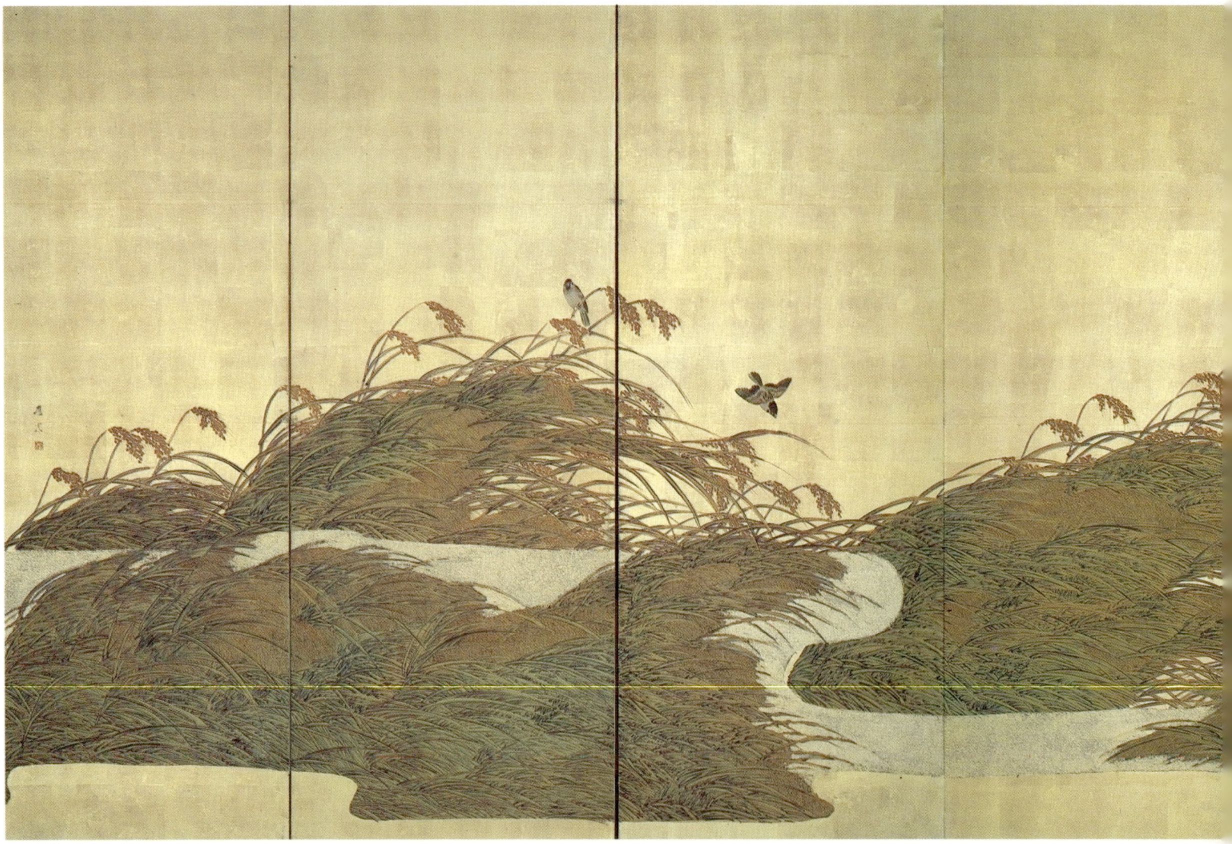

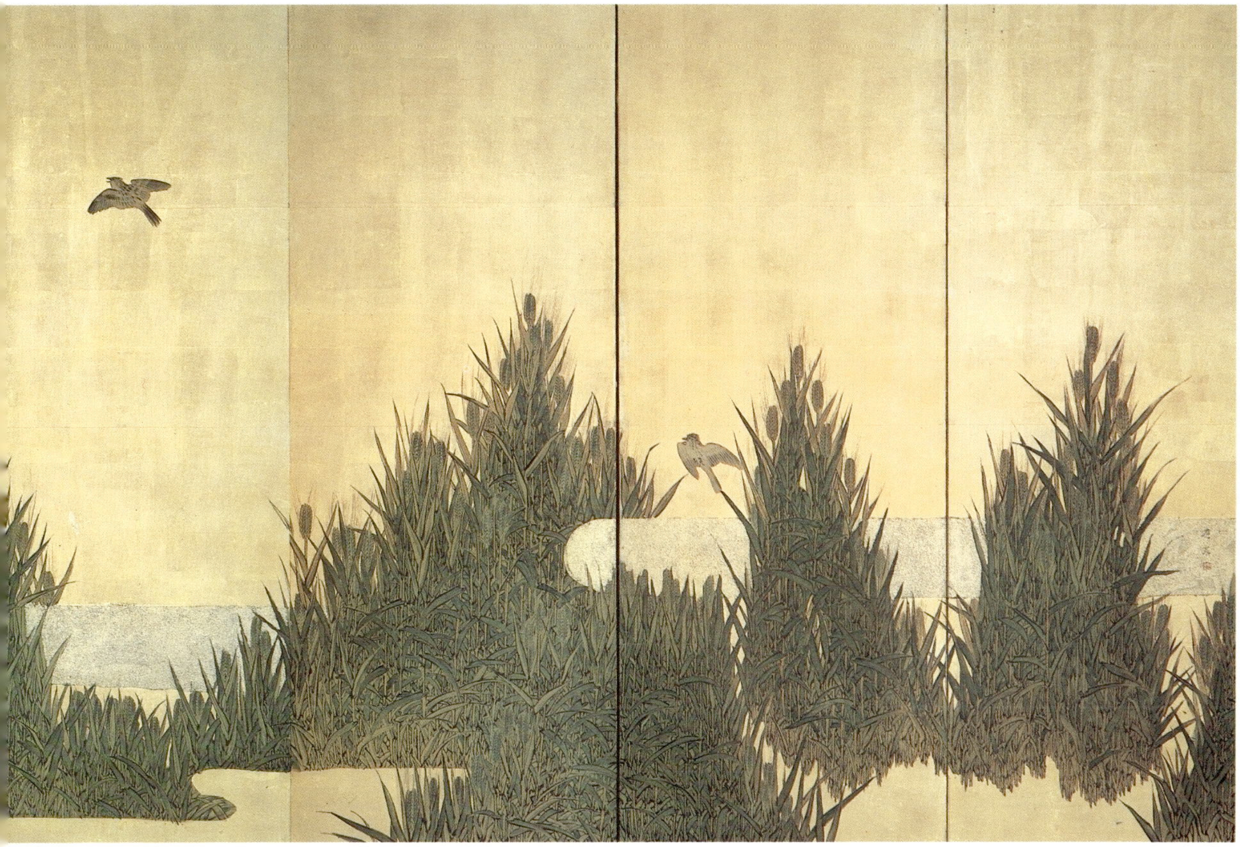

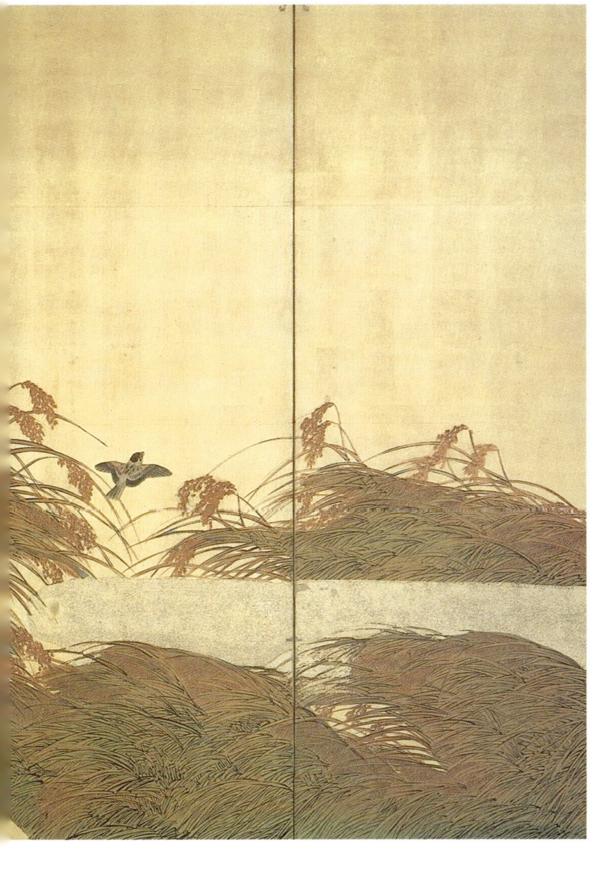

49
Maruyama Ōshin (1790 – 1838)
Rice and Barley
Pair of six-fold screens
Color with gold ground on paper
Each 156.7 x 362.6 cm
(61$^{11}/_{16}$ x 142¾ in.)

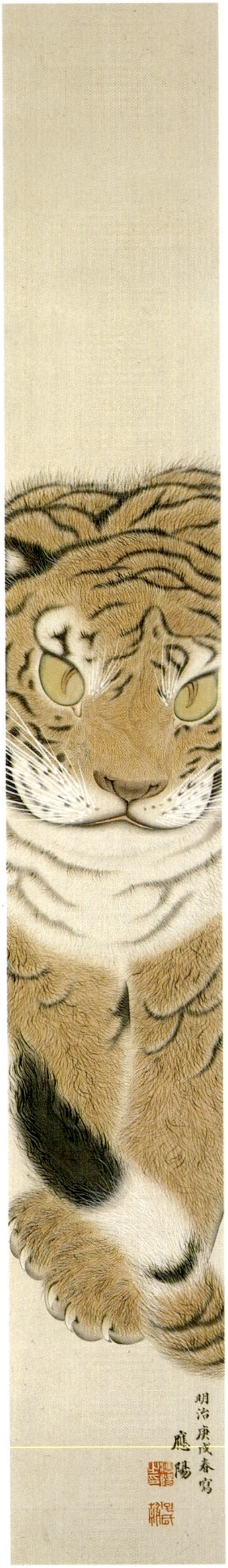

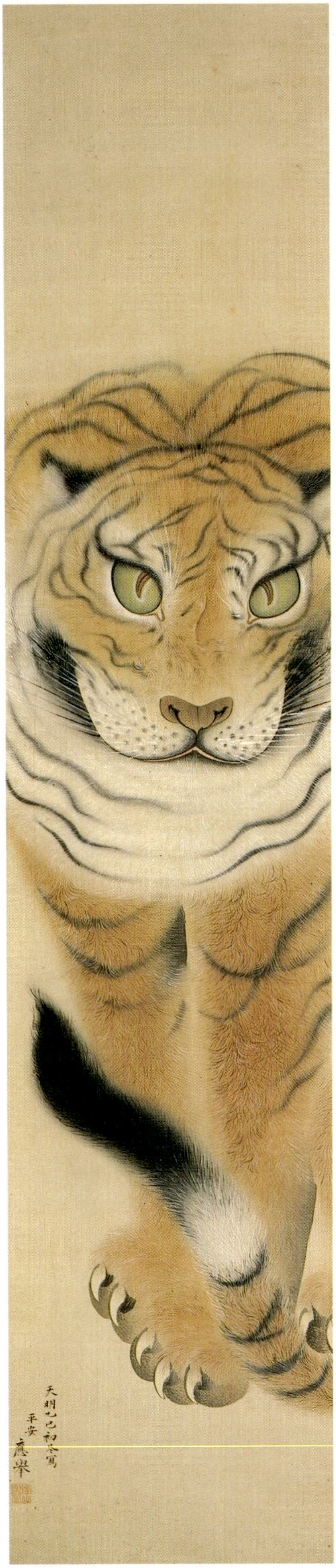

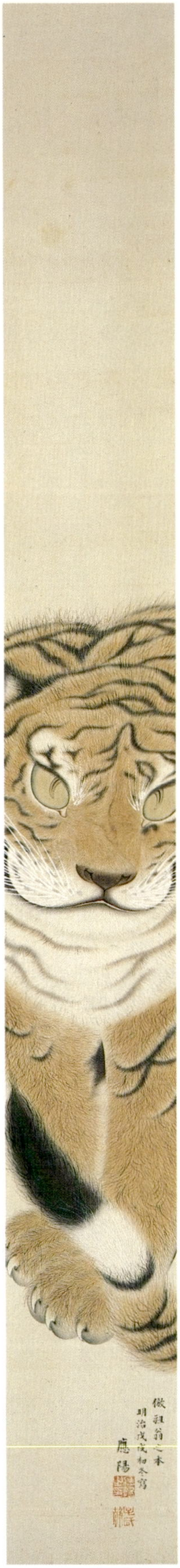

50
(left)
Kunii Ōyō (1868 – 1923)
Tiger, 1898
Hanging scroll
Color on silk
127.2 x 15.7 cm
($50\frac{1}{8}$ x $6\frac{3}{16}$ in.)

51
(center)
Maruyama Ōkyo (attrib.) (1733 – 95)
Tiger, 1785
Hanging scroll
Color on silk
114.1 x 25.3 cm
($44\frac{15}{16}$ x $9\frac{15}{16}$ in.)

52
(right)
Kunii Ōyō (1868 – 1923)
Tiger, 1910
Hanging scroll
Color on silk
108.0 x 15.6 cm
($42\frac{1}{2}$ x $6\frac{1}{8}$ in.)

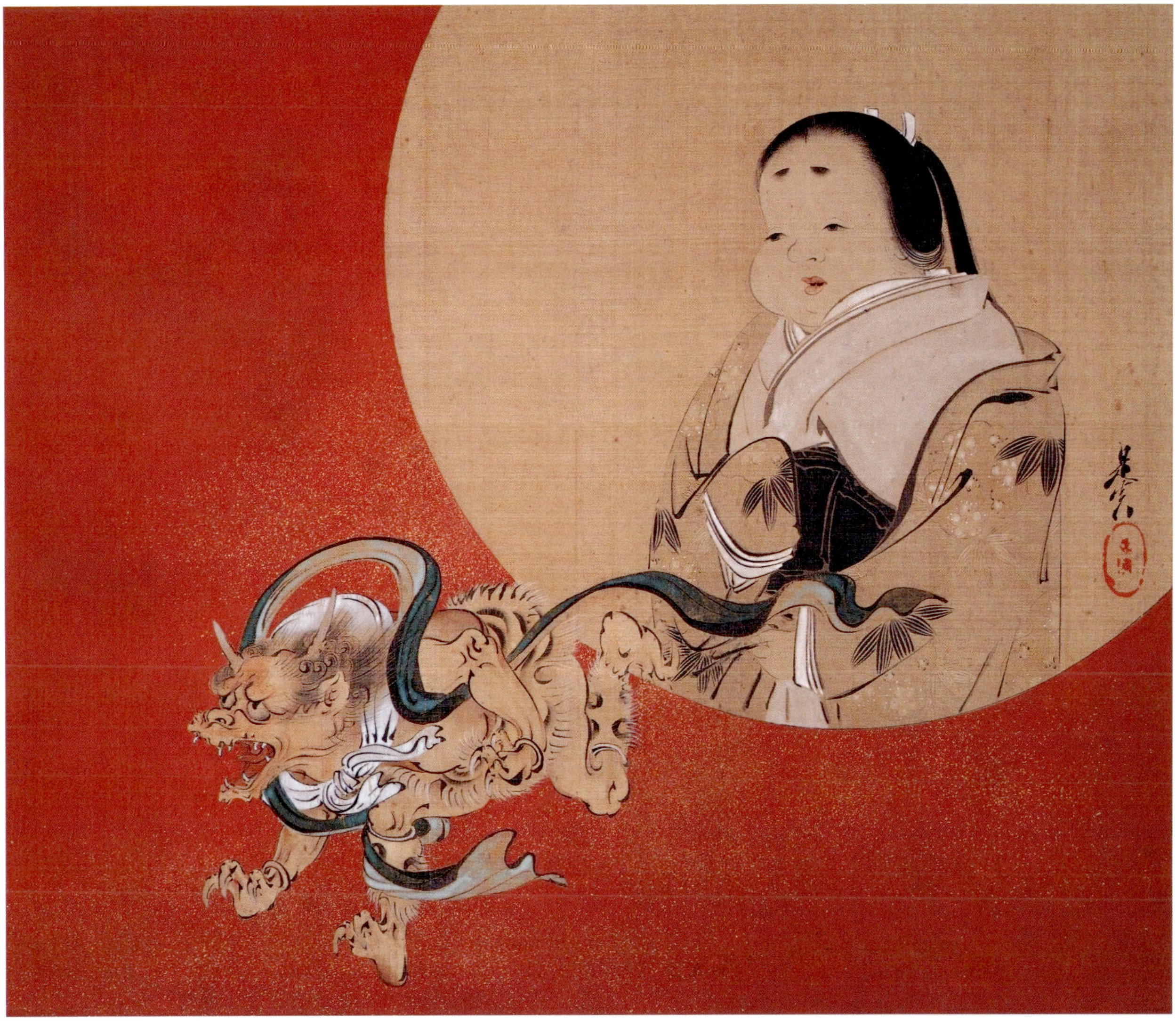

53
Shibata Zeshin (1807 – 91)
Otafuku and Demon
Hanging scroll
Color on silk
43.8 x 52 cm
(17¼ x 20½ in.)

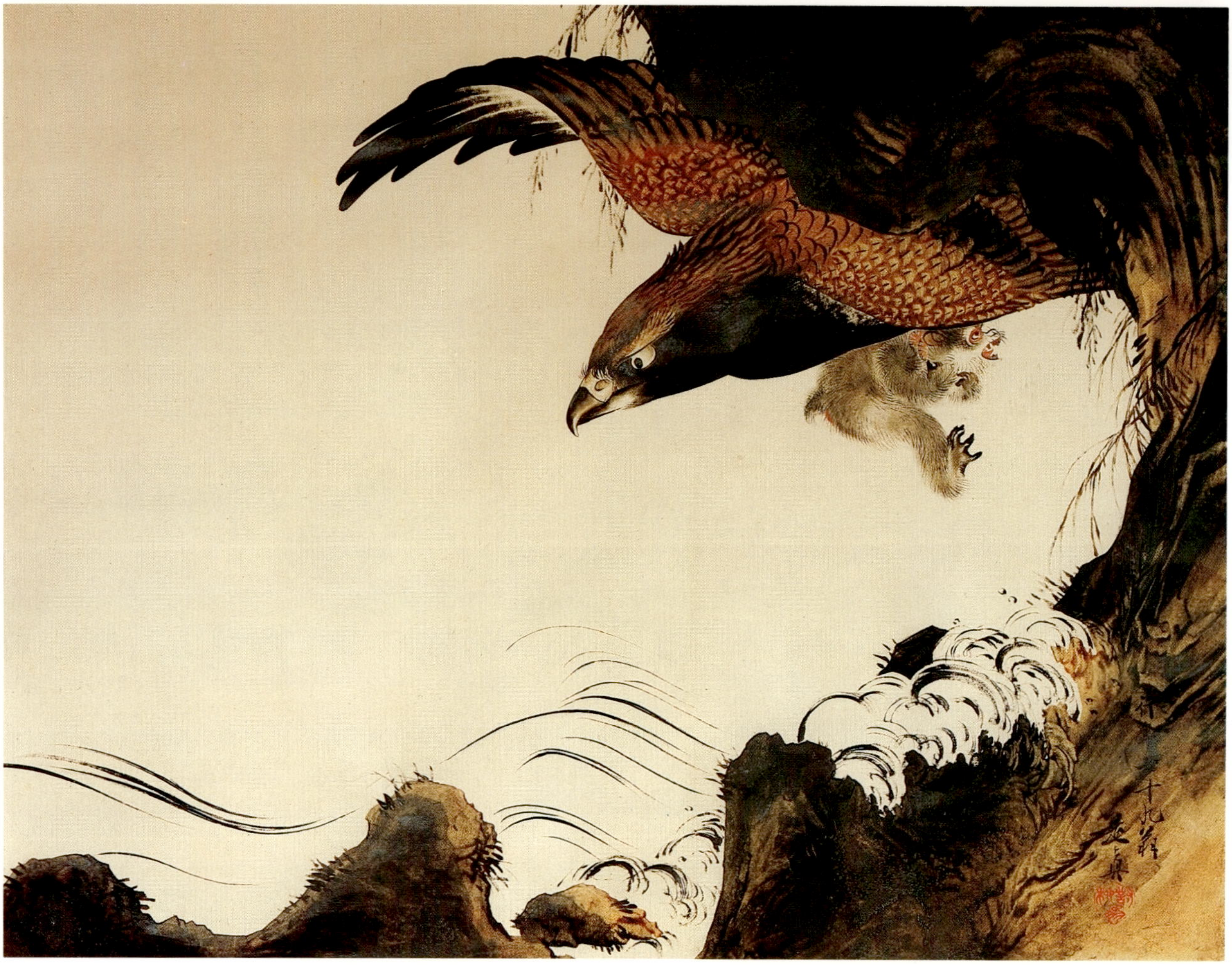

54
Shibata Zeshin (1807 – 91)
Hawk Carrying off a Monkey, 1885
Hanging scroll
Lacquer on paper
38.4 x 49.9 cm
(15⅛ x 19⅝ in.)

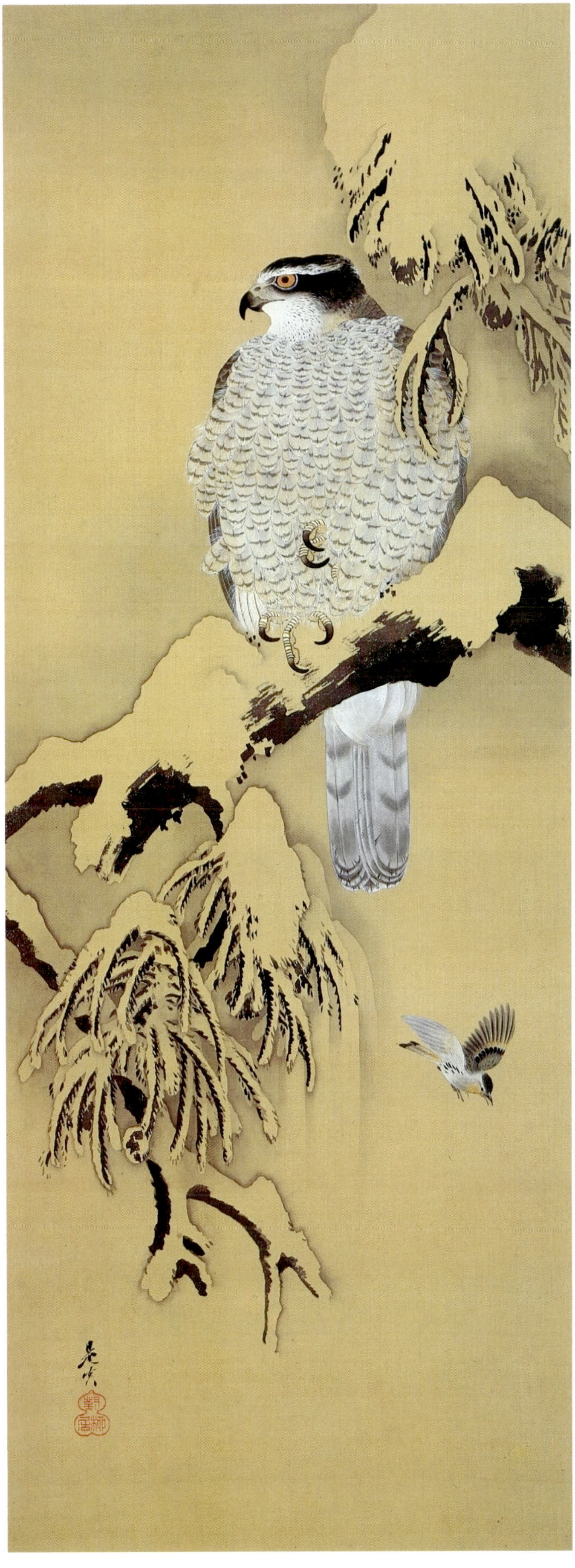

55
Shibata Zeshin (1807 – 91)
Hawk Perched
on a Snow-covered Branch
Hanging scroll
Color on silk
109.2 x 40.8 cm
(43 x 16$\frac{1}{16}$ in.)

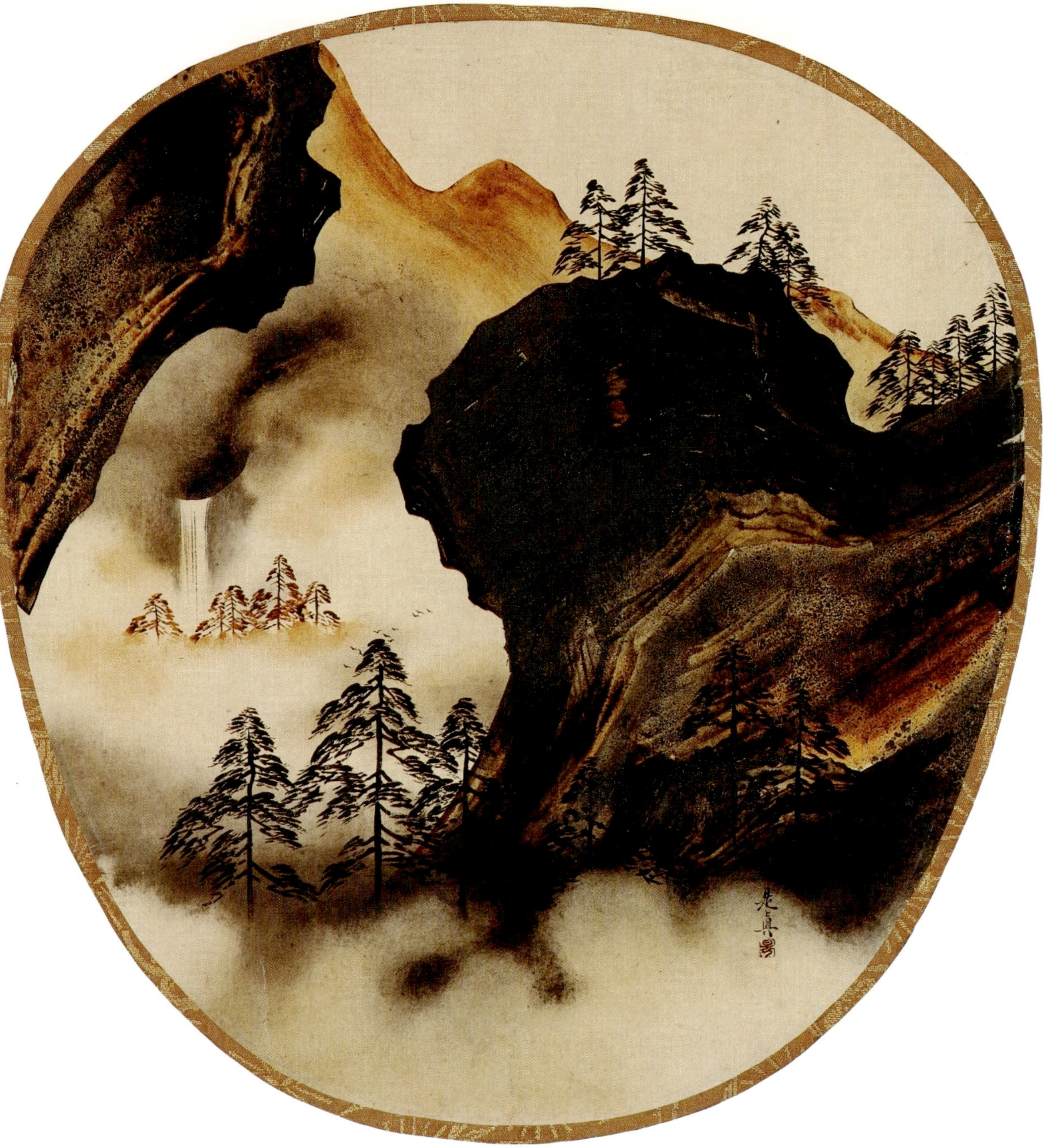

56
Shibata Zeshin (1807 – 91)
Landscape
Hanging scroll
Lacquer on paper
26 x 21 cm
(10¼ x 8¼ in.)

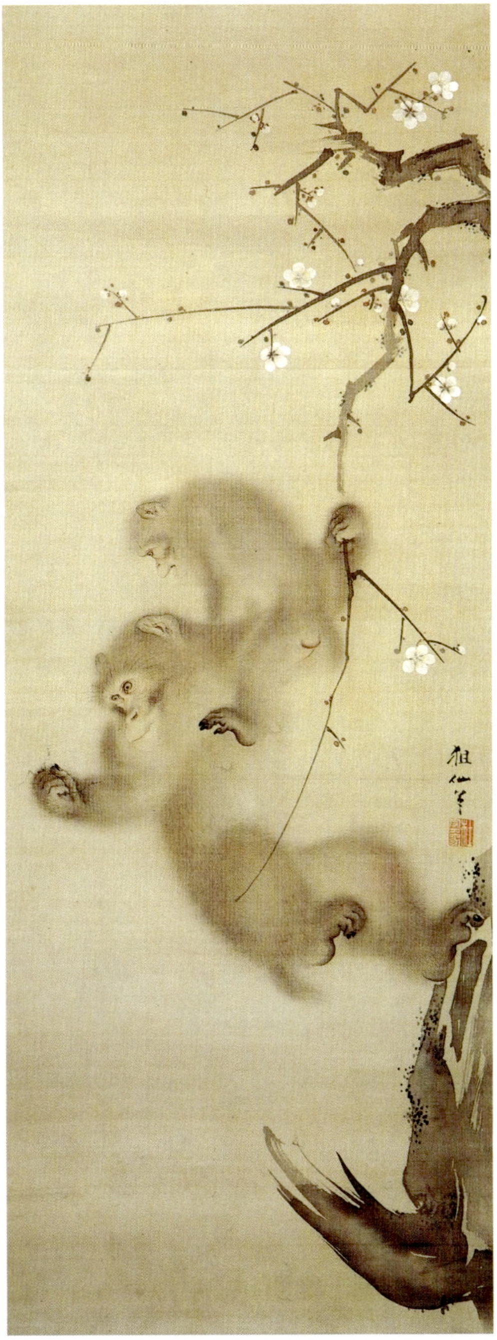

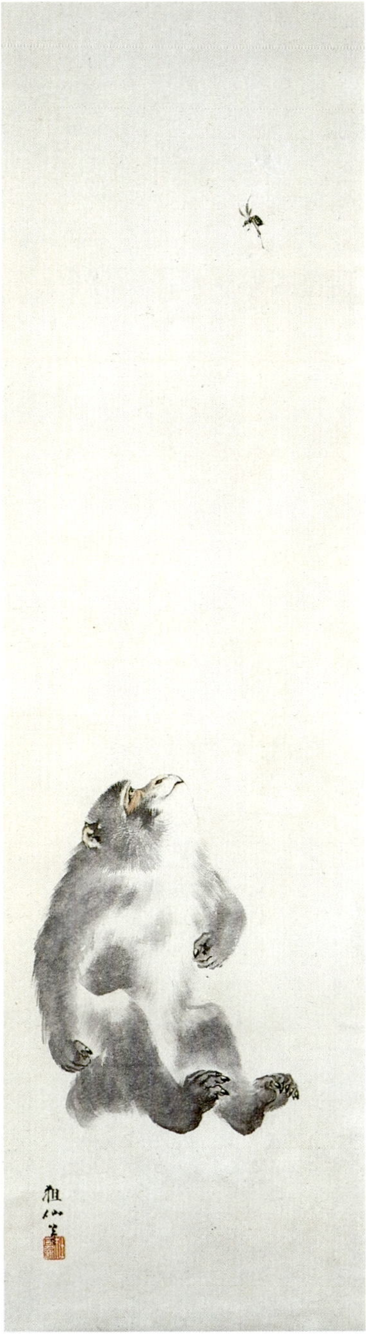

57
Mori Sosen (1747 – 1821)
Monkeys and Plum Tree
Hanging scroll
Ink and color on silk
89.8 x 33.6 cm
(35$\frac{3}{8}$ x 13$\frac{1}{4}$ in.)

58
Mori Sosen (1747 – 1821)
Monkey and Wasp
Hanging scroll
Ink and color on paper
103.4 x 29.0 cm
(40$\frac{11}{16}$ x 11$\frac{7}{16}$ in.)

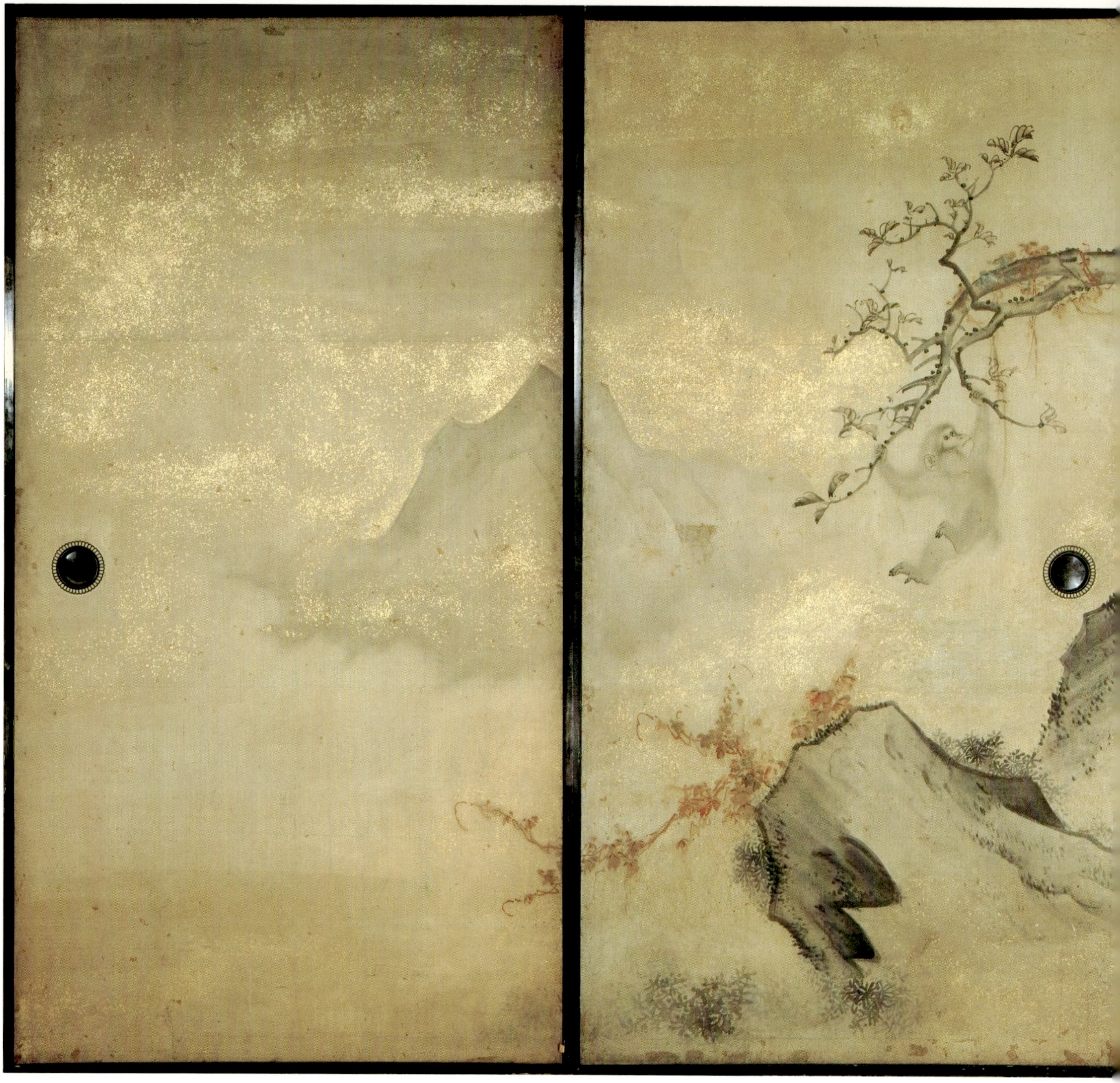

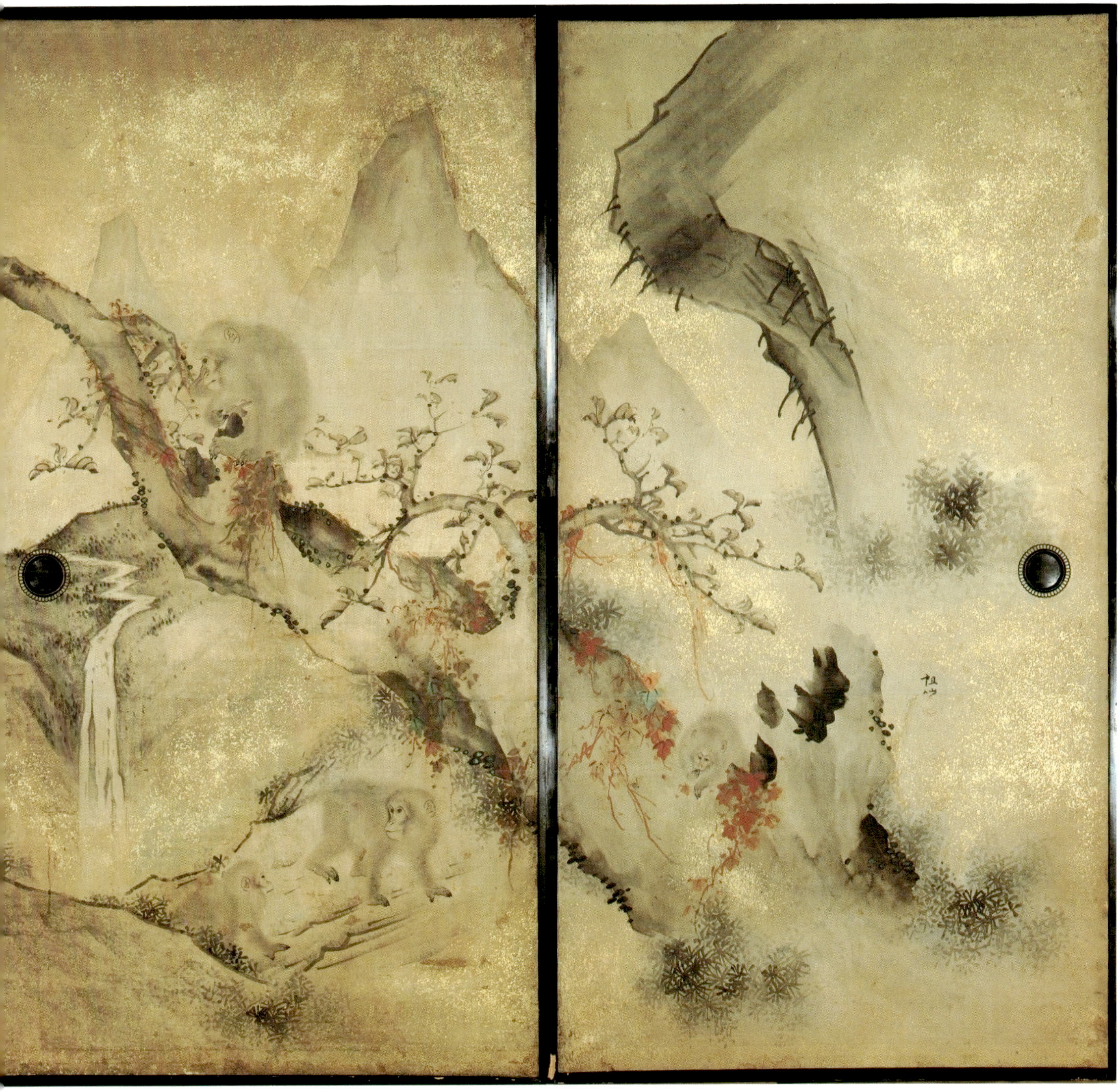

59
Mori Sosen (1747 – 1821)
Monkeys in an Autumn Landscape
Four fusuma panels
Color on paper
Each 172.0 x 92.5 cm
(67¾ x 36⁷⁄₁₆ in.)

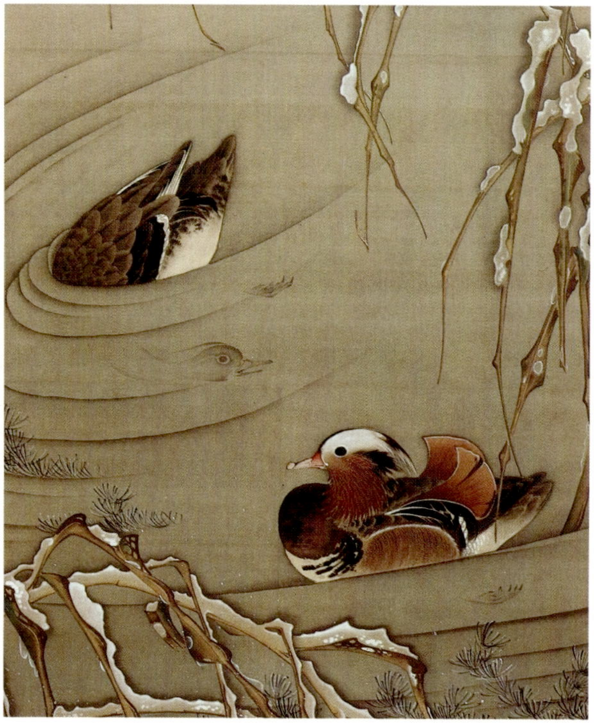

The history of Japanese painting is dominated by the rise and decline of various schools that were established or revived by professional artists of particular merit. But in the eighteenth century there appear several painters who do not fit into one particular tradition or another; they rejected or transcended the training they received or seem to have taught themselves. These artists invented their own visions and produced work that was often ignored or ridiculed in its time. But in their search for self-expression, the productions of their eccentric genius hold great appeal for modern man. Their appearance was made possible by the eighteenth century's iconoclasm, loosening of class barriers, greater affluence and freedom to travel, and quest for novelty, but as with all great artists social conditions do not fully explain the directions these painters took.

The central position of Ito Jakuchū (1716–1800) in this collection is illustrated by the collection's name: Shin'enkan. Shin'enkan was the name of Jakuchū's studio. Translated literally the syllables mean "house of the faraway heart." Born the son of a prosperous greengrocer, Jakuchū retired from the family business at forty to devote the rest of his life to painting. It is recorded that he began his study under a Japanese Kanō School teacher and then studied old Chinese paintings, but that he eventually turned to a close observation of nature for inspiration. His color paintings of birds and flowers are so exactingly painted and their colors so rich that the effect is often overpowering. The exceptional range of Jakuchū works in the Shin'enkan Collection allows one to follow his development all the way from a relatively early painting in color (*Cranes*, plate 60) to a masterwork in ink done in the last year of his long life (*Eagle*, plate 67).

In *Rooster, Hen, and Hydrangeas* (plate 64), a particularly large painting, he combines an almost obsessive realism with an overwhelming richness of color; the amorous play between the rooster and hen electrify the composition. In *Grapevines* (plate 61), an early ink painting, he imbues knotty grapevines with a twisting energy. In *Figures, Birds, and Flowers* (plate 65) he paints birds, flowers, and people in a special wash technique, *sujime-gaki,* he is credited with having invented. His *Tiger* (plate 62) is based on a still-extant Chinese folk painting, but Jakuchū's tiger is more alive than its model and infused with a zany playfulness as well. The wild and obsessive side of Jakuchū is not better illustrated than in *Birds, Animals, and Flowering Plants* (plate 66), a pair of "mosaic screens" composed of more than 80,000 tiny squares, most of which consist of one square of color inside another. This technique is known in only two other Japanese paintings, both attributed to Jakuchū. Here the effect is of a riotously colorful fantasy land of real and imaginary birds, animals, and plants.

Soga Shōhaku (1730–81) was a celebrated eccentric whose most representative works are in ink, many of which have a turbulent spontaneity of great power. *Cranes* (plate 68) is a comparatively restrained work by Shōhaku, but its mastery of ink tone and line and the piercing expressions on the faces of the three cranes reveal his unique manner.

Little is known of the artistic career of Katsu Jagyoku (1735–80), and *Crows and Plum Tree, Rabbits and Pine Trees in Snow* (plate 69) is his only known extant painting. In both screens a dark ink wash is laid down to suggest a winter day. The tree trunks and branches are left in reserve so that the unpainted paper becomes highlights and piled-up snow. As a final step the artist has spattered white pigment over the entire surface. The unrestrained brushwork and exhilarating conception are a testament to the spirit of individualism that flourished in eighteenth-century Japan.

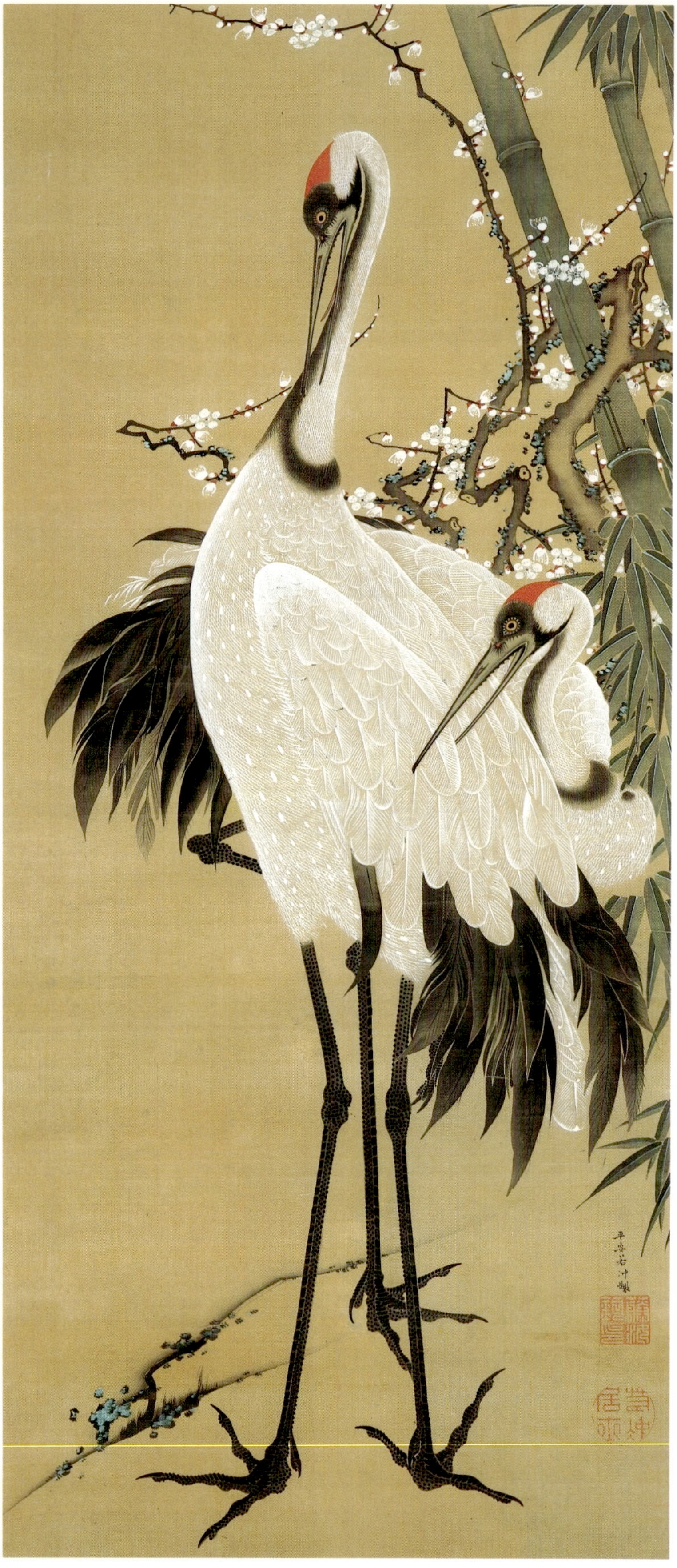
平安若冲擬

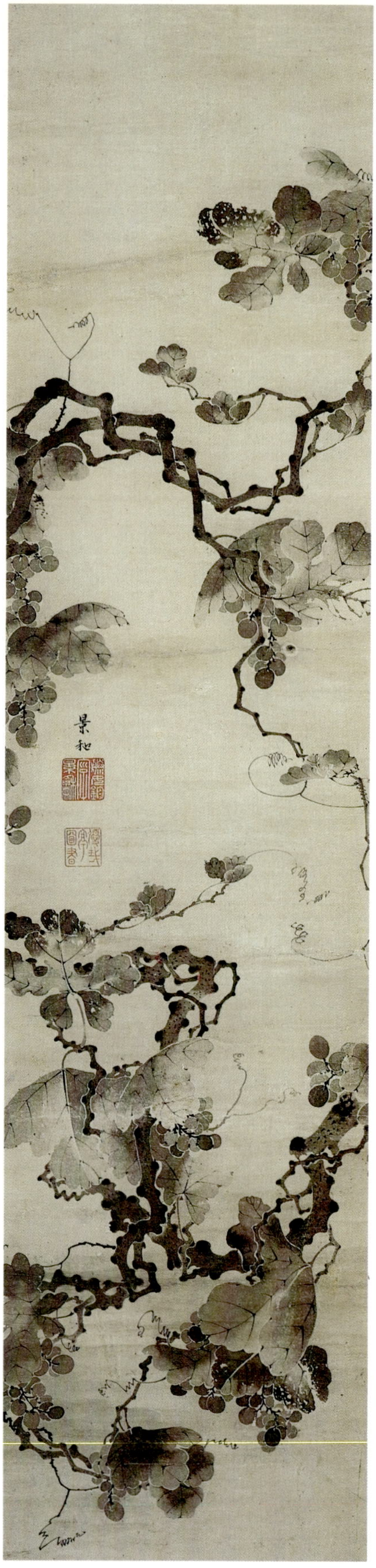
景和

60
(far left)
Itō Jakuchū (1716 – 1800)
Cranes
Hanging scroll
Color on silk
112.6 x 49.8 cm
($44\frac{5}{16}$ x $19\frac{5}{8}$ in.)

61
(left)
Itō Jakuchū (1716 – 1800)
Grapevines
Hanging scroll
Ink on paper
118.8 x 28.5 cm
($46\frac{3}{4}$ x $11\frac{1}{4}$ in.)

62
(right)
Itō Jakuchū (1716 – 1800)
Tiger, 1755
Hanging scroll
Color on silk
130.3 x 71.4 cm
($51\frac{5}{16}$ x $28\frac{1}{8}$ in.)

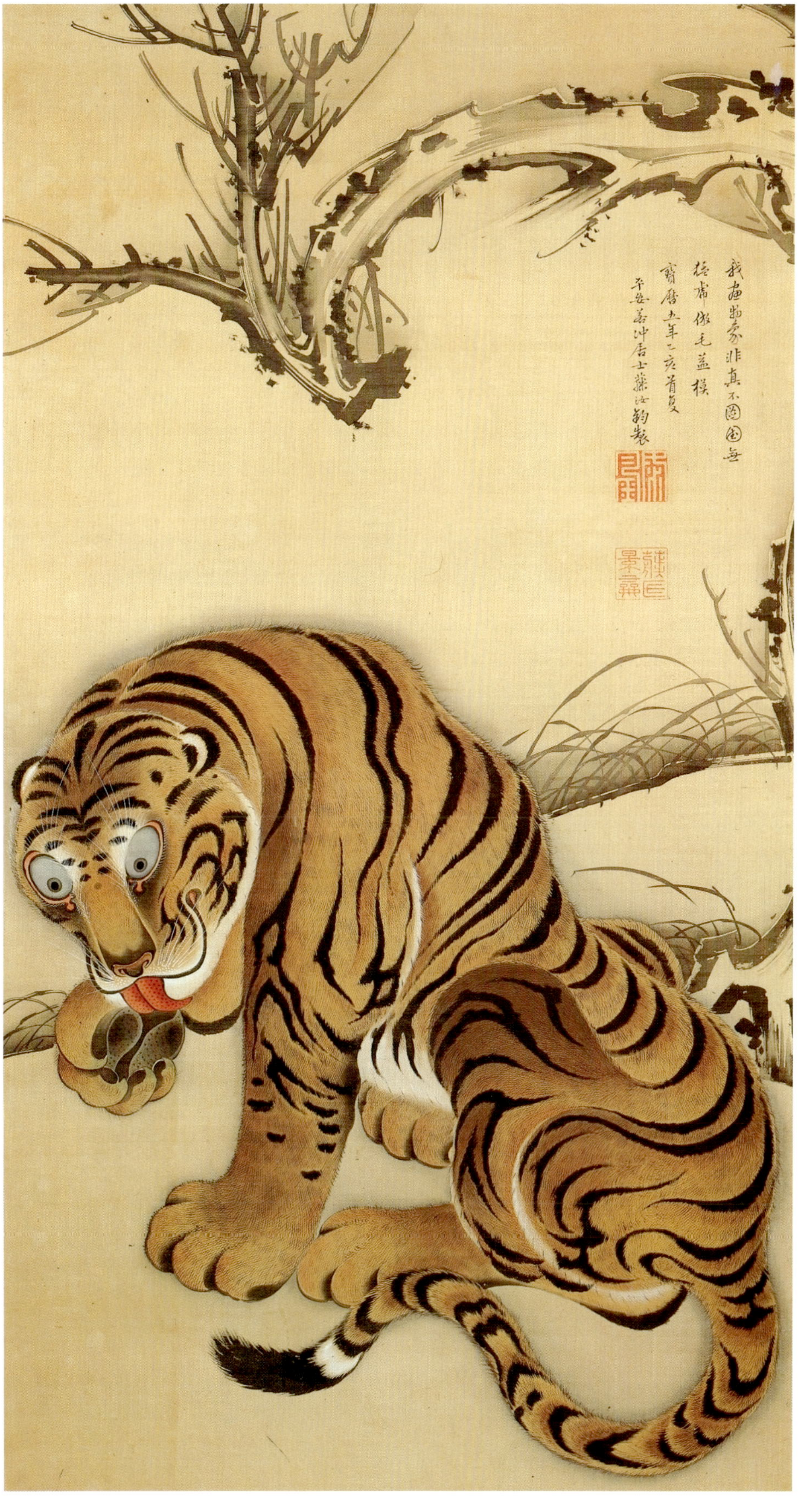

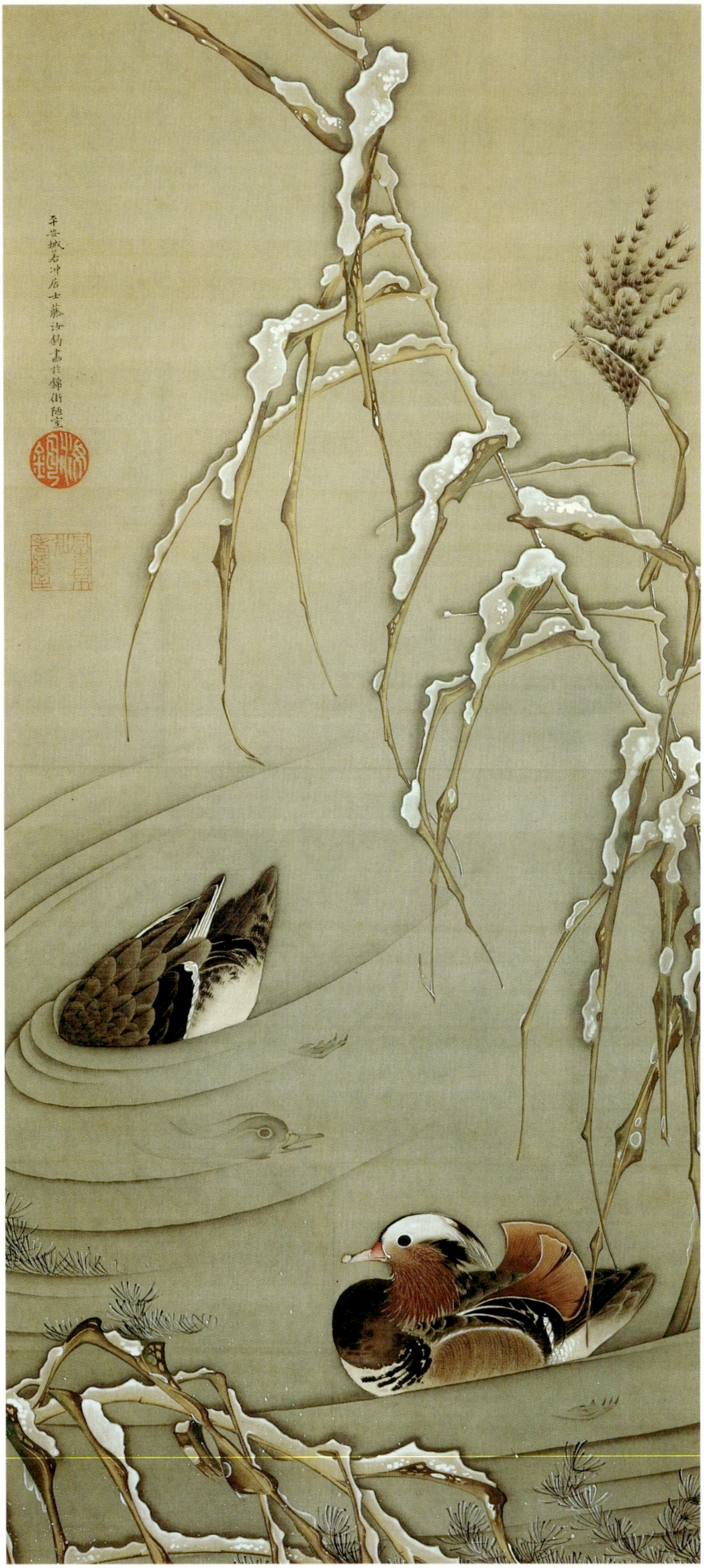

63
(left)
Itō Jakuchū (1716 – 1800)
Mandarin Ducks
amid Snow-covered Reeds
Hanging scroll
Color on silk
110.7 x 51.5 cm
(43⅝ x 20¼ in.)

64
(right)
Itō Jakuchū (1716 – 1800)
Rooster, Hen, and Hydrangeas
Hanging scroll
Color on silk
139.4 x 85.4 cm
(54⅞ x 33⅝ in.)

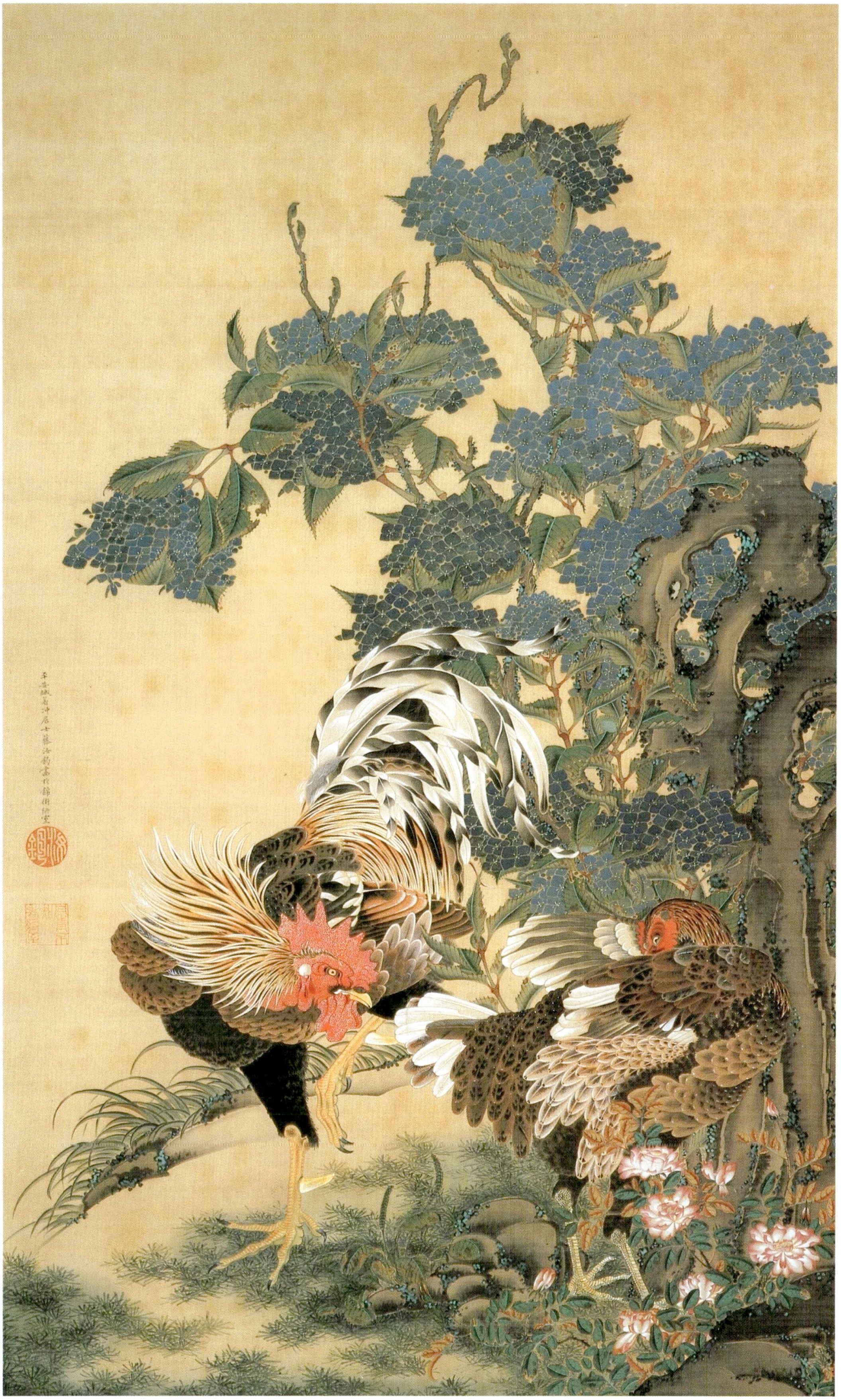

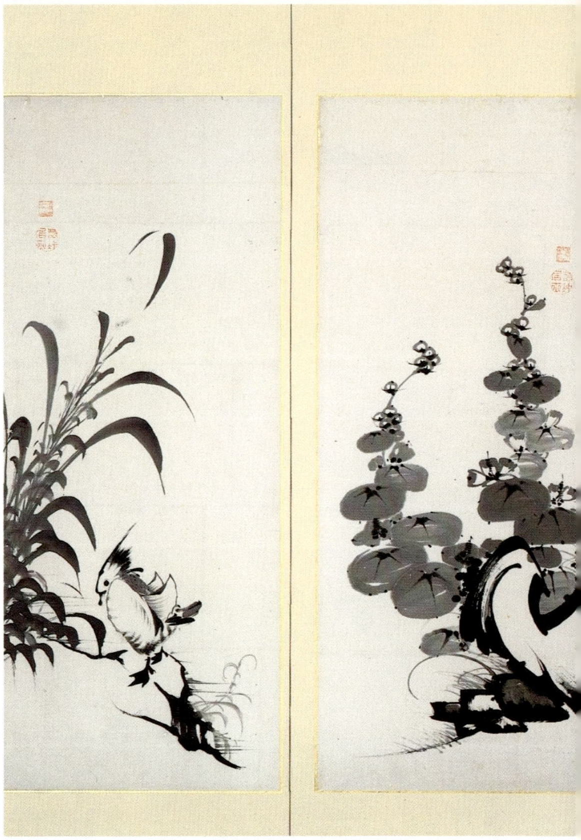

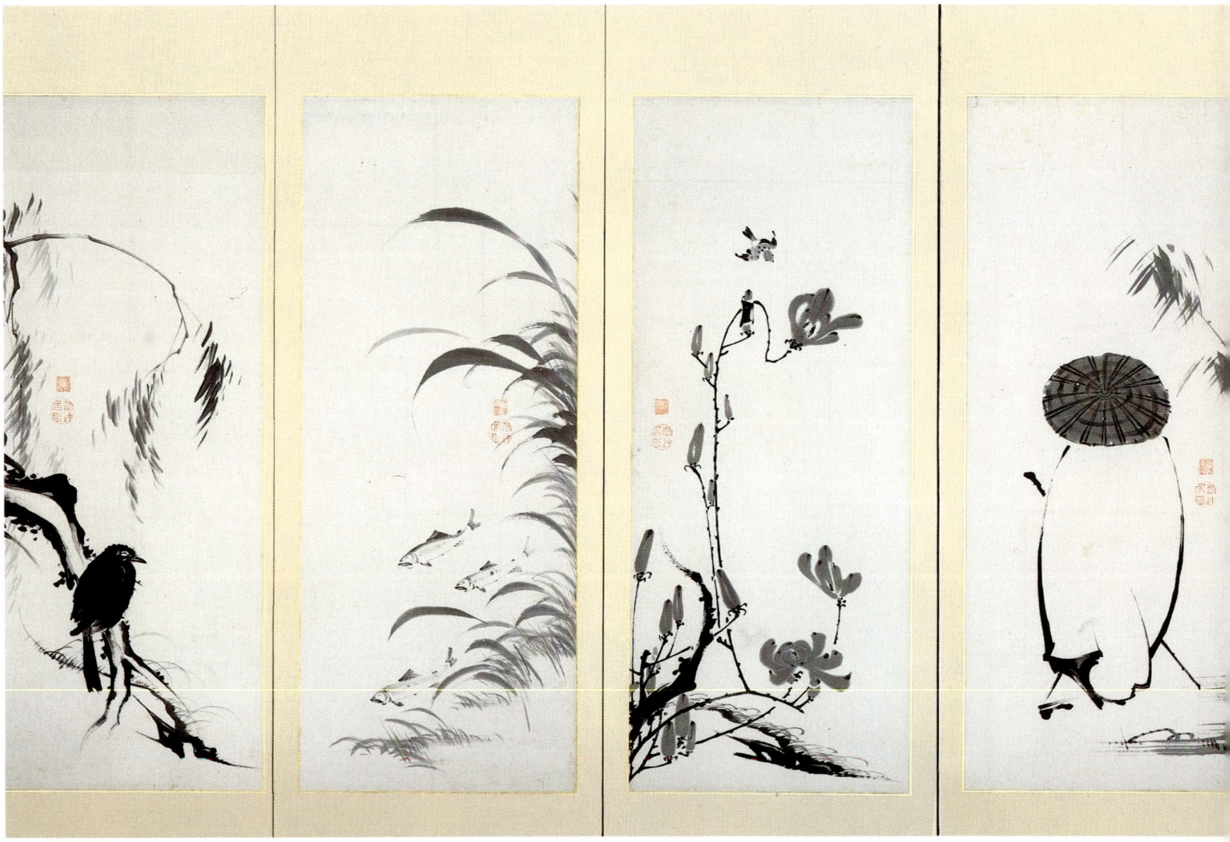

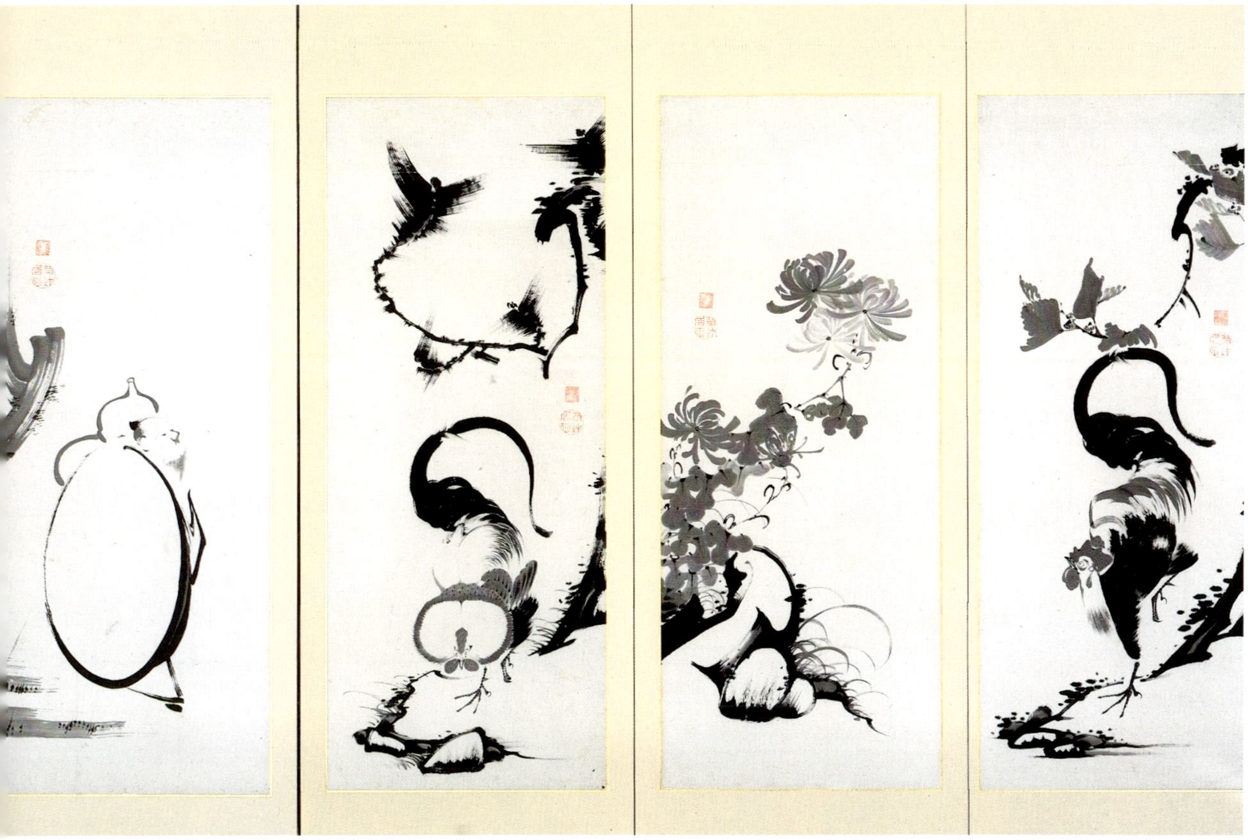

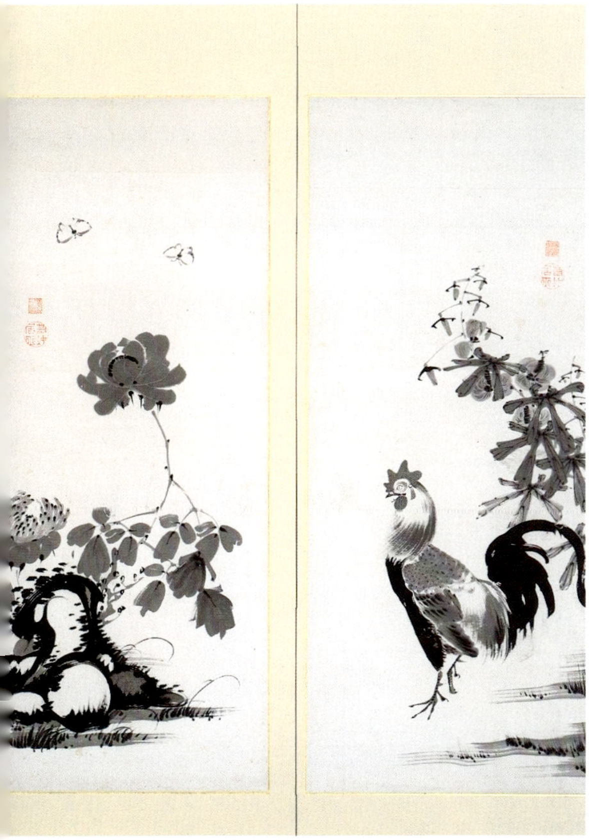

65
Itō Jakuchū (1716 – 1800)
Figures, Birds, and Flowers
Pair of six-fold screens
Ink on paper
Each panel 127.5 x 52.6 cm
($50^{3}/_{16}$ x $20^{11}/_{16}$ in.)

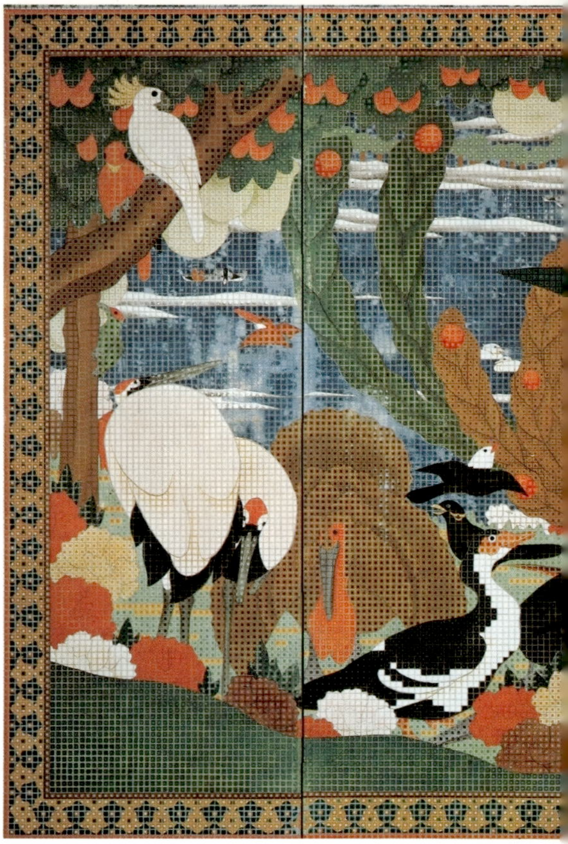

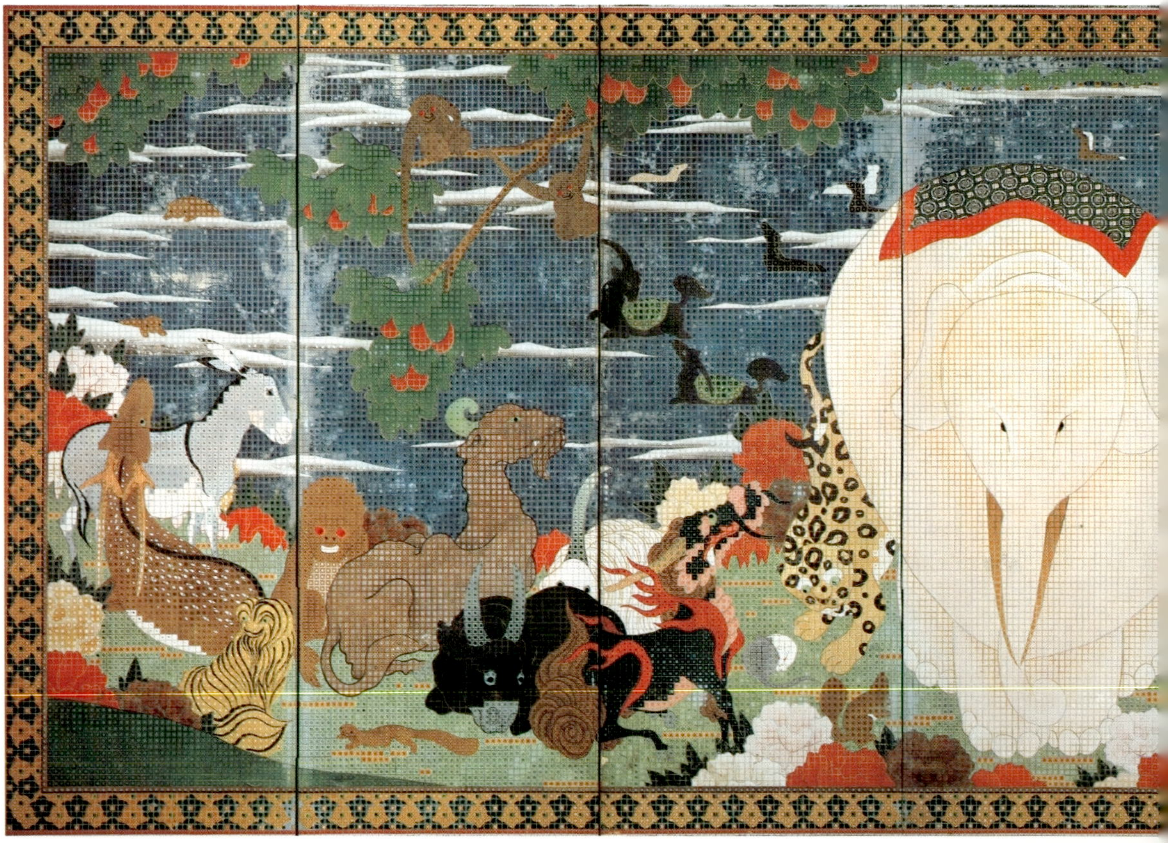

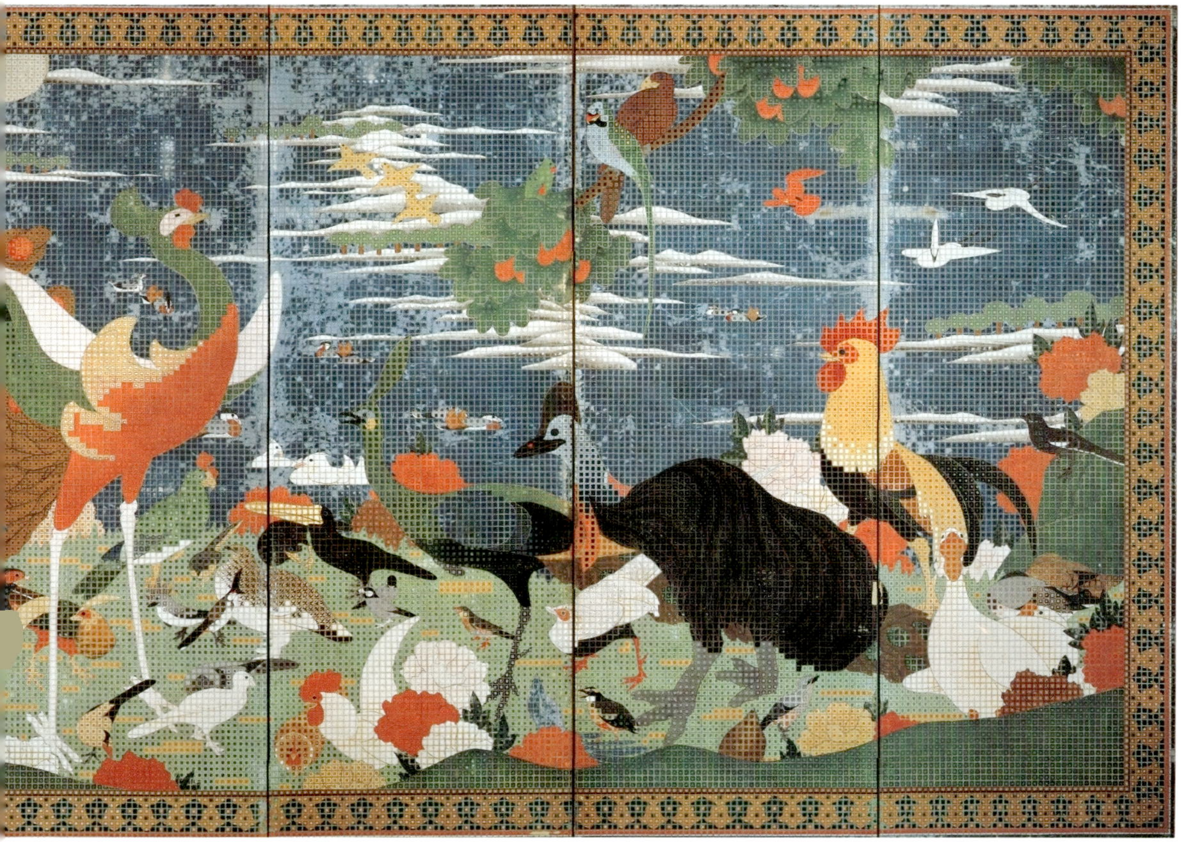

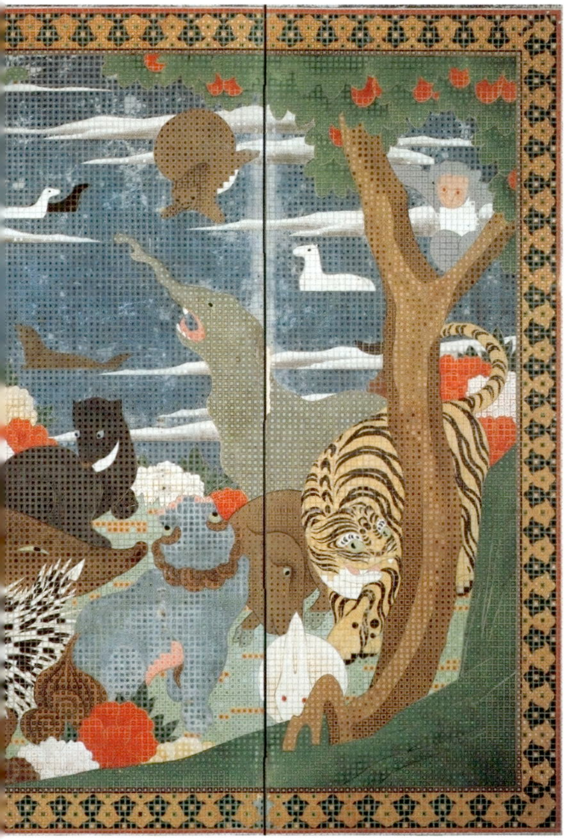

66
Itō Jakuchū (1716 – 1800)
Birds, Animals, and Flowering Plants
Pair of six-fold screens
Color on paper
Each 167 x 376 cm
(65¾ x 148 in.)

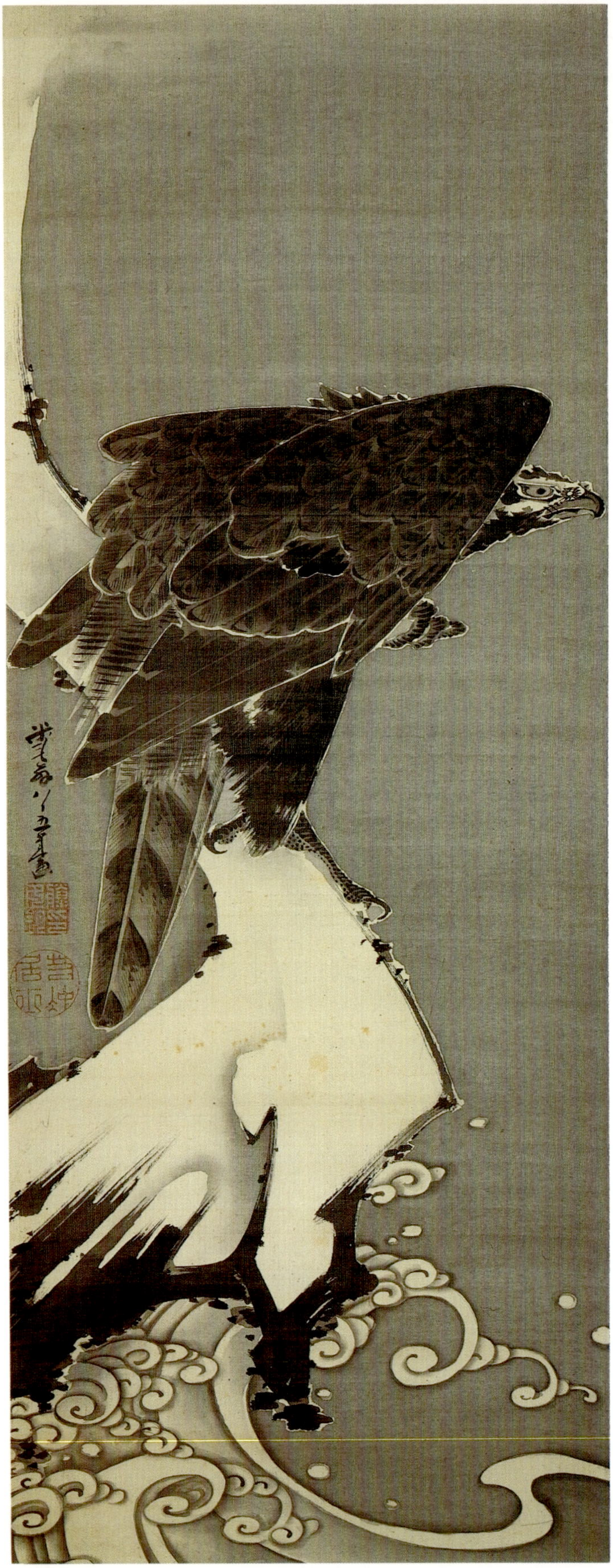

67
Itō Jakuchū (1716 – 1800)
Eagle, 1800
Hanging scroll
Ink on silk
102.4 x 40.3 cm
(40⁵⁄₁₆ x 15⅞ in.)

68
Soga Shōhaku (1730 – 81)
Cranes
Hanging scroll
Ink and color on paper
122.4 x 52.5 cm
($48\frac{3}{16}$ x $20\frac{11}{16}$ in.)

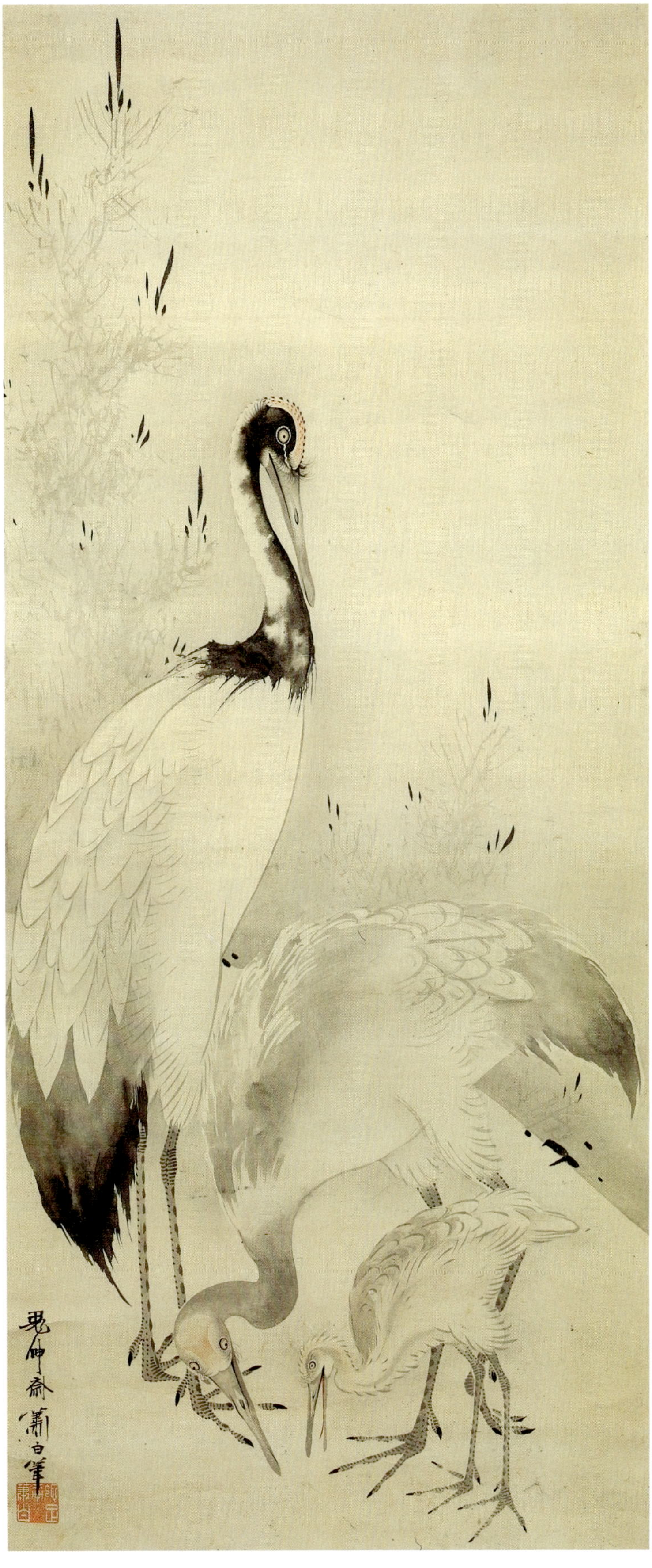

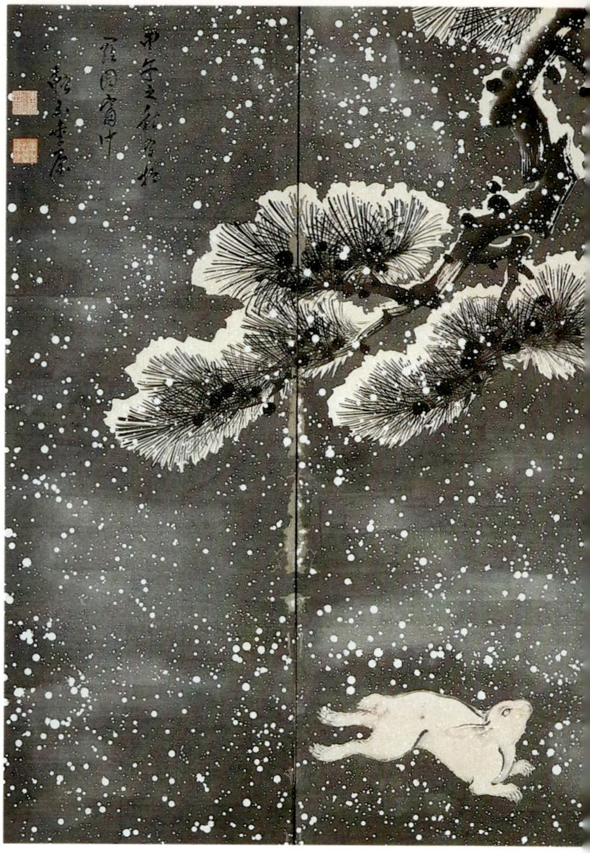

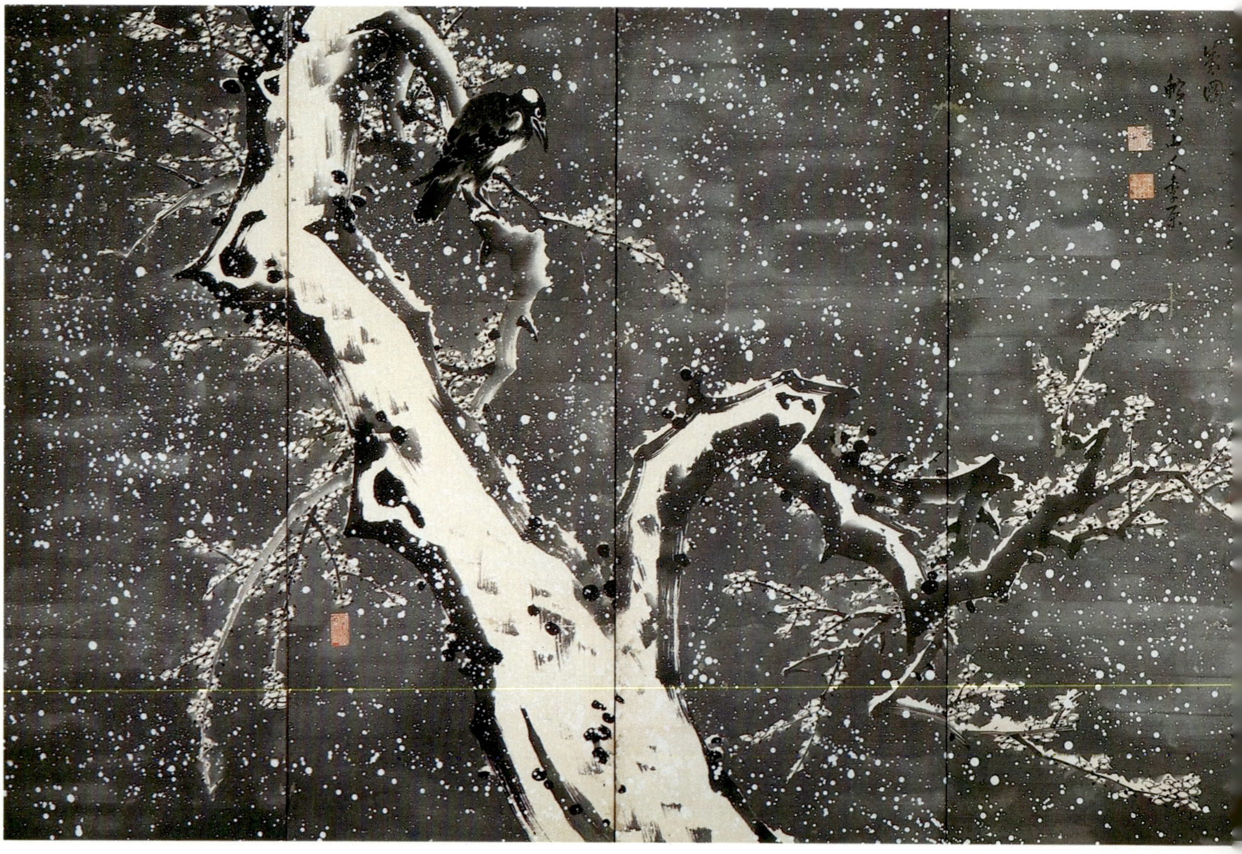

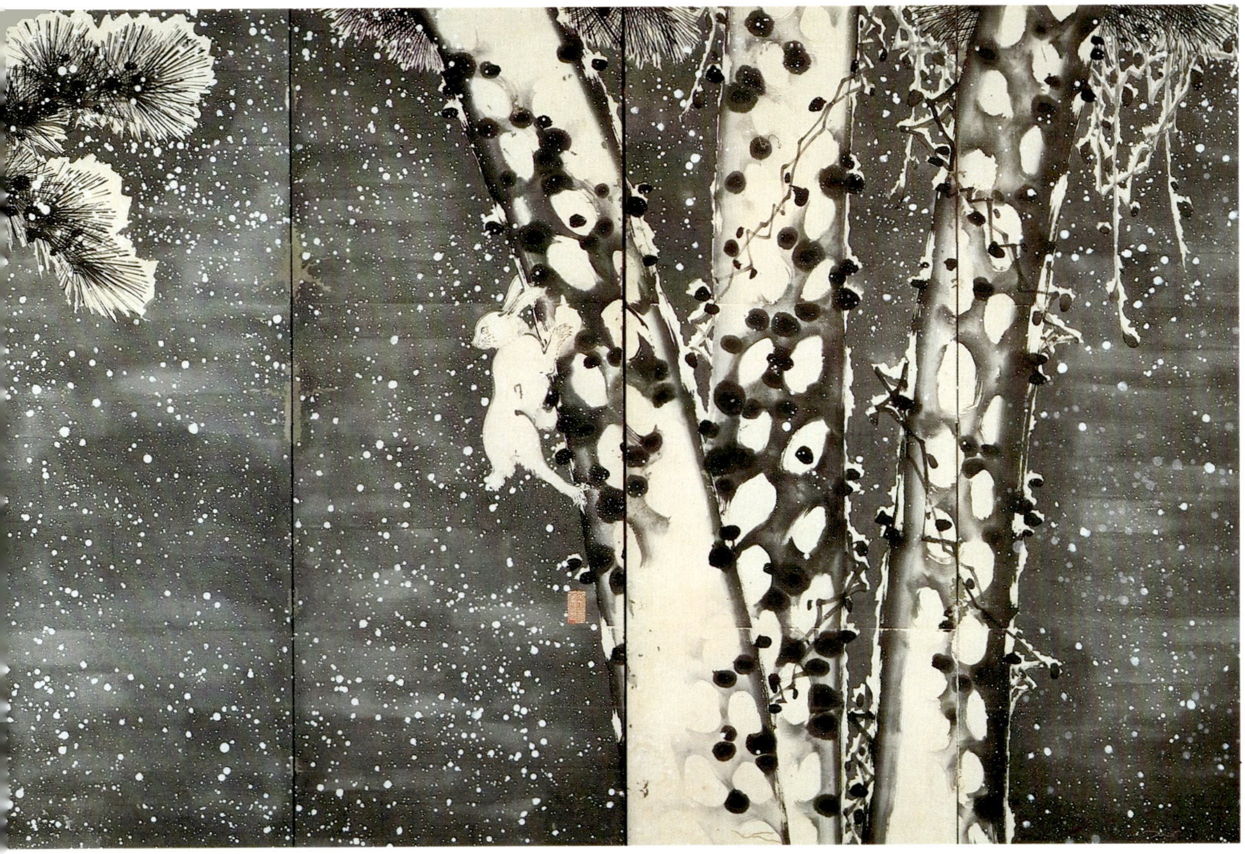

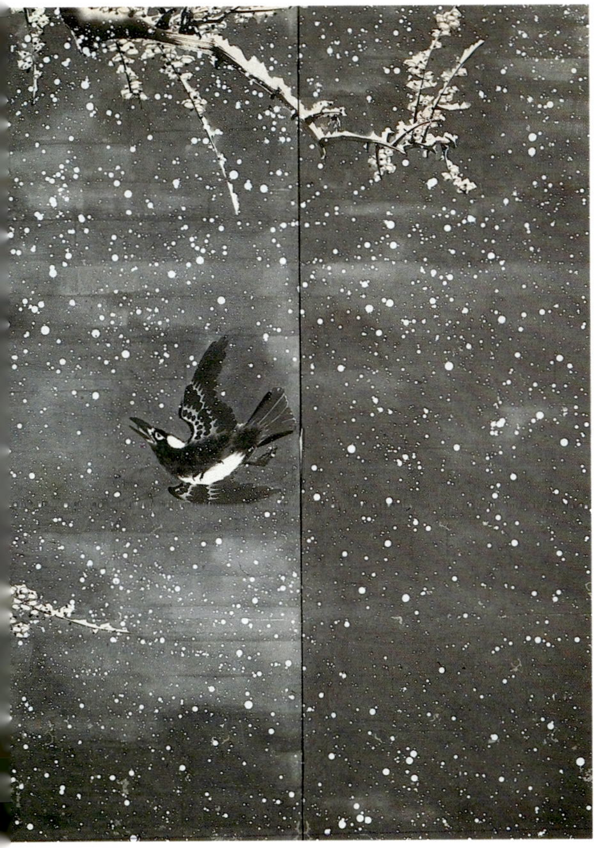

69
Katsu Jagyoku (1735 – 80)
Crows and Plum Tree,
Rabbits and Pine Trees
in Snow, 1774
Pair of six-fold screens
Ink and white pigment on paper
Each 153.8 x 353.0 cm
(60⁹⁄₁₆ x 138¹⁵⁄₁₆ in.)

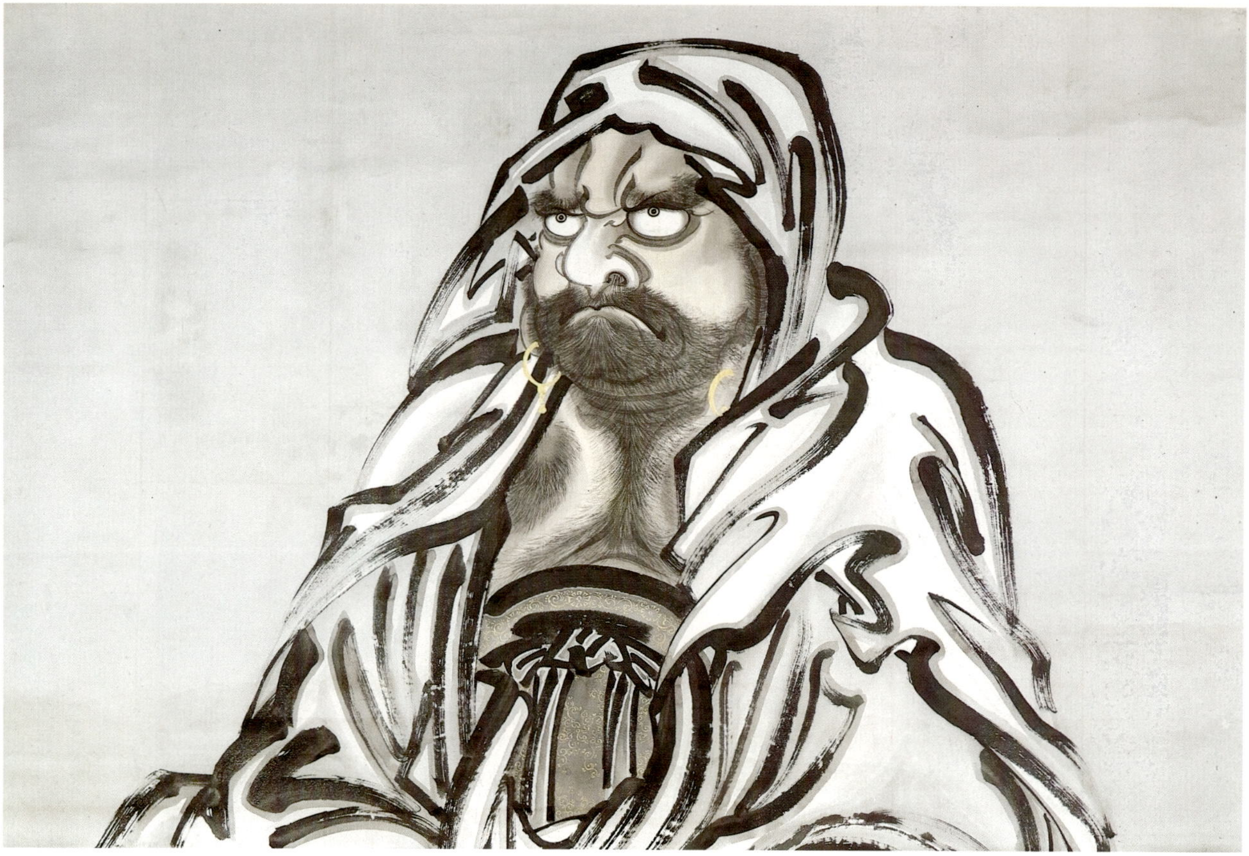

70
Kawanabe Gyōsai (1831 – 89)
Daruma, 1888
Hanging scroll
Ink and color on paper
121.5 x 183.5 cm
(47 13/16 x 72 1/4 in.)

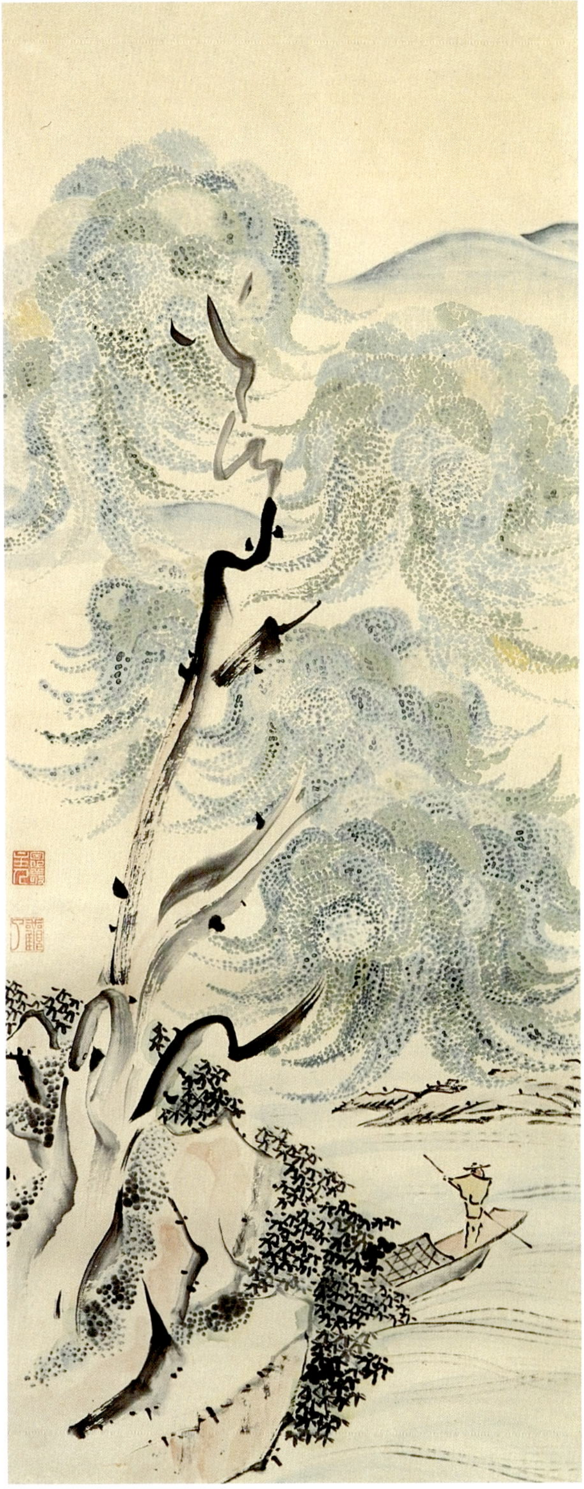

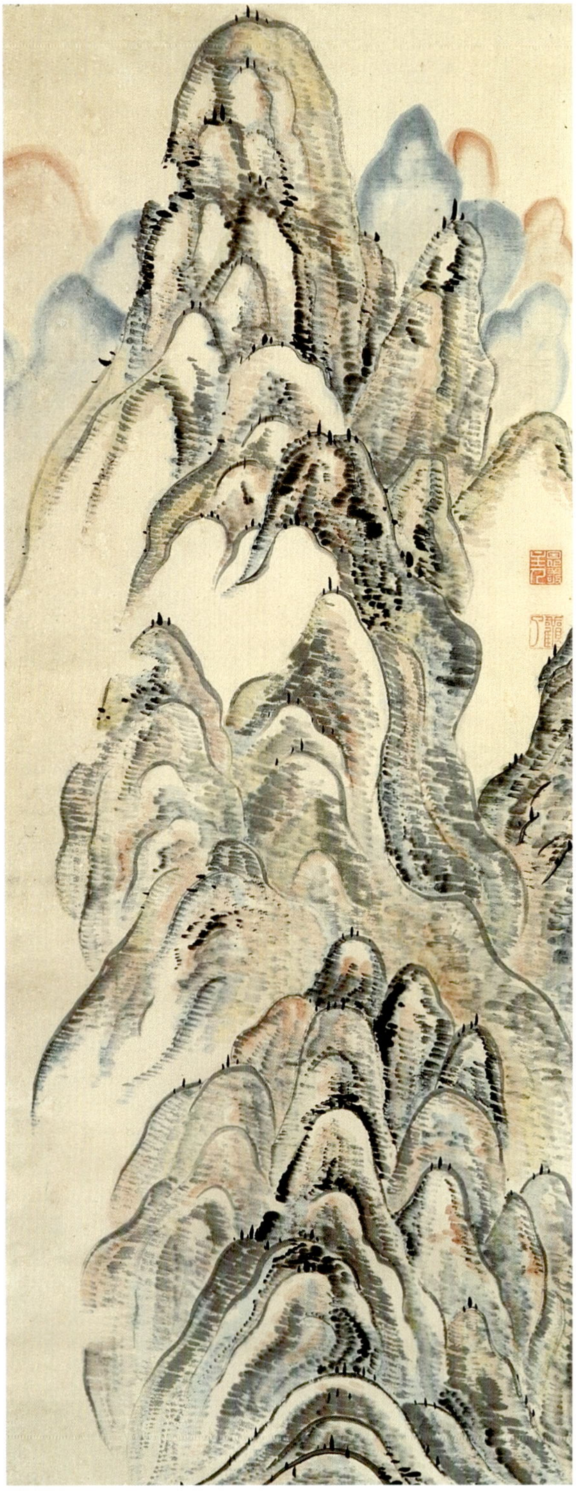

71
Ike Kanryō (1753 – 1830)
Summer and Autumn Landscapes
Pair of hanging scrolls
Ink and color on paper
Each 130.3 x 52.3 cm
(51⁵⁄₁₆ x 20⁵⁄₈ in.)

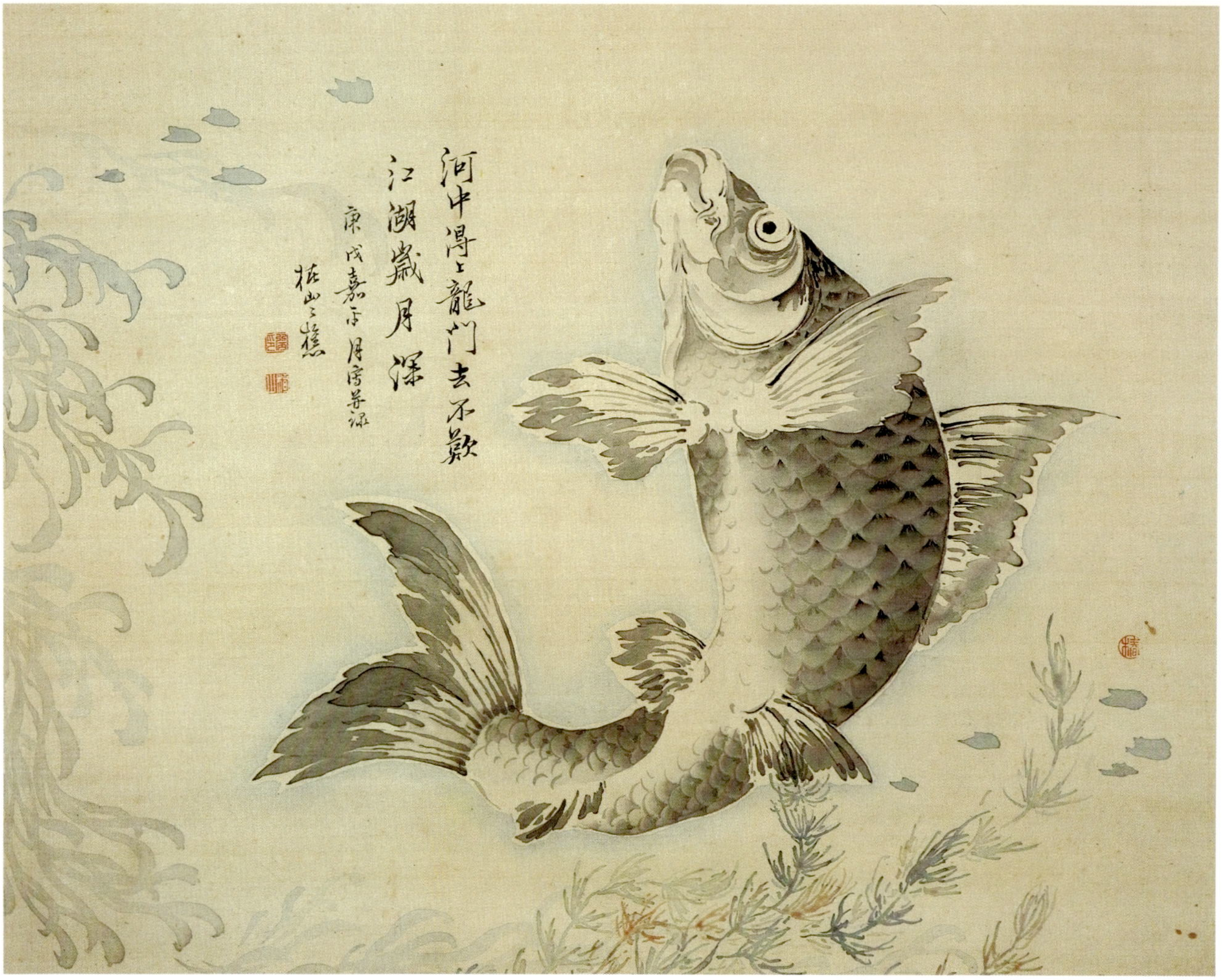

72
Tsubaki Chinzan (1801 – 54)
Carp, 1850
Hanging scroll
Color on silk
55.0 x 69.9 cm
(21 11/16 x 27½ in.)

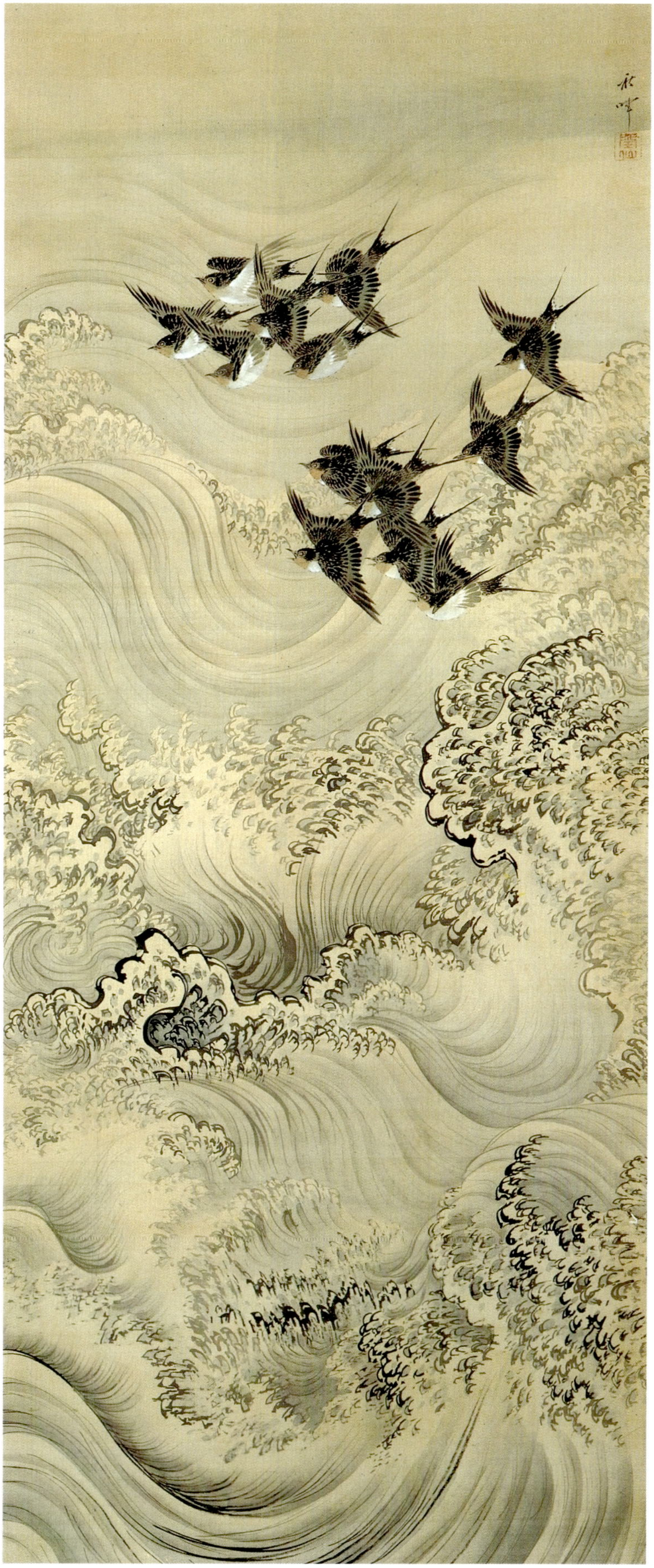

73
Okamoto Shūki (1807 – 62)
Swallows and Waves
Hanging scroll
Ink and color on silk
130.3 x 56.1 cm
($51\frac{5}{16}$ x $22\frac{1}{8}$ in.)

Index of Artists

Supervisors and Trustees

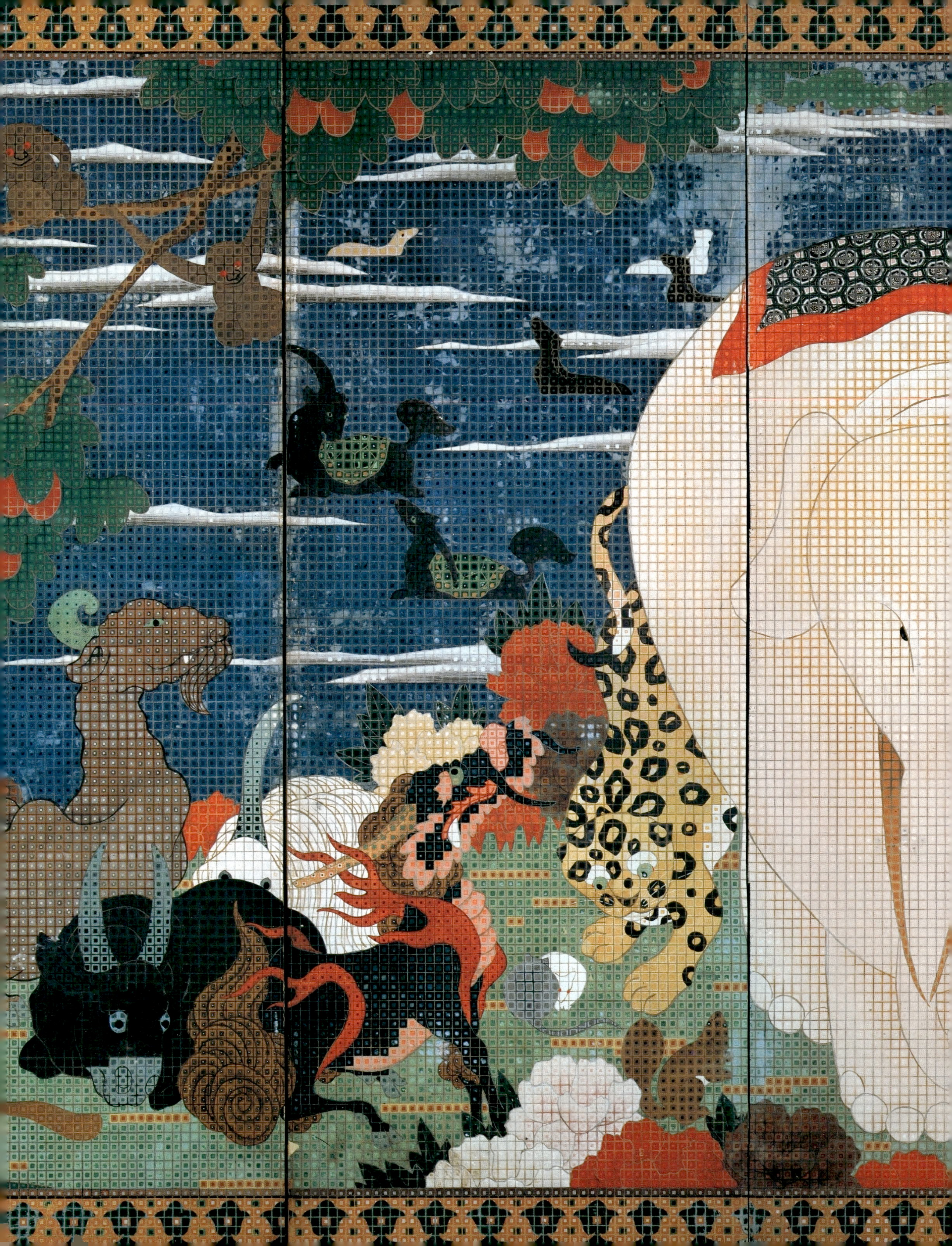